Gender and policing

Gender and policing
Sex, power and police culture

Louise Westmarland

WILLAN
PUBLISHING

Published by

Willan Publishing
Culmcott House
Mill Street, Uffculme
Cullompton, Devon
EX15 3AT, UK
Tel: +44(0)1884 840337
Fax: +44(0)1884 840251
e-mail: info@willanpublishing.co.uk
website: www.willanpublishing.co.uk

Published simultaneously in the USA and Canada by

Willan Publishing
c/o ISBS, 5824 N.E. Hassalo St,
Portland, Oregon 97213-3644, USA
Tel: +001(0)503 287 3093
Fax: +001(0)503 280 8832
e-mail: info@isbs.com
website: www.isbs.com

First published 2001

ISBN 1-903240-70-0 Hardback

British Library Cataloguing-in-Publication Data

A catalogue record for this book is available from the British Library

Printed and bound by T.J. International, Padstow, Cornwall

Contents

List of Tables

Preface and acknowledgements

This book draws upon and updates research originally conducted for a doctoral thesis and without the help and support of a number of people during that process, it would not have been achieved. Dick Hobbs, as my PhD supervisor, was a constant source of advice, guidance and inspiration. He not only said that his door was always open, but that I should regard him as 'the last stop before the Samaritans'. Other members of staff at Durham who also provided invaluable support include Dave Chaney, Nick Ellison, John Tierney and Robin Williams. During my time at York, whilst the writing process of the book was continued, Anne Ackroyd, John Forrester and Steve Yearley, amongst others, helped by providing bibliographic references and opportunities for work, rest and play.

In addition, several people discussed and commented upon conference papers, articles and chapters in draft, including Richard Collier, Simon Blyth, Jennifer Brown, Sandra Walklate, Jim Sheptycki, Dave Wall, Adam Crawford and Malcolm Young. Betsy Stanko provided useful advice by suggesting a number of changes to the original format of the book and I would also like to thank Laurie Taylor for constantly asking me when it would be finished, in addition to giving me the confidence to think it ever would. Brian Willan has helped in the final stages of preparation of the manuscript, and without the cooperation of the two police forces that provided access, the research would not have even begun. Thanks are due to the many officers who gave freely of their time, opinions and in some cases friendship during the fieldwork, especially Elaine Taylor, Stephanie Yearnshire and Brian Douglas.

Finally, I would like to thank my family, for supporting me in many different ways for the duration of my academic career so far, and my colleagues at the Scarman Centre, including Rosemary Barberet, Tina Skinner and Chris Wilkinson. Most of all, thanks to Keith for being a great friend and debating partner.

Louise Westmarland
November 2001

Chapter 1

Policing and gendered bodies

Police officers embody the authority of the state and are afforded certain powers with which they are expected to preserve the peace, maintain social and political order and fight crime. To carry out these functions they wear a uniform and carry certain 'tools of the trade' such as handcuffs and truncheons, symbolising their legitimate right to use force. In carrying out their duties it is expected that bodily strength may have to be used to facilitate certain tasks. Despite the potentially physical nature of these activities and the increasing popularity of the study of 'the human self as an embodied agent' (Turner, 1996:6) however, it seems that the police have not been analysed in terms of the body. Indeed, there appears to be a significant lack of empirical research to complement the growing number of theoretical studies concerned with embodiment and gender, such as Bordo (1997), Davis (1996), Hausman (1995), Mackenzie (1998) and Scott (1997). 'Lived' experiences of men and women in the police, acknowledging differences in the ways they are embodied, have been ignored to date. This book will explore connections between police culture and the significance of gendered bodies on the street and throughout various specialist departments. To support this analysis, extensive ethnographic data are provided which illustrate the way force and strength are used as officers 'contract in' with their bodies, or choose to withdraw from certain encounters. Indeed, as personal and professional status in the police is largely dependent upon showing 'bottle', choices concerning the use of their physicality are especially significant to our understanding of police work. In effect, the way gendered bodies create a situation which perpetuates beliefs about certain occupational roles being designated either 'male' or 'female' is explored. Similarly, gendered identities, which take 'genitalia to be the definitive sign of sex ... essential to the symbolisation of reproductive sexuality' (Butler, 1990:109–10) will be explored. One of the ways this will be carried out is by analysing 'masculinity' and 'femininity' as a require-ment in different fields of policing, through an examination of how the police deal with child abuse, domestic violence and sexual offences.

As a result of 'bringing the body back in' (Frank, 1990), therefore, this study analyses two interdependent areas of contention, the first of which is the debate surrounding differential deployment and gender. Since the official integration of women officers into the main police organisation there have been discussions about what they are actually doing in the police, what they should be doing, and how efficiently they are doing it. In the past this discussion has tended to be within the context of what Heidensohn describes as the 'Is it working?' approach (1995:104), which has examined the often fragmented and ineffectual organisational policies designed to create 'equality of opportunity' for women officers (see for example, Jones, 1986, Anderson, Brown and Campbell, 1993). In terms of the force and strength element of this debate, however, which usually reflects upon whether women are physically capable of carrying out the policing mandate, personal autonomy and the body as a repre-sentation of the gendered self seem to have been disregarded. As Walklate argues, there has been 'an absence of a debate around policing as a gendered task' (2001:149), leading to policewomen finding themselves in ambiguous positions regarding their careers. As 'specialists', simply by merit of being women, they are encouraged to work in departments dealing with supposedly gendered issues such as domestic violence, and may feel that this is where their talents can be used to provide the best possible service for the abused. Due to normative social and cultural expectations, the issue of embodiment has been ignored here too, although many of the tasks officers are required to carry out in their specialisms are linked to gendered bodies and their erotic and sexual identities. As authors of works on the body and sexuality have suggested, these issues are now believed to be more intimately connected than pre-viously presumed (Pringle, 1992, Butler, 1997, Halford, Savage and Witz, 1997). Similarly, in policing, occupational roles are constructed due to assumptions about embodied expertise, such as the ability to care for children due to being able to give birth, or the ability to fight due to some aspect of male strength. Hence, this study uses the gendered body to illustrate the way force and anatomy are determinants of competence in the police.

A second area of contention this work will examine, in addition to the debate about differential deployment, is the way men and women experience their bodies in a gendered social order, 'under the constant critical surveillance of others' (Davis, 1996:115). Empirical evidence from field observations of the reality of 'lived' policing will be used to reflect upon various theoretical studies which are concerned with the 'problem of the body in social life' (Turner, 1992:31). As the analysis contributes to the debate about social theory and the body it considers the effect of gendered bodies in various situations, such as in the patrol car, and by observing the investigation of certain crimes. Consequently, as part of the ethnographic tradition, it interprets not only the actions but also the shared meanings of police officers by reflecting upon their 'world view', motives, values and beliefs, to examine the various gendered ways of enacting policing. In addition, in terms of participant observation and the analysis of police culture, it will provide the first British study of its type, concentrating on gender as a central focus.

As indicated above, previous studies which have described the daily activities of the police have tended to ignore the importance of the body as an analytic concept (Holdaway, 1983, Reiner, 2000, Fielding, 1994), whilst theoretical discussions (Butler, 1990, Seidler, 1997, Shilling, 1993) have not been tested empirically. As Watson suggests, this is because the sociology of the body has 'privileged theorising of "the body"; bracketed out the individual; and largely ignored practical experiences of embodiment' (2000:51). Given the emphasis on various aspects of physicality and the apparent significance of personal strength in debates about gender and policing, it seems that this is a serious omission. It has been recognised for some time, however, in fictional representations of police activities, that upon arrest suspects become 'bodies' as they enter the domain of the police car, van or cell. This transitional process, which Young describes from an anthropological perspective as being based upon binary opposites, allows officers to distance themselves from the 'prisoners' by giving them derogatory titles such as 'prigs' and 'scumbags' (1991:111). Furthermore, in order for officers to manage their workload whilst abiding by certain 'rules' (Smith and Gray, 1983:171), suspects are dehumanised, slotted into coded offence categories and treated with reference to culturally accepted biases. In terms of normal practice, this means that 'drunks' picked up by the police may be classified as 'incapable', or alternatively capable and hence 'disorderly', depending upon their behaviour as a result of the amount of alcohol they have consumed. Arrested 'bodies' are usually assigned a certain status along a continuum of passivity and danger. In addition, dirty and 'disgusting' bodies, in the case of sex or drug offenders, are in diametric opposition to the bodies of women and children, who are seen as being in need of moral or physical protection. Gendered bodies are also significant, as this book will show, because the 'stripped' body, in the conducting of searches, and the contained body, in the event of imprisonment, require special attention to prevent allegations of sexual impropriety.

As Stanley and Wise argue, within sociology feminism has had an impact upon various fields including 'crimes of violence towards women and children' (1993:186-7). In addition, some feminists have concerned themselves with epistemological questions such as the 'rejection of Cartesian binary or dichotomous categories as supposed descriptions of social life' (ibid:137). Indeed, due to dissatisfaction with 'both biologically essentialist and social constructionist analyses of the body', Scott (1997), amongst others, has argued for the establishment of the body as 'an agent in its own right, rather than as unintelligent, static and passive' (Maynard, 1997:9). Furthermore, as a result of the critiques of certain anti-essentialist approaches to the study of gender, it has been suggested that social constructivism has ignored the body, leading to problems with explaining any connection whatsoever between biology and the social. As McNay argues, however, it is important to analyse differences within 'monolithic sexual differences' because 'the female body and the feminine gender are not radically discontinuous as the sex/gender distinction implies' (1992:23). Similarly, in his discussion of embodiment and social theory, Turner reviews theoretical approaches to the body and acknowledges the lack of productive empirical research in the area (Turner, 1996:1). His description of the history of the sociology of the body claims certain changes in Western industrial societies have led to new directions in the nature of labour and consumption. He argues that the machismo of young, working class men, which 'no longer has a direct functional relevance', has meant that what was once the 'labouring body' has now become the 'desiring body' (ibid:2). In essence, these men now carry out hard physical work, not as an aspect of paid employment, but to produce the toned body. Further, as Hobbs suggests, 'violence is an enduring, emphatically masculine resource' (1995:29), and policing, particularly for young men, may be regarded as one of the few remaining non-military occupations with a requirement for physical, bodily power and the possibility of mortal danger.

It seems that policing has traditionally been an occupation where physical, violent labour has been accepted, required and valued. Numerous studies have illustrated the importance of participants being perceived as being able to 'handle themselves' (see for example Fielding, 1988, Uildriks and Mastrigt, 1991, Heidensohn, 1994). Just as the growing consumer interest in 'keeping fit' is said to be relational to class and gender, in terms of an indication of financial status and availability of leisure, in the police the body as 'physical capital – a possessor of power, status and distinctive symbolic forms' (Shilling, 1997:88) is connected to being able to effect difficult, violent arrests. Consequently, as policing is somehow dependent upon physical abilities such as running, climbing and fighting and is potentially a legitimate outlet for aggression at work, it could be seen as an example of what Turner describes as the 'culture which recognises the body is a project' (1996:4). In a discussion of the changing styles of the female figure across time and cultures however, Bartky argues that although both men and women exercise, 'Today, massiveness, power, or abundance in a woman's body is met with distaste. The current body of fashion is taut, small breasted, narrow hipped and of a slimness bordering on emaciation' (1997:132–3).

In terms of his thesis on the body as a consuming self and representational being, Turner highlights the process whereby bodies are disciplined by consumerist desire, whilst emerging medical technologies provide 'new opportunities for democratisation and authoritarian control of the human self as an embodied agent' (1996:6–7). Once again, however, it could be argued that this process is linked to gendered bodies, as Young suggests that women are not normally judged in terms of their physical fitness. She is critical of the traditional approach which suggests that although most men are by no means superior athletes, 'The relatively untrained man nevertheless engages in sport generally with more free motion and open reach than does his female counterpart' (1990:146). Furthermore, the assumption that women 'often approach a physical engagement with things with timidity, uncertainty and hesitancy' (ibid), as they lack confidence and trust in their bodily abilities, is, she says, due to a certain self-consciousness in women and an 'objectified bodily existence' – meaning that 'to open her body in free, active open extension and bold outward directedness is for a woman to invite objectification' (1990:155).

Agency and structure

Theories of embodiment and the study of gendered roles and identities in the police cannot be discussed without reference to control and autonomy. If the body can be a representation of the self, through which 'value and meaning is ascribed to the individual by the shape and image of their external body' (Turner, 1996:23), it could be argued that an occupational culture which emphasises the need to produce quantifiable results and 'confront the threat of sudden attack from another person' (Reiner, 2000:88) will be especially dependent upon the outward appearance of the body. As police officers' uniformed bodies are used as the signifier of the legitimate power to stop and detain suspects and the means by which the arrest is effected, even in nonviolent situations, this is of special relevance to individual status and sense of self. Studies that have examined police culture and competence, such as Holdaway (1983), Smith and Gray (1983) and Fielding (1994), have described tests of 'manhood' relating to arrests, which in turn lead to peer admiration. Where arrests are classified as dangerous or requiring athleticism, it is apparent that there are important qualitative judgments being made about men's bodies as powerful agents capable of physical intervention. On the other hand, women's bodies are generally disregarded as enforcers in police cultural analyses, with the exception of Young (1991), but as the evidence in this book this book will suggest, they are of great significance to the police as topics of erotic interest. Existing studies of the police, with a few exceptions where reference is made to unusually 'manly' women, their bodies are ignored, which is in contrast to the general interest in the female body, as in the literature on anorexia, 'looking good' (Turner, 1996:23) and medical technologies.

As noted earlier, Heidensohn classifies some of the previous studies focusing on women in the police as 'Is it working?' research (1995). She describes the ways in which women officers have been alleged to be controlled and constrained in their careers, and as Walklate suggests (2001), being 'encouraged' to go into departments dealing with women and children. This leads to their skills being undervalued and their prospects for promotion blocked because they are not engaging with so-called 'proper policing'. One of the issues this book addresses, therefore, is 'differential deployment', by challenging the notion that women are unable to choose certain specialties whilst being manipulated into areas concerned with empathy, families and sexual offences. Just as it is acknowledged that women and men cannot leave their bodies, and that their uniforms cannot fully disguise or negate their gender, evidence will be presented in this study that although certain 'roles' are designated male or female, due to the gendered body being regarded as a qualification, the situation regarding human agency is rather more ambiguous. It is argued, for example, that although some police roles are supposedly gender neutral, as physical attributes such as muscular strength are not required for the tasks involved, they are symbolically 'gendered' due to other, more subtle cultural nuances.

In terms of controlling the body, Davis argues throughout her discussion of the 'objectified body' and cosmetic surgery that women are 'agents ... knowledgeable and active subjects who attempt to overcome their alienation, to act upon the world themselves instead of being acted upon by others' (1996:115). In another debate about the way women are 'alienated' from their bodies, Young suggests that despite the effects of a male-dominated culture, 'many women identify their breasts as themselves' (1990:192). Furthermore, due to the possibilities of the 'plastic body', she asks, 'Why shouldn't a woman choose perfect breasts?' (ibid:201). As Martin points out, however, it is debatable to what extent women can escape their 'bodily mode' (1989:199), which is especially relevant within a 'male' environment such as the police. In a discussion grounded in Cartesian dualism, Church outlines the debate which she narrows to 'two equally problematic alternatives – a conception of ourselves as something wholly distinct from our bodies … and a conception of ourselves as identical to our bodies' (1997:86). She uses the ownership and selling of bodies to illustrate her argument that it is perfectly possible to sell '*parts* of our bodies – organs, parts of organs, skin, hair and so on' (ibid:95 original emphasis) but prostitution and paid pregnancy create the notion of the selling of 'more of oneself'. So although we can choose, 'we do not have the right to prostitute ourselves' because the selling that presupposes legitimate ownership simultaneously undermines the very possibility of ownership (ibid:96). As Edwards observes, prostitute women 'demarcate and rigidly define quite precisely … thereby placing boundaries around certain parts of the body' (1993:89). She discusses the exploitative nature of prostitution in the light of evidence that these women claim to 'retain their autonomy and private space' whilst 'segmenting and selling parts of their bodies as commodities' (ibid), which highlights the issue of autonomous agency and women's embodiment (Mackenzie, 1998:122).

It could be argued, therefore, that the 'absent body' as Turner describes it, in terms of the problem of structure and agency (1992:67), is central to the debate about gender and differential deployment in the police. As he says, if the idea of sociology is regarded as a study of action, a social theory of the body is necessary because 'human agency and interaction involve far more than mere knowledgeability, intentionality and consciousness' (ibid:35). Connell also suggests that 'the concern with force and skill becomes a statement embedded in the body', due not only to the structure of class relations, but also to the structure of power in gender relations (1987:85). Furthermore, as Giddens argues, understanding the individualised agent in embodied terms is vital in relation to competence because 'routine control of the body is integral to the very nature both of agency and of being accepted (trusted) by others as competent' (1991:57). One of the reasons this type of approach has been absent, however, according to Turner, is that structuration theory has ignored the 'nature of the agent in agency' (1992:67), simply treating the body as a subject for the natural sciences, and as a 'rational choosing disembodied "man" [researchers] have ignored the importance of feeling and emotion in social action' (ibid:68). Consequently, sociological views of the body have tended to view the 'meaningful character of social action from the standpoint of the social actor', thus avoiding the 'corporeal side of human action' (Turner, 1996:36).

In summary, it is argued here that in policing, as in other occupations which may or may not require physical strength, such as agriculture and medicine, there is a 'between-men culture' which has been structured to exclude women (Irigaray, 1993:45). Irigaray argues that to demand equality is a 'mistaken objective', however (ibid:12), because men and women are not equal and differences should be recognised (ibid:84). In order to move on from traditional epistemologies, therefore, which regard emotions as 'disruptive and subversive of knowledge' (Stanley and Wise, 1993:193) 'inimical to the production of reliable and rational knowledge' (Scott, 1997:115), it has been suggested that empiricism should be discarded. In their rejection of the value of 'objective scientific' observations, Stanley and Wise suggest that feminist ontologies should 'include emotionality as the product of culture' rejecting 'Cartesian binary ways of polarising reason and emotion' (1993:193). As a result, there could be analyses in which 'the body can be a source of the alternative perspective which leads to a more complete and adequate understanding' (Scott, 1997:115).

Method

In essence, this study aims to complete some parts of the picture concerning what is known about the relationship between policing and gender. It focuses on those areas that have been discussed and theorised previously, such as differential deployment and the gendered nature of tasks, in addition to the relationship between the body and policing. Unlike many previous studies, however, rather than drawing upon what the participants say they feel or do, the research was conducted primarily using ethnographic principles, with policing as a site for 'an ethnography of the body and body work' (Coffey, 1999:61). As Wolcott suggests, every ethnography is unique and 'no particular one can be singled out for having set the standard for all that follow' (1999:110). Hence, no single study 'past or present will ever serve as a suitable one-model-fits-all' (ibid), and in this study there was some deviation from a 'classic ethno-graphy', in the strictest sense of the term, in places. Supplementary material was gained through interviews, focus groups and statistical analysis, where this illustrated or supported the ethnographic data, although not in some mistaken attempt to triangulate the data – as Gomm, Hammersley and Foster argue, 'denial of the capacity of case study research to support empirical generalisation often seems to rest on the mistaken assumption that this form of generalisation requires statistical sampling' (2000:104). The ethnographic part of the research was in the general sense participant observation, in that the researcher accompanied and observed officers, but at times was unable to remain outside the scene completely. Instances where 'help' was needed or demanded by officers on patrol, or the researcher was mistaken for a police officer, are examples of this situation.

So although this study claims to be based on 'participant' observation, to suggest that a researcher can ever access all areas of police life is problematic. A number of factors come into play which restrict the ability of the ethnographer to capture a 'true' or empirically testable set of findings. As Brown argues, the 'insider/outsider' status of any researcher will affect not only the data members of an organisation such as the police will allow to be gleaned, but also the way the study is conducted (1996a:180–5). In addition, other factors such as gender, age, class, and arguably, the body, in addition to some elusive element best described as 'trustworthiness', also come into play. Even 'full' participants, or what Brown would describe as 'inside insiders', in the case of police officers such as Holdaway (1983) and Young (1991), discover how difficult it is to be 'part of the scenery' to make colleagues forget that they might be recording incidents or remarks. 'Outside insiders' such as academic researchers have other barriers to overcome and as this study was about gender and policing, and the researcher was a woman entering a male-dominated world, problems with being fully accepted were multiplied. This includes resentment about the focus of the research being viewed as 'women' which created animosity from female officers who did not wish to be 'problematised', and from male officers who saw it as giving an already supposedly privileged minority more attention. Further, a female researcher entering a male world raises questions of plausibility and the 'various layers of *vraisemblence*' (Atkinson, 1990:39 original emphasis) that it is possible to construct due to their status as 'other'. In her discussion of fieldwork with the police, Hunt argues that a researcher always brings with 'him/her certain features which the subjects interpret in culturally prescribed ways' (1984:283). She explains how it was necessary to gain credibility in her study of American police officers by being able to shoot accurately and behave fearlessly. In a similar way the fieldwork for this book has involved certain tests of appropriate allegiances and 'bottle' (see Westmarland, 2001).

Another problem which has been identified previously by researchers is that of 'accessing male and female worlds within a culture' (Warren, 1988:15). As Golde suggests, certain cultural expectations have restricted women who attempted to conduct studies in male-dominated environments (1986 in Lee, 1995:57). In addition, the police service has been described by Punch as an 'institutional obstacle course' and in order to gain access it is necessary 'to penetrate the minefield of social defences to reach the inner reality of police work' (1993:184). In this study some of these difficulties have been confronted by entering the world of supposed danger and excitement in order to view the police carrying out their daily activities. Previously women have not conducted ethnographies of the police in Britain focusing on gender as part of the research process. Perhaps this is partly due to what Hobbs describes as the 'machismo as well as a veil of eccentricity' which is afforded to fieldwork (1993:62). Due to the high level of trust which needs to be fostered for the successful completion of an ethnography, the culture in which the researcher chooses to participate has to be reasonably accessible to the fieldworker. As the police are predominantly male this has created barriers in the past for women needing to become 'part of the scenery'. In terms of the collection of valid data, permission for access to a group such as the police needs to be negotiated not only at an organisational level but also on a daily, personal basis. In order to do this successfully, as Norris argues, in the 'observer-as-participant role researchers often have to share many elements of the everyday lives of police officers' (Norris, 1993:126) and the study will be dependent upon the extent to which this is achieved.

In order to provide as full a picture of gender and policing as possible, two largely separate case studies were conducted over a period of three years, leading to the analysis of data for this book. Two contrasting police forces allowed access to their officers and facilities with approximately six months spent researching each organisation. During this time nothing was officially 'off limits', although certain strategies were employed in order to prevent some scenarios or information being discovered by the researcher, as might be expected. The first of the two research forces is one of the smallest in the UK, having approximately 1,300 officers. Its patch covers a large rural geographical area, with a relatively low population and two or three 'hot spot' towns or cities. In contrast, the second research force is one of the largest metropolitan forces outside the capital in the UK. It has over 3,000 officers and an even larger geographical area to police, in addition to a high population, a large city and a number of densely populated conurbations. With this large urban density often comes a high level of social deprivation, and the main city in the research force's area had been in receipt of numerous urban regeneration initiatives.

In terms of the case study method itself, the aim was to become an 'informed stranger' by conducting interviews and focus group discussions prior to the ethnographic observations commencing. Due to logistical difficulties with arranging these events in the original order, however, in the first force, which was the smaller of the two, the interviews and focus discussions were conducted at the same time as the researcher was involved in participant observation activities. Most of the observations were conducted during weekend night and evening shifts and so a weaving together of information was possible during the interviews and focus groups, where experiences of the researcher on patrol could be used to inform and facilitate the discussion at the university, where the officers came for these discussions. Approximately 35 officers took part in the discussion groups and 26 interviews were conducted with officers from all ranks, from probationer to chief constable in the smaller research force. In addition, all women in promoted positions in this police force, which amounted to only eight officers, were interviewed and 70 hours of field observations were conducted in this first phase.

In the second research force, the larger one, about ten formal interviews were conducted. These were restricted to key managerial personnel and were generally aimed at finding out about the organisation itself. The bulk of the work with the larger, metropolitan force was therefore conducted on the streets in a closer approximation to traditional ethnographies, where researchers become immersed in the world of the participants. Around 360 hours were spent observing officers during evening weekend shifts and accompanying officers in specialist roles, such as members of firearms teams. These observations were conducted in three contrasting geographic areas within the force and in each place a shift or relief became the focus. On each occasion that this group of officers were on duty for their weekend of night shifts, the researcher accompanied them. This had certain advantages. First, the researcher was viewed as 'interested' in them, and was prepared to continue per-severing, as they saw it, with weekend nights for six months. Second, they could ask about the other shifts in other areas of the force, comparing their workloads, practices and so on. Third, the officers became more used to the researcher and she could understand the group dynamics, having watched their behaviour and activities on a number of occasions. In addition, one of the areas was chosen for a one month intensive observation in December, which the police often claim to be their busiest period, as it includes Christmas and New Year. During this part of the study, every night shift was observed and each officer in this sub divisional area was observed to some extent.

These methods were employed in order to observe 'gender in action' on the streets, in the patrol car and police van. Research on the tasks officers are assigned has traditionally been based on what people believe they do whilst at work. Women and men have been asked in previous studies if they think they are asked to deal with 'violent incidents' or cases involving children more than their male or female colleagues (Jones, 1986, Anderson *et al*, 1993). Although this type of discussion is conducted here, in later chapters of the book, it is informed by observations of the officers. Workers in any occupation might believe themselves to be dealing with lower status work, and hence to be disadvantaged when applying for promotion, so to accept individuals' beliefs about the type of work assigned to any particular group – especially in an organisation such as the police where competitive advantage is often gained through 'talking a good arrest' – could lead to false impressions of the situation. Hence, another part of the analysis is concerned with the number and types of arrests officers make and whether this can be related to gender. Force data are analysed from the second, larger force, for one sub divisional area, first by yearly arrest rate, then by month and finally by type of offence. Although this was a small sample of around 100 officers, and not really in accordance with traditional ethnographic tradition, it provided some further evidence to inform the 'differential deployment' debate. As arrests are very often counted as the 'product' of policing, in managerial terms, and women are said to be excluded from the full range of operational tasks, records of arrests giving gender of officer and type of offence were used to provide some substance to the 'What are women doing in the police?' debate.

Overall, therefore, this book draws upon a largely ethnographic study of women and men on patrol. It concentrates on the 'gender' of tasks and duties, beliefs about what is women's and men's work in the police, and the behaviour and actions of officers on patrol. It aims to show that the apparently restricted level of promotions for women in the police, and the way they are said to be denigrated and given the lowest status tasks, can be challenged by observation, by accompanying officers on their daily work and by asking them for their reasons rather than the outcome of their actions. Finally, the book aims to provide an explanation for the organisation of gendered activities and structures in the police. This evidence is from specialist posts or departments where few women can be found. 'Traditional' male departments such as those concerned with cars, guns and horses are investigated, and the reasons women do not apparently choose to pursue this career path are analysed. Throughout the book, evidence is taken from the numerous 'conversations' conducted in police cars, vans and canteens. In addition, there are observations conducted when potentially dangerous situations led to the researcher experiencing the full range of 'police' emotions such as fear and disgust, and others where the true extent of extreme boredom officers suffer is felt.

Scope of the book

In Chapter 2 the significance of gender and the 'natural' skills women possess is discussed regarding career choices and the irresolvable tension between discrimination and difference. This is a wide-ranging discussion of women in specialist posts, and several areas which are often classed as 'women's work' in the police are examined here. 'Structural' constraints which may include policies or practices discriminating against women are examined. As the argument challenges the accepted wisdom that women are subjected to 'differential deployment practices' (Anderson *et al*, 1993) as 'policemen are overtly and consistently hostile towards women in "the job" ' (Young, 1991:193), two questions are posed. First, what is the extent to which women are working in certain specialist departments consistent with their gender, as national statistics suggest (HMIC 1996), and second, to what extent does the existence of 'macho cop' culture in the police have an effect upon these career choices? There are two separate sections in Chapter 2. The first is devoted to women both as offenders and the victims of crime, and the way the police deal with domestic violence. In the second section, cases involving children and juveniles are examined for evidence of differential deployment. Then in Chapter 3 the way sexual offences are processed is analysed. An in-depth examination is conducted of the way child sex abuse is regarded as an area of expertise in which women are 'natural' experts. This is supported by an investigation of some of the mistakes made in the Cleveland Inquiry (Butler-Sloss, 1988). Hence, the analysis highlights the very special and potentially alienating levels of knowledge that are required to conduct investigations involving children and sexual offences. It seems that due to the tendency of police forces to provide sexual offences courses to women officers only, male detectives may find themselves ill-equipped to deal with child victims of sexual abuse. As children are often referred to the Family Protection Units for this reason, and much of the work involves sexual offences, only women officers in these specialist teams gain the necessary skills and expertise. On the other hand, the limited number of men in these departments find themselves dealing with the perpetrators, the 'husbands and boyfriends'. They hence take the role of enforcer, making the arrest and gaining the credit, but leaving the 'emotion work' to women colleagues.

Chapter 3 also provides evidence of the way women officers choose to join the Family Protection Units (FPUs) to gain investigative experience. In some of the group discussions which are analysed, they indicate that supervisors have told them that an attachment to the CID might be forthcoming after they complete their period of duty in the FPU. Ambitious women, tempted by the chance to get out of uniform and into some sort of specialism, or simply wishing to escape anti-social shifts, state in Chapter 3 that the FPU work is undervalued and that some of their male colleagues regard them as 'social workers'. Despite this lack of regard, and acknowledgement of the dedication expressed by the women in these interviews, it is clear that they find the work stressful in terms of caseload and content. As the work is dependent upon confidentiality, it is not discussed with colleagues from outside the units. Uniformed patrol officers and those working in specialties such as the CID are therefore largely unaware of the work the FPU conduct and the load they carry. In addition, some general patrol work is discussed in this chapter, with reference to the way men and women gain the necessary experience to join specialist departments, and the opinions of male officers towards female supervisors is explored.

A slight change of focus which leads into Chapter 4 is concerned with the way uniformed patrol or 'beat' work is carried out on a daily basis. One of the aims of this chapter is to explore the status of certain tasks in general policing activities. In the main, patrol work is not regarded as depending on high levels of expertise by officers on the ground, despite being regarded as one of the core activities with which the rank and file are engaged. Patrol work, often on foot, is the place all police officers begin their working lives, and the crux of the differential deployment debate is illustrated here. As a low status activity, it can be used as a marker within the hierarchy of tasks in order to place women and men along a continuum of skill and professional regard. Women's promotion has said to have been blocked in the past due to prejudice and discrimination by supervisors. As they fail to gain experience and a good 'arrest portfolio', their achievements are viewed as inferior by members of interview panels. As these panels are often composed of men, working by male rules in a 'masculine' organisation, it has been suggested that women are disadvantaged.

In order to test these allegations empirically, this book asks two questions at the beginning of Chapter 4: first, whether women are deployed differently on patrol, and second, if women are constrained by their gender in the police, to what extent could it prevent them from making arrests? Officers were accompanied on patrol for extensive periods, their actions analysed, and their arrest patterns collated. Qualitative data are supported in this chapter by a small-scale comparison with quantitative material which reveals the arrest patterns of men and women in one of the sub-divisions. Officers' daily working lives are observed and described, showing some potentially catastrophic events as they were patrolling one of the busiest and supposedly most dangerous areas in Britain. Attitudes towards danger are explored in this chapter with reference to the way supervisors may be deploying men and women differently. Evidence is evaluated in the course of the analysis, which considers this supposition and the way technology such as computerised control rooms might negate this process.

In Chapter 5 this focus upon gender is moved to the study of the problematic nature of masculinities through an examination of certain specialist posts which are usually occupied by men, such as those concerned with cars, guns and horses. The discussion is about officers in 'rarefied' posts, who are removed from low status patrol work, and allowed to act 'as men', as opposed to an increasingly 'feminised' version of the police. These officers have the right to use force as a strategy. In the case of the mounted branch, for example, this involves using their elevated position on top of 'two tons of horseflesh' to move crowds. Firearms officers have the ultimate in terms of power and lethal force, and the men in cars, calling themselves the 'cruisers', have high-powered vehicles which are constantly updated in an attempt to outmanoeuver the 'scumbags'.

In this penultimate chapter, four categories of stereotypically masculine attitudes are examined; the first being the way the concept of professionalism is used by police managers to encourage certain behaviour within the ranks. In certain circumstances this is used by these officers to justify or excuse their actions when they are less satisfactory than could be normally expected. In the next category, which is competency, the way men attempt to be adequate, if not necessarily 'perfect', police officers, is discussed. In the third category, examining sexuality and power, the way men bolster their heterosexual image and prowess by discussing women's bodies, pornography and their sexual activities, compared with their inability to deal with cases of sexual assault or 'perversion', is analysed. In the final category, the concept of heroism is used to examine the way men in the police behave towards women, children and victims of accidents and brutality whilst maintaining their front of masculinity.

The concluding chapter reflects on the way gendered bodies are regarded as being so significant in policing, and compares theoretical approaches with the 'lived experience' of the participants outlined in the study. Indeed, as the material which is to follow is primarily ethnographic data, it begins where other studies mentioned earlier, such as Turner (1996), Mackenzie (1998) and Scott (1997), have ended. By emphasising the importance of the gendered body and recognising that men and women, even as neuter police 'officers', cannot leave their bodies, the analysis develops a number of key themes in the existing 'cop culture' literature. It differs in comparison to those by 'malestream' writers such as Reiner (2000), Young (1991) and Hobbs (1988) because gender is placed at the centre of the analysis. In addition, it is an extension of work by feminist writers on the police such as Heidensohn (1995), and those who have examined equality of opportunity in the police such as Anderson *et al.* (1993) and Jones (1986), as it highlights the importance of the hitherto 'absent body' (Turner, 1992:67). In summary, this book provides a 'dirty fingernails ... and battle-scarred' (Hobbs, 1993:49), empirical examination of various approaches to the study of embodiment and police culture which have previously been discussed without the benefit of ethnographic observation or analysis.

Chapter 2

Gendered specialists: dealing with women and children

Various studies analysing the way women are employed in the police have portrayed them as occupationally segregated and marginalised. Research by Anderson *et al.* (1993), Jones (1986), Young (1991) and more recently, Walklate (2001), suggest that female officers are often relegated to 'low status' departments dealing with women and children. One explanation for this situation is that it can be attributed to traditional structures within the organisation and another to the existence of a 'cult of masculinity' (Smith and Gray, 1983:91). Analysts concerned with the workings of the police machine, such as Holdaway (1994) and Hoyle (2000), have debated this relationship between structure and culture. Hence this chapter will be concerned with the first of these two main strands of the debate as an explanation for what appears to be a situation that disadvantages women in the police. It will be explored by comparing policies and statistics with what happens in practice, and whether there is any evidence to support the notion that organisational structures are gender specific. In later chapters there will be an evaluation of the evidence supporting the existence of a 'macho cop' culture and the effects of subtle nuances of police behaviour upon 'gendered' policing. Evidence collected during fieldwork observations of officers working in specialist posts and incidents involving work traditionally associated with women officers is analysed there. This will compare structural elements such as policies, statistics and the literature on promotion and deployment with the views of the officers themselves. The discussion will also consider the fieldwork data to see whether it supports the commonly held belief that as the organisational majority is male, policing is dominated by masculine ideologies, and these combine to create an oppressive, 'male' environment.

Structural constraints

Organisational structure can be differentiated from 'culture' in that it is more concerned with how the organisation operates regulations or controls, which attempt to direct how working arrangements are enacted. Aspects of these rules are then adopted by other members of the organisation, converting them into policies, practices and ways of working, subject, of course, to the influence of occupational culture. Examples of this in the police would include promotion procedures, the rank system and equal opportunities policies. Organisational structures create a framework for the way people behave, although this is often subverted by individual actors. These structural constraints can also be viewed in a more abstract way, as Young describes women in the police being assigned 'structural marginality' (1991:191). Here he is using the term to describe the way male hierarchies in the police create oppositional categories, with women situated quite firmly outside the male cultural domain. Indeed, throughout his discussion of women in the police, Young attributes great importance to 'prestige structures'; he uses them to support field observations that men are hostile to women in the police and that women can never compete or achieve full parity in the police service.

More tangible elements of police structure are working practices, recruitment policies, and selection for promotion, specialist posts and training. These can be examined for evidence of gendered assumptions which may perpetuate themselves and provide justification for practice. An example would be that as women do not apply for the traffic department, they are assumed not to be interested in this type of work, and so there is little point in trying to recruit them. As this implies, structural and cultural elements relating to practices and policies are constantly informing and reinforcing each other, and so are difficult to separate. Structured sets of rules about behaviour inform organisational culture and the way they are arranged can affect the way certain groups of workers are perceived. It has been suggested that these organisational structures, informed and controlled by masculinist cultural ideals, continue to sustain certain barriers in the police, affecting the progress of women officers. A range of studies have asserted that female officers are treated unfairly due to their gender, despite equal opportunities legislation.

One of these studies is by Martin, who questions the impact of equal opportunities policies on the daily lives of women officers. She interviewed nine women constables and 25 male officers of various ranks from a UK police force. She found senior officers 'embarrassed' because there were no promoted women officers in the division in which she was conducting the interviews (1996:514–5) and argues that the implementation of the force's equal opportunity policy had led to some women officers believing they were coerced into joining 'traditional all-male' departments following their probationary period. Despite this, four of the nine women constables interviewed were working in departments dealing with sexual and child abuse. Martin concludes, therefore, that despite this area of work often being viewed as 'women's work' and 'low status', compared to traditional CID posts, there are reasons for women to choose this type of work. She says that it allows them to remove themselves from the more 'competitive' areas of male-dominated areas of police work and to escape shift work and generally 'hated' uniform (1996:517).

In another study, both male and female officers were asked why they had not applied for promotion in the past three years. Women tended to reply that they were too young in service or felt that they lacked experience, and 17 per cent of women (compared to just 5 per cent of men) said that they had not applied for promotion due to *'potential conflict with domestic commitments'* (Holdaway and Parker, 1998:52 original emphasis). A significant group of women also said that they had difficulty in working the hours required to obtain promotion, and that they had to work harder than their male colleagues to 'achieve a parity of acceptance' (ibid). Little had been done to encourage women's career development and, despite controlling for length of service, women reported receiving 'significantly less encouragement than men from their immediate supervisor, senior officers and colleagues' (ibid:54). Over a quarter of the men interviewed by Holdaway and Parker said that policies such as part-time working should be discouraged and over half believed that 'most women leave the service in order to get married and have a baby' (ibid:55). Senior officers apparently did not believe women were contracted and employed in the same way as men and believed they were not making a life-long commitment to policing (ibid:56). As a consequence, Holdaway and Parker argue, these ideas form constraints to women officers' opportunities for advancement and experiences at work, leading to 'strengthened and sustained unequal opportunities within the research constabulary' (1998:56).

One of the reasons women are prevented from applying for advancement and transfer into specialist posts is said to be 'differential deployment'. Unfair sexual discrimination occurs because the 'operational tasks women officers are asked to perform and their access to deployment and promotional opportunities' is limited (Brown, 1998). Further, this leads to a cyclical process defining women in the police within certain roles and capabilities. In a study of their structural representation and operational tasks, Brown used a questionnaire to ask about perceptions of task assignment and career opportunities, in terms of their own and opposite gender. Her results showed that women were over-represented in community relations and training departments and that over 60 per cent of male officers who responded to the questionnaire believed themselves to be 'dealing with violent offenders' more often than their women colleagues (1998:271).

Another study surveyed officers in a metropolitan force to explore the 'procedure adopted by one large, metropolitan force to handle grievances arising from breaches of the force's equal opportunities policy' (Brown and Gillick, 1998:122). They argue that one of the problems with the implementation of equal opportunities legislation in the UK police is related to the 'liberal, gender neutral' philosophy most have adopted. In effect, the authors argue that this philosophy encourages the belief that, 'women who can do a job equivalently to men should be given the opportunity to do so but implicitly accepts that the norm for the job is still based on a male model' (ibid:123). Further, they suggest, the mechanism to rectify problems under the equal opportunities legislation, namely the grievance procedure, had not been used. According to independent research, by 1992, three years after Home Office Circular 87/1989 had recommended their introduction, fewer than one third of officers had the confidence to use the system. Research in the first half of the 1990s into the grievance procedure, argue Brown and Gillick, has revealed that officers have little confidence in the policy or procedure for complaining about the lack of implementation of equal opportunities policies, bullying or harassment. Their results showed that whilst there had been a decline in the number of male supervisory officers in the force they studied in the first three years of the1990s, women supervisors had maintained their position, perhaps illustrating that 'equality policies have benefited women compared with men' (1998:127).

Despite this evidence that things may be improving slightly, in that the position of female officers is not deteriorating, in general it is difficult to deny that a range of difficulties exist for women in the police. However, to what extent organisational structures have contributed to sexual discrimination, and to women officers' position as an occupational minority, is debatable. In the past Jones argued that a set of 'unwritten selection criteria' existed (1986:129), limiting the number of serving women officers to a level which is acceptable to the male hierarchy and believed to be operationally viable. One of the changes which appear to have occurred since Jones' study is that more women applicants are being appointed. In 1994, for instance, 78 per cent of applicants were male and

22 per cent were female; from this group, however, only 8 per cent of the men were appointed, compared with 12 per cent of the women (HMIC 1996). Although the number of women joining the police service in England and Wales was increasing significantly, from 4 per cent in 1971, to 9 per cent in 1981 and 13 per cent in 1993 (HMIC 1996), their promotion, particularly to the more senior ranks, did not keep pace in relative terms. It has also been reported that even prior to the integration of women's departments into the main police organisation, proportionately less women were being promoted to supervisory positions. Even with increasing numbers of women constables being recruited during the second half of the 1970s and early 1980s, promotions for women continued to wane; for example, there were fewer women inspectors in 1982 (129) than ten years earlier in 1971 (134), according to Jones (1986:101). As the Home Office figures for 1995 show, however, there was an overall increase in the number of women in all promoted ranks in the first five years of the 1990s, and the percentage of women sergeants serving in provincial forces in England and Wales (excluding the Metropolitan Police) had almost doubled, rising from 4 to 7 per cent by 1995 (HMIC 1996) and to 9 per cent in 2000 (Home Office, 2000). Perhaps most significantly, in the highest ranks the promotion of women officers accelerated, as appointments of the first female assistants, deputies and chief constables occurred in various police forces throughout England and Wales. In effect, although figures are not statistically significant, the three women chief constables in posts in 2000 represent 6 per cent overall and the 12 women assistant chief constables constitute 8 per cent of the total.

The occupational structure statistics reported by HMIC in 1996 showed that once women began to compete for supervisory posts they achieved promotion more quickly than men. If the 837 women who were serving as first line supervisors in provincial forces in 1994 had progressed through the rank structure at the same pace as their promotion to sergeant, gender ratios in the police hierarchy would have been radically transformed. There is some evidence that this did happen, with a 24 per cent increase in the number of women inspectors in four years, rising from 153 in 1990 to 200 in 1994 (HMIC 1996) and to 394 by mid 2001 (Home Office, 2001), which is 7 per cent overall. A report drawn from some preliminary research for this book supported this statistical trend, as in 1994, in a small rural force, two female officers were promoted to sergeant, from a pool of approximately 150 women. At the same time, three men were promoted, from an establishment of about 1,200 male officers. As only these two women were qualified to apply, having passed the requisite exam, this represents a 100 per cent success rate. On the other hand, the three men who became sergeants at the same time were drawn from a pool of 124 qualified to apply, which is 4 per cent. Furthermore, all the women officers serving in the force had been promoted to sergeant earlier in their careers and at a younger age than those from their male cohort (Westmarland, 1999).

More recently, as a percentage of the police service in 2000, women represented around 17 per cent of the total number of officers in England and Wales, with just over 20,000 female officers in total (Home Office, 2000). This represents a steady increase in numbers over the decade, as in 1990 there were only approximately half this number with 10,837 serving women officers (HMIC, 1996:85). One of the questions that need to be addressed, however, regarding differential deployment, is what women officers are actually *doing* in the police in terms of tasks which are reasonably quantifiable, and one place to start is the specialist departments which seem to recruit women more than men. This is partly a historical legacy because in the UK, until the mid 1970s, occupational segregation was perfectly legal, with female officers having a separate rank structure within their own departments. Women were often located in a physically separate part of the building, with their own offices and changing facilities, and a similarly segregated set of tasks to carry out. These duties were concerned with children, women suspects and sexual assaults. Once integration took place all officers were required to be prepared to carry out exactly the same tasks and duties, with some minor exceptions relating to decency in the searching of suspects. It has been argued, however, that that certain types of cases – equating to those of the old 'policewomen's' departments – are still being imposed upon women in the police; and they persist due to the 'dirty work' being left to men whilst the system '"ghettoises" women's issues' (Walklate, 1995:119).

It seems, therefore, that women are confirmed as a structurally marginalised group of workers, segregated from 'real' policing, due to their prominence in certain specialist departments. It has been argued that women have been kept in their 'rightful' place and away from 'danger' on the streets fighting crime, in the 'safe' environment of familial violence and sexual abuse. This is associated with the public/private nature of women's skills and, Walklate has suggested, a series of complex organisational mechanisms allow police forces to maintain that they are an equal opportunities employer whilst specialist posts in areas such as domestic violence are usually occupied by women. As shown above, she argues women are kept away from 'proper policing', staying in symbolic locations that require sympathetic, supportive listening and communication skills. In a Home Office classification of departments dealing with 'Child, Sex, Domestic', for example, in ten forces grouped together with the larger research force studied for this book, in 1993, from a total of

273 officers, 199 were women and 74 were men at a time when around 13 per cent of the overall officers were women.

So the argument is that women find it difficult to achieve promotion in the police because they are prevented from gaining experience in certain key departments which are considered to be essential for success. Whilst they are being kept busy with a myriad of often difficult-to-solve problems such as domestic abuse, their male colleagues are gaining experience in the CID, conducting murder enquiries, becoming 'known' in the right circles and generally building up a portfolio that will help at promotion interviews. As Westmarland and Yearley illustrate (2001), male officers were much more likely to 'tell a good war story' at interviews for selection to the CID. Their observations of selection interviews revealed that this resulted in male applicants being given higher 'scores' on their interview performance and were more likely to be successful. Meanwhile, women officers can receive 'further, specialised training' related to the duties with which the officer may be employed in areas such as domestic violence, child abuse and sexual assault, according to a report on the position of women in Britain (HMSO, 1991:65). Hence, with reference to differential deployment of women police officers, there are three main questions to be posed regarding structural issues. First, why does there seem to be an assumption that dealing with sexual matters or those concerning children is 'women's work'? Second, do perceptions surrounding weight and body strength define the type of tasks to which women are assigned? Third, are they being permitted to enter certain specialist areas of policing on a quota basis, in order to present the illusion of equality?

As mentioned in the introduction, the aim of the first part of this chapter is to look at evidence supporting the notion that there are structures within the police which perpetuate certain gendered practices regarding deployment. It has been suggested by previous studies that these structures which are said to control women officers come from two sources. First, the 'management' as a traditional, patriarchal, quasi-military group of men, hostile to women, which strives to perpetuate clearly drawn lines dividing masculine and feminine. Second, men who are encountered on a daily basis by policewomen during their working lives, either as colleagues or 'customers'. Male colleagues being resentful of encroachment into their exclusive power domain has been examined to some extent in the literature, but with the exception of Dunhill (1989), Heidensohn (1995) and Stanko (1994), very few studies have looked at power differentials between women officers and 'service users' – suspects and victims of crime. Hence, three areas with which female officers are traditionally associated will be discussed here: dealing with women, especially those who have been the victims of domestic violence, cases involving children, and in the next chapter, sexual crimes.

Dealing with women

Women are said to be constrained throughout their careers due to male structural controls and one of the ways this is illustrated is that they become gendered specialists in the field of 'domestic' assault. The main reason this is said to have occurred is that it is a result of the publicity surrounding the unsympathetic treatment of women who were the victims of violent or sexual assault in the home. This became a call for change, and 'dedicated' units were created in almost all police force areas. This strategy became fashionable and regarded as 'best practice' in this area in terms of deterrence and prevention, with various initiatives featured in police practitioners' journals and magazines. Many of the studies which were discussed in these publications were instigated by Home Office circular 60/1990, which directed forces to improve their responses to domestic violence. At the same time, in the academic field, feminists were writing about the inappropriate treatment of female victims by the police and women's groups and organisations were campaigning for change. In particular, there was a call for female victims to be dealt with by women officers, whom, it was suggested, would be more empathetic.

Throughout the1990s women were recruited into domestic violence units, sometimes called 'Child and Family Protection Units'. Forces across the country competed to be seen as leaders in novel methods of responding to domestic violence. As the political agenda changed towards the middle and end of the decade, however, visible crime fighting with 'proactive' street-level policing became more important. In most forces there was a trend towards non-uniform, supposedly invisible 'service' and headquarters posts being swept away, in order to fulfill the call for more 'bobbies on the beat' and more officers in the 'crime' squads. Consequently, some of the domestic violence units were disbanded, and new methods had to be found to deal with disputes in the private sphere of the family. In force areas where the dedicated, specialised units were closing, which included one of those studied for this book, police managers now had to devise an alternative to cope with the problem of high numbers of recurring domestic assaults. A solution needed to be found which would protect women, so that forces could not be accused of inactivity, yet had a minimum cost in terms of police or other agency resources. In the UK some forces turned to evidence from the well-known

Minneapolis experiment, where sample groups had been used to assess the effects of policing policies upon the incidence of domestic violence. Further evidence, from other studies, was also drawn upon to formulate policy; for example, some research suggested that by the time the average domestic dispute came to the attention of the police, the victim had suffered violence for an average of two years (Dobash and Dobash, 1979, Pahl, 1982) resulting in as many as 35 previous assaults (Horley, 1988). In addition, intra-relationship murders were often shown to have had a long history of requests for assistance from the police, so arresting the perpetrators of domestic assaults came to be recognised as the most 'successful' long-term strategy. As a result of these studies, and most crucially the Minneapolis experiment, which concluded that men who had been arrested following an assault were much less likely to re-offend, more legal intervention was advocated in the UK. One reason for this was that following a number of replication studies in America and Canada, a study of the 'victim protection-offender arrest' model was conducted in collaboration with the Metropolitan Police, in 1985 (Edwards, 1989), which was also to be influential in police policy making.

Rubbish calls

As Hoyle explains, this research by Edwards led to Home Office recommendations in Circular 1990/60 that officers should 'arrest perpetrators where there is evidence of an offence' (2000:65). Although domestic violence was more firmly placed in the operational domain it was still regarded as being peripheral to 'real policing' by some officers. It has been well publicised that the police find calls to domestic disputes frustrating due to their often inconclusive outcome, referring to them as 'rubbish' work. From her comparative study of women police in the UK and US, Heidensohn says that 'Highest values still attached to those who caught serious villains in both systems, and "domestics" were seen as rubbish work' (1995:220) It could be suggested, therefore, that calls which are regarded as low status would be assigned to women officers as the 'natural' specialists in such matters. Indeed, from her research Heidensohn argues that the increasing numbers of female recruits and their larger role in work connected with rape and domestic violence has meant that issues which rely upon a high level of public confidence in policing have become more important due to the association of women officers with these areas of work (ibid:219), although in the USA, skills training was becoming less gender specific. Empirical evidence collected during the fieldwork carried out for this book support Heidensohn's assertions, as very few police officers, either male or female, were heard to make positive remarks when the control room directed them to domestic disturbances. Despite their apparent lack of popularity, however, when calls come through via the patrol car radios with 'reports from neighbours of a fight in progress' they take precedence over any jobs waiting for that particular crew. This is because incidents involving violence and the possibility of personal injury are prioritised. So calls over officers' personal radios from the control room operator stating 'I have a report of a violent domestic at … ' or, '… woman caller requesting assistance … boyfriend/husband smashing the house up', or '… a phone call from child at … parents fighting … ' would be regarded as urgent. In such cases, these jobs are issued to the crew in the patrol car, and the control room 'puts a delay' on the various other calls. Sometimes, if there is an outstanding routine job such as an attempted burglary, the operator will inform the crew that they are clear to deal with the domestic as the operator will telephone the people who are awaiting their attention, to tell them it may be some time before they are visited. Hence the so-called 'rubbish work' actually provides a diversion from much of the repetitive daily routine of statement taking and looking at windows that would-be burglars have attempted to break open.

One argument supporting differential deployment of women officers could be that control room staff view domestic assault as the type of work women should be directed to attend. In the six months of observation of the second larger police force, however, there was a large subdivision dubbed 'domestic city', and this was not the impression gained. 'Domestics' tend to receive high priority, and given the relatively small number of women on shifts (about 1:5) and the demands of the workload, especially in the evenings, the flexibility which would allow control room staff to differentiate on the basis of gender does not exist in practice. In addition, although police officers genuinely seem to dislike calls to violent incidents in the home, there are situations in which force and strength are seen as the main skills necessary and these situations would be regarded as physically tough and demanding. Common examples of this include drunken husbands or partners refusing to leave the house, or trying to gain entry to premises by force. This problem of trying either to eject, or to keep out, violent men is not one that officers view as a 'softer' aspect of policing. Indeed, many of the calls are attended using blue lights and sirens and are regarded as high-adrenalin cases. Even on occasions when the perpetrator has disappeared, male officers often see it as their role to comfort the woman who has been abused and to drive around the locality looking for the perpetrator. On one occasion during the fieldwork there was a case where a woman's ex-partner had caught a live fox, and left it to strangle itself, by hanging it from an exterior door handle with a rope, causing the woman a prolonged period of high anxiety as she was trapped in her house until the police arrived. In situations such as these, the male police officers seem to regard their role as hero-protector. At one incident, where a man was arrested following threats of violence, he was told, whilst complaining about being taken to the police cells, 'Well, this'll teach you to go picking on women then, won't it?' (male PC, 1995).

In general, therefore, it is suggested here that dealing with female survivors in domestic disputes is not necessarily regarded as the domain of women officers. On the other hand, this is not to say that women are never deployed in certain ways in operational situations, especially regarding crimes involving sexual assault. In addition to the structural/ career and management element of alleged constraint, however, a protective 'care and control' attitude has been alleged to exist in the police towards women officers which affects their deployment. In physically dangerous situations, previous ethnographic accounts have suggested that the male police hierarchy attempts to censure the sexual morals and actions of the female minority (Holdaway, 1983, Smith and Gray, 1983, Young, 1991). In his description of the way women are denigrated and categorised, for example, Young recounts the various unflattering and sexually explicit names policewomen are given. He goes to great lengths to show that highly insulting so-called 'terms of endearment' are used by the men to keep female colleagues 'marginalised' whilst they attempt to control them (Young, 1991:242). Women officers encountered in the course of the fieldwork seemed well aware of these attempts to exert a controlling influence over their private and sexual lives. In general this appears to be more pronounced for women who are unmarried, divorced or separated, and those known to be experiencing marital 'difficulties'. Various nuances of sexual 'availability', or potential availability, en- courage the apparently accepted norm of women being coerced and controlled by male officers on the shift. In a study completed before the one quoted above, Young's description of police life recounts the authority the organisation had over officers' partners. Within living memory the wives of male officers were not allowed to be employed outside the home without the permission of the divisional super- intendent. In one case an officer was disciplined for failing to 'control his woman because she was working as a teacher' (1984:87). So although these regulations are now obsolete, women officers are still much more 'visible' and noticeable in terms of relationships and liaisons, because they are in a minority ratio of approximately 5:1 in general shift work, and often younger than the average age of the male officers with whom they work. The male majority have more opportunities to discuss the women's appearance, bodies and general demeanor amongst themselves. More specifically, in close working partnerships such as traffic patrol, there have always been allegations of sexual 'misbehaviour' since the integration of male and female officers. It is alleged that because two officers work closely together and are generally out together in a car, in some sort of bizarre reenactment of 'marriage' sexual liaisons are possible and often advantage is taken of the freedom this affords. A woman officer who had worked in the traffic department explained that she always arranged a social evening with her husband and her current working partner and his wife or girlfriend, to dispel suspicions, through 'everyone getting a look at each other'. Another officer, an experienced woman sergeant, explained about sexual politics within her shift, saying that one of the new, young and attractive probationers was being targeted as a 'conquest' by some of the men on the division. From observing her behaviour it was obvious that this fairly naive new recruit was flattered by the attention, but as the older, more experienced officer pointed out,

> She doesn't realise it yet, but in this job word gets around, and wherever she goes after this, they'll hear about it. I want to say to her, watch out, you'll regret what you're doing here (female sergeant, 1995).

Another example of women having to be careful about their 'private' lives and morals was revealed when driving through the city with a policewoman one night. On passing a thin, lanky youth walking along a footpath, she started laughing and said,

> See him? I had a dream about him the other night. I dreamt I was going out with him and the bosses found out. Can you imagine it? What they would say? (female PC, 1995)

She was laughing as she recounted that she thought the dream had been the result of her remembering having arrested him a couple of weeks previously, and in response to her cautioning him about anything he said being written down and used in evidence, he had said, 'Fancy a shag?'

A similar story of a fear of being associated with the 'underworld' was told by another woman officer encountered during the fieldwork. She said she had recently been in a restaurant with a female friend and they had found themselves on a table near to some members of a locally notorious gang. A couple of 'the lads' had come over to their table saying to her, 'Here – don't I know you from somewhere?' Her friend, a nurse, being unaware of their suspect identity had said, 'Well, I work at the General Hospital'. Both women were therefore assumed to be nurses, and members of the gang stayed at their table for a chat, one of them remarking to the policewoman, 'Oh yes, that's where I know you from, you've probably stitched my wounds at some time or other'. As the policewoman told her friend that she wanted to leave the restaurant as quickly as possible after this, they asked for the bill and were told it had already been paid. She had found it difficult to insist to the restaurant owner, who was worried about upsetting 'the Gang', that she should pay for her meal. She said that she would have found it difficult to justify to her senior officers allowing the criminals to pay, but at the same time she did not want them to become suspicious. Another policewoman was confined to desk duties inside the station because her boyfriend had been arrested for fraudulently conducting mortgage agreements, the case involving a wide-ranging and complicated investigation connected to the gang.

Such paternal controls by the managerial hierarchy can be presented as care and concern for women by their supervisors. It is likely that female officers will find themselves in more potentially compromising situations, given that men often expect to pay in social situations and are recorded as involved in crime much more than women. In the restaurant scenario described above it is unlikely that a male officer would have found himself in a similarly compromising situation. In the next section various aspects of surveillance, including monitoring of sexuality, strength and certain aspects of clothes, body, hair and make up, will be examined as illustrations of the way women are monitored by their colleagues. However, to finish this section on organisational structures, some evidence will be discussed that suggests women themselves may be choosing certain areas of police work in which to specialise. This counterbalances the earlier assertion that female officers are being denied access to certain posts and directed into others through male police structures. An example that was encountered during the fieldwork was a woman sergeant who helped to set up a domestic violence unit in one of the forces studied, in the late 1980s. She said that she had been invited, as a female officer with over 20 years' experience, to be in charge of the new set-up in her area. Having just failed the preliminary part of a driving course which aimed to prepare her to transfer into a traffic department, this seemed to be an inviting option. She explained that she had not been allowed to stay for the main part of the advanced driving course because,

… I didn't get on with my instructor, and I was sent home after only a week (female Sergeant, 1995).

Despite this disappointment she said her time in the Domestic Violence Unit (DVU) had been enjoyable, and she recounted, with obvious satisfaction, that she once had to 'hit a violent husband who refused to be locked up for hitting his *own wife* in his *own home*' (fieldnotes 1995). In this case it seems that she had failed to complete her driving course due to male expectations and a personality clash, but was asked to run the DVU, a classic example of keeping women in their traditional place. This could be analysed as a stereotypical case of men protecting their own traditional working arenas – fast cars, exciting chases, life out on the streets, impersonal yet measurable. In effect, this would serve to persuade women that their arena or 'expertise' should be caring, personal, dealing with problems which will have at the very least, a protracted and possibly unsatisfactory conclusion. In a care or control, personal versus private debate, this case would fit neatly into Reiner's definition of cop culture developing as a 'patterned set of understandings that help officers cope with and adjust to the pressures and tensions confronting the police' (2000:87). As shown in various ways throughout the discussion so far, police culture is not famed for being woman-friendly and there are many examples from the fieldwork throughout this book which support this view. However, having examined some of the ways management structures work to control and constrain on the basis of gender, evidence will now be analysed which suggests that the situation is more ambiguous than has been claimed in the past, at least regarding structures in the police which constrain women's career choices. In some areas of police work, it will be argued here, women officers are more able to choose, have autonomy, and use their 'femininity' to achieve control of their careers than has been claimed previously.

Woman-friendly structures

The extent to which women have to mask their 'femininity' or behave in masculine ways to achieve success in the police is an interesting debate. In the US a study showed how women officers working in patrol situations tended to adopt certain gendered roles. These styles were classed as feminine, semi-masculine, masculine or neutral, and were adopted in order to blend into the system (Wexler, 1985). Young's ethnography of police culture also recognises the woman officer who is not regarded as traditionally attractive and adopts overly masculine characteristics to deflect unwelcome attention from male colleagues. He acknowledges, however, that this stereotypical 'burglar's dog', as he describes this type of officer, may not be typical, as there is a newly emergent group of women in the police. He describes this latter type as '… competent new policewomen', explaining that they are educated, feminine, attractive and professional (1991:240–1) which poses structural difficulties for the male police hierarchy and challenges certain aspects of the masculine occupational culture. In effect, structures cannot cope with this 'new strange breed' of women officer, who is independent, unwilling to 'blend in' and more capable and competent than many male colleagues and so cannot be denigrated in the way the previous group were. This type of officer was encountered during the fieldwork for this book. They revealed during discussions and interviews that they were not only free to choose specialisms and work in traditional areas of male dominance, but that they were being positively encouraged. As one explained,

> I was working in the custody suite as a sergeant one day and I was called up to headquarters. It came as quite a shock, I was *told* I would be working with the Chief Constable, as his staff officer, and promoted to inspector (female Inspector, 1995).

Another woman, in her early thirties, recounted a similar story,

> One day I was working away in my department as a DS, quite happy, you know, and the next I was off to London as a special assistant on a special job, top fraud stuff, with automatic promotion (female Inspector, 1995).

Although this may seem to suggest that male structures are still controlling these women, especially as they both point out that they had very little choice, they are examples of women being promoted, taken into previously male, specialist areas. They did not indicate that they were likely to refuse such as good chance for promotion or to feel they were being 'constrained' or manipulated. Another woman who had been working in the CID explained,

> I needed a move for personal reasons so I went to see the Superintendent and it was agreed that I could have an attachment to the Public Order Group. I went for a fitness test and got on (female PC, 1995).

In addition to these women who had been moved to specialist areas or departments, during the fieldwork with the larger research force three patrol officers were observed working part time, and several others had young children whose personal circumstances had been taken into account when their duties were arranged. One of the part-timers said,

> When I came back after my second baby, we sat down and worked out a shift system which would benefit them and me. So, because my husband's in the CID, I can come in on Saturdays, he looks after the kids, and they find it quite useful to have a woman around to deal with searching the young lasses – there's lots of shoplifters (female PC, 1995).

In general, a similar view of the situation was offered by the officers responsible for the management of personnel issues. One of these police managers explained that when women return from maternity leave,

> We organise a mutually agreed system with the woman, if this can't be done, it's a failure on the part of management. When women return – whether they want to work part-time – I have them in to find out what would suit them best – it might be a nine to five office job, or maybe shifts to fit in with their partner (male Inspector, 1995).

He went on to say that flexibility was necessary on both sides: 'It's no good her coming to me and saying, "I'll only work every other Wednesday morning" '. But in general he said they always sort out a mutually acceptable situation. Of course, the women for whom this arrangement had not been successful were not available to interview as they would have left the organisation, although the impression from other women officers whose opinion was sought was that the system is generally fair. This view was confirmed by some of the women who were working and managing the care of young families. Most were married to police officers, and one said,

> …and we've arranged our shifts so that it means we can cover the nights, and then we have some help, but it works quite well (female PC, 1995).

As the evidence from the final part of this section shows, some women are being offered high-status transfers to departments dealing with public order, serious crime and offering high flying promotion opportunities. In addition, compromises were seen to be available for women returnees and those wishing to work part time. This is not to say that the situation is completely satisfactory and evidence will be provided in the discussion on specialisms which will show that ultimately power often remains with men in the police. However, before embarking upon a discussion of who deals with certain cases that may be 'gender specific', there needs to be a definition of what these categories of 'children', young people or juveniles mean. People who can be classed as 'non-adult' come into contact with the police for many, diverse reasons. They can be divided into at least four groups, with some of them being in more than one category, including children and young and/or 'vulnerable' victims; child and juvenile offenders; young people or juveniles who are perceived as needing 'control' and those in need of care, not necessarily having committed any offence. In a similar way to cases involving domestic violence, many calls to the police to deal with children result in 'no further action', and very often are not associated with a crime; the police are called by the public to act as social controllers, perhaps in a warning or preventative way, or as carers, when no-one else seems to be available to fulfill this role. As the Audit Commission noted in their study of the way duty time is allocated, about 10 per cent of police work is concerned with nuisance and anti-social behaviour. This is a relatively large percentage when compared to 'crime' accounting for 30 per cent of calls to the police. One of the main examples the Commission cited was 'youths congregating on street corners' and the most common issue raised at public consultation meetings was found to be 'juvenile nuisance and anti-social behaviour' (Audit Commission, 1996:20–21). In addition, members of the public who were questioned by the Audit Commission researchers said their top priority for improving community safety was 'better parental discipline' and for 40 per cent of those interviewed, police presence on large housing estates was regarded as the 'main priority' (ibid:15).

In the following section, several examples of these reported attitudes will be examined and it will be argued that even if work with young people and children is regarded as gendered work, the 'appropriate' role may be viewed as 'masculine' rather than traditionally carried out by women. In other words, much of the routine work concerning children which was observed during this study was unrelated to any offence, but still tended to be of a paternalistic, controlling nature, rather than exclusively care and hence 'feminine'. Of course, there are exceptions to this approach, as Chapter 3 will show, where cases of sexual abuse are discussed. In general, in carrying out the average workload of routine policing, contact with children and young people is not confined to women officers.

'Natural' expertise

The obvious place to look at officers who are regarded as 'official' specialists is within the Child and Family Protection Units. In the smaller, rural force investigated for this study there were several of these across the various subdivisions. In most cases these units consisted of an office with a couple of desks and an identifying notice on the door. In general it was female officers who were working in these departments, often not very long out of their initial two-year probationary period, being supervised by women with slightly longer service. Once an initial familiarisation period has been worked in a unit, they attend a training course, usually at force headquarters, with input from 'outside' professionals such as doctors and psychologists. In addition, they learn specialist interviewing techniques, such as the preparation of video evidence, from police trainers. In terms of day-to-day operation, the units receive referrals from uniformed patrol officers, the CID, social services and calls from members of the public, which can be diverted to their confidential extension number. As the units are only open during office hours, requests for their attention are normally passed by paperwork or from the control room; individual forces often have a system of printed forms which are completed by the patrol officers and sent up to the Unit, or they may be telephoned following a request by personal radio from a patrol officer. In addition, an answering machine service is available out of hours and at weekends, although there is emergency cover. Callers to the general police telephone number are diverted to this extension to leave a message if the operator thinks it is appropriate, or a senior officer can authorise a member of the team to be called from home, if something is thought to be urgent or serious enough.

An exact description of the type of incident which falls within the remit of a child protection unit is difficult to define precisely, due to the diverse nature of the work. A general question about the type of cases they deal with elicits replies from officers such as; 'All sorts' or 'Everything really', 'Anything to do with children – sexual abuse, neglect, supporting social services', but from field observations they seem to be primarily concerned when it is clear that classifiable offences have been committed, and when they perceive the Crown Prosecution Service (CPS) will be interested in taking the case forward. In particular their workload seems to be significantly concerned with sexual assaults, although some units will only deal with 'familial' sex, others with any offences against children, by strangers, or otherwise. As the following table shows, the two research forces investigated here have a large number of women officers in child protection. As these departments are the visible and public part of the police organisation dealing with matters concerning children, they are often used as an example when occupational marginalisation is discussed in the police. As the officially designated experts, women are back in their 'policewomen's' departments and, worse, they are now supervised by men, so even the autonomy of self rule is lost to them. It is necessary to question the relationship between this evidence of segregation and the supposed oppression of female officers, however, to determine whether 'male structures' are preventing equality of opportunity.

Evidence that appears to 'fit' too neatly with stereotypical assumptions needs to be investigated in more depth. It is widely believed, for example, from published figures on police specialists, that matters concerning children are dealt with by women officers. This type of work is acknowledged to be to be low status because it is the opposite of crime fighting, focusing on care and rehabilitation. It also seems to have been assumed that women have been placed in the child protection units as a result of male beliefs about their competencies linked to their 'natural' mothering abilities, despite women officers often being discouraged from having children of their own due to the demands of shift work. In order to investigate this situation, it is useful to compare it with the picture in traditional bastions of male power such as the CID. Data from the

Table 2.1: Child and family protection unit structure

Research force 1	(Total number of officers employed: 1,377)	
	1 Inspector (MALE)	1 Sergeant (MALE)
	1 Constable (MALE)	1 Sergeant (FEMALE)
	13 Constables (FEMALE)	

TOTAL: 3 Males (1 Constable) 14 Females (13 Constables)

Total: 17 officers (14 Constables)

Research force 2	(Total number of officers employed 3,581)	
	1 DC Inspector (MALE)	2 D Inspectors (MALE)
	6 Constables (MALE)	6 Sergeants (MALE)
	17 Constables (FEMALE)	

TOTAL: 15 Males (6 Constables) 17 females (17 Constables)

Total: 32 officers (23 Constables)

personnel department of one of the forces being discussed here, allowing for the fact that at the time these figures were recorded (1995) the male officers outnumbered the women 10:1, and had younger service profiles which may prevent them from applying for specialist posts, show that a significantly lower percentage of female applicants to the CID were successful. Only 12.5 per cent of the women applying for CID were successful, whilst for men it was 35 per cent. Statistics such as these seem to provide one explanation for the lack of promoted women – restricted deployment, through a lack of experience – which is so well established in the literature on gender and the police. Evidence from 'male' departments in Chapter 5 and statistics from the Home Office confirm suspicions about an organisation which is male-dominated, with women only superficially integrated, controlled by traditional, masculine structures. More in-depth ethnographic research on the general position of women in these departments dealing with children supplies further evidence. Applications for departments that are traditionally regarded as female specialisms are almost exclusively from women and if men do apply, they are regarded with suspicion by their colleagues. In these departments men sometimes find themselves experiencing role reversal, confined by their female officers, either as assistants who wait in the office answering the phone, accompanying the women officers when male perpetrators, 'the husbands and boyfriends' are arrested, or taking over the interviewing of the accused in rape cases. From field observations of case loads, a significant percentage of the resources available for child and family protection seem to be taken up with sexual matters, with neglect and physical abuse being regarded more as the domain of social services, rather than the police. In the next chapter it will be shown that sex offences, unlike general neglect, are almost always regarded as police work, and quantitative data will be used to support the assertion that their level of casework is substantial.

Offending children

In addition to the officers who are designated as 'experts' in the protection units, there are many instances in ordinary patrol work where children may be encountered. Generally, resources and deployment patterns do not permit individual matching of officers and incidents, and just as domestic incidents are regarded as routine work for patrol officers, both male and female, calls from the public about children or young people are regarded as ungendered. An example of this is a call from a resident, usually on a housing estate, about children causing a disturbance outside, for one of a variety of reasons. Over a period of months of fieldwork, it was seen that these calls have a seasonal cycle. Beginning in late August, requests come from local residents to stop 'kids climbing trees for conkers' or 'collecting wood, setting fires and knocking on doors for money', or 'letting off fireworks', through to 'throwing snowballs'. As one busy and frustrated police officer remarked after being sent to see some children throwing sticks at horse chesnut trees, but causing no harm,

> I'm sick of these type of calls – it's what kids *do*. Someone ought to say something about it. We've got better things to be doing (male PC, 1995).

Another very common call to the police regarding children, particularly in the early evening, is known as 'missing from home'. Worried parents telephone the police to report their child failing to return home at the expected time. Due to the extremely common occurrence of these calls, unless there is some unusual or seemingly sinister element to the call, or the child is very young (under ten years old), this will be regarded as fairly low priority. Some officers will take other calls before going to this type of incident, on the basis that the child may turn up before they reach the house. Thus they can avoid listening to the story and filling in a complicated form, which must be written out by hand each time a child is reported missing. For 'regular runners' who reappear without fail, this is regarded as pointless. Another regulation which is supposed to be ad-hered to by the police is a check to see whether the child has returned, so that the name can be removed from the 'missing' register, and the police officer must see the child alone to question them about their whereabouts whilst away from home. From fieldwork observations it is argued here that this is not a task which is regarded as work especially reserved for women officers. Even in cases involving young female teenagers, whose parents suspect them of running away with older boyfriends, and express fears about under-age sex, coercion or 'moral' concerns, the task is still viewed as one involving paternalistic, informal control and general policing. Due to the limited number of women, officers who attend 'missing from home' cases are usually male, and were observed usually to conduct themselves as surrogate fathers, uncles or elder brothers, reassuring the parents that the child will soon return and promising to reprimand them when they eventually come back. At one of these incidents in the early evening a boy aged 12 had been 'missing' since lunch time. He arrived as two male police officers were comforting his mother. She was crying and asking the police officers what they thought might have happened, as the older of the two police officers took hold of the boy, pushed him into the hallway and launched into a lengthy session which consisted of several variations of,

> Do you think it's clever to get your mother in a state like this? She's been worried to death. Do you know what happens to kids like you? You start by staying out, and next thing you're down the police station – in the *cells* – and it isn't very *pleasant*. Is that what you want? (male PC, 1995)

At intervals the boy attempted to answer these rhetorical 'questions', but the officer cut him short with, 'Don't tell me lies, I don't like people who tell me lies'. At the end of the five minutes or so, during which the officer shouted continuously at the boy, who was staring at his feet, he was ordered upstairs, and he ran to do as he was told, relieved that his ordeal had ended. Later, in the patrol car, it was explained that police officers have to be capable of 'role playing'. The one who had reprimanded the boy added, 'Young cops, you know, they can't do it', inferring that his age and experience gave him an advantage. On another occasion, a young girl was reported missing, and her mother said she thought she might have gone to her boyfriend's house. As she was only 13, worries were expressed by her parents about her having sex with him, and the police officer replied that he would 'Go round to see the lad and have a word'. Again, this work is viewed as controlling men and boys, and so it is regarded as masculine, not one in which a policewoman might be specifically requested, despite the fact that sexual offences are usually handed over to women officers. In a similar way, young shoplifters, and to a lesser extent burglars and car thieves, are viewed in a paternalistic way by the police. At one incident, a male officer gave two young girls, aged 13, a thorough telling off about their morals, what their parents would say when he took them home, and how stupid they had been, for stealing a lip gloss from a shop. He had already explained to the store manager, privately, that no action would be taken against the girls because the amount was too small for the Crown Prosecution Service to proceed; so they were taken home to their respective parents, to tell them what had happened. At the second girl's house the parents were out, but the officer obviously felt it was his duty to make sure they punished her. On the way home she had been trying to put the blame onto the other girl and she became quite agitated, saying she had been bullying her, making her take the things from the shop; so at a convenient point the police officer stopped the car and turned round to face her, saying,

Look, I can get nasty if people don't tell me the truth, I don't believe that for one moment – everyone tries that excuse, it's the oldest one in the book. Don't tell me lies because I don't like it. It's natural to try to find excuses, but it's better to tell the truth (male PC, 1995).

To follow this up he telephoned the parents later, explaining that the girl had blamed her friend for the theft, saying that she had been 'made to do it'; but in his opinion this was a lie, and their daughter must take responsibility for her actions. As the value of the stolen lip gloss was minimal, this may seem to be rather strenuous police involvement, but the police officer viewed it as necessary to prevent further offences. He said that he thought the parents were taking a rather too forgiving stance with their daughter, who knew what she was doing, but was blaming her friend. In his opinion, the girl was misleading the parents, and he needed to sort the matter out, so that she would be punished by the parents and dissuaded from doing it again.

So the fieldwork suggests that work with young people or juveniles is not regarded as a specifically female domain. Despite previous studies suggesting that it is regarded as 'women's work', on patrol this does not seem to be the case. On the other hand, specialist posts in the area of child 'welfare' are disproportionately occupied by women officers. As Table 2.1 shows, where men are working in departments dedicated to children, sexual and domestic matters, they tend to be in a supervisory position. However, moving from the specialist roles to the general, previously accepted ideas that women officers deal more frequently with children are challenged on two main grounds. First, patrol officers cannot choose their own jobs – they are called to the next incident and usually it will be male officers who attend – and second, the work is seen as being of a masculine, paternal type, rather than any sort of 'mothering'. Even in cases where very young children are involved, and they are viewed as victims rather than offenders, male police officers immediately deal with the situation, and were not observed suggesting that a woman officer should take the call. An example which illustrates this was an occasion when a call came into the local police sub station from a woman who claimed her ex-husband had not returned her son following an access visit. It was early evening and two male constables who had just come on shift were preparing to go out on patrol. After taking details from the mother they went to the address she had given and found the man with his new partner and baby, caring for the toddler who was the subject of the call. He was aged about 18 months and clinging to his father, who wanted to keep him for 'just one more night'. Despite his protestations, the officers were quite insistent that the child must be returned to his mother, and took him and the child to her house in the police car. When the father returned to the car, having deposited the child with the mother, he was upset, because she was 'drugged up' and their little boy didn't want to stay with her. Sitting in the back of the police car, the father, who was a former army officer, started crying, which made the male police officers uncomfortable. One of them said to him,

> Oh come on mate, it can only get better, get yourself back in the army, and the culture; get into married quarters and you'll get custody. Your new girlfriend, she seems alright; do it the legal way (male PC, 1995).

On another occasion a call came in which was described by the control room as a 'domestic over children', which is usually a dispute involving custody. Arriving at a large block of high-rise flats, two male officers went upstairs and were invited into a living room full of people, with every seat occupied and two young boys sitting on the floor near the door, looking dejected. A woman pointed to them and told the officers,

> I've no room for them and *he* said he was having them for the weekend. My sister's been beaten up by her husband so I've said her and her four kids can stay here, and *they've* just arrived back (fieldnotes, 1995).

She went on to explain that their father, her ex-husband, had sent the two boys, aged eight and ten, to walk across the rough side of the city in the dark, to find their way back to their mother at 10.30 pm. It was not strictly a police matter, but the boys look so dejected and unwanted, and as the mother claimed to have no money for a taxi, the officers agreed to take them back to their father. As they left the flat she repeated to the boys, accusingly, 'Well, *he* said he wanted you', apparently for the benefit of the assembled room and police officers. Having driven across the city to another estate of dilapidated tower blocks, the officers found the father, who said that he usually had custody of the children, but claimed to have given his wife some money to look after them for the weekend, saying, 'Now her sister's turned up, she doesn't want them'. Although the two young boys were shivering, hungry and aware that neither of their parents wanted them, and the family environment seemed less than ideal, the two male police officers simply dealt with the situation as it was presented to them. At no stage in this matter was there any suggestion that a woman should be called to deal with the children.

On other occasions during the fieldwork, 'juveniles', of around 15 or 16 years old, were arrested on suspicion of committing crimes such as burglary, taking cars, or absconding from secure accommodation. In all of these instances, they were simply dealt with as another 'customer' for the system by male officers. Young suspects are not interviewed without an 'appropriate adult' being present, but once this person arrives, the process of fingerprinting and bail procedure simply advances as with any other case. Police officers seem to regard these young offenders as a 'good catch'. They fit into their scheme of the control of young people, who, they seem to believe, are a major problem for society. This may be influenced by what the Audit Commission identified as the public demand for action against 'prolific' offenders.

As with domestic violence cases, women officers were not specifically diverted from their routine tasks because of their gender. There was one exception observed during the fieldwork when patrolling in a personnel carrier with two women officers and a male sergeant. A man was standing at the roadside beside his car, indicating that he wanted to speak to the police. The van stopped and he came round to the window and said that he had nearly knocked a couple of young girls over, as they had just run in front of his car. He pointed around the corner in the direction they had gone and rather unwillingly, the sergeant driving the van said he would go to speak to them. The two girls, aged about 14, were sitting on a bench in a small paved area. At this point, without anything being said, the two women officers got out of the van, went over to the teenagers and made notes of their names and addresses, what had happened, where they had been and so on. It was quite late at night, after licensed premises closing time, and when the women officers got back into the van they agreed that the girls seemed unusually apologetic. The older of the two officers seemed disapproving and she remarked to her colleagues,

> I bet those two have told their parents they're at each other's house tonight, because it's far too late for them to be out. I've got a good mind to ring them up (female PC, 1995).

A few weeks later, this officer, who had been in the policewomen's department prior to integration, was observed arresting two boys, aged about 13, and insisting to the custody sergeant that they should be charged with the offence of 'drunk and disorderly' to the muted surprise of other officers in the room, one of whom confided later that most people would have regarded it as the lesser charge of 'drunk and incapable'. She also expressed disgust when the sergeant, later that night in the van, told a member of the public who was being 'difficult', to 'fuck off' through the open window, and turning to me in the back of the vehicle she asked,

Do *you* have to put up with language like that from the men you work with? (female PC, 1995).

When the opportunity for the researcher to speak to this woman privately on another occasion arose, she said that she regretted the closure of the policewomen's departments, and used to enjoy the work they were allocated and the freedom and autonomy they enjoyed. She also said that she had applied to work in the force's Child Protection Unit but had been rejected as unsuitable. On another night, the younger policewoman who was working with her when the incident above occurred expressed the view that this colleague represented the 'old style' policewoman, which perhaps explained her readiness to view work with young girls as her domain.

As this was the only example observed of women 'self selecting' to deal with children or young people, it seems reasonable to concur with the findings of an ethnography conducted in Northern Ireland, which stated that throughout the fieldwork in the Royal Ulster Constabulary, there were no recorded instances of policewomen being deliberately sent to deal with children (Brewer and Magee, 1991:51). On the other hand, there is evidence from other studies which analysed the quality of women's deployment experiences, in which the 'traditional' activities of female officers are described as being associated with women victims and offenders, children and juveniles. One study was conducted by Jones (1986) and in the section she devotes to the duties women are allocated she makes brief mention of children, saying that women were more readily available to interview them because they were often assigned to 'inside' station duties (Jones, 1986:69). Her study was conducted some years ago and, with the exception of sexual offences, Jones does not really provide any evidence to support the claim that women are deployed differently. Her evidence relies upon the work that women officers are *prevented* from doing, including violent physical incidents and 'unpleasant' or dirty jobs. This does not necessarily support her case that women are therefore dealing with children whilst not engaging in these other tasks. Indeed, throughout the section Jones devotes to differential deployment, upon which the main thesis of her book is based, (1986:69–79) there is relatively little empirical evidence to show that women are called upon to deal with children more often than men. This may be linked to her earlier assertion that there was 'ample confirmation' (ibid:69) from interviews and observational work, although this was limited to about 10 hours in total. This may not have been enough to provide evidence showing that supervisors were sending women to traditional activities concerning children and juveniles. It could also represent a view of the role of policewomen in the early 1980s.

Similarly, in her 'construction of a picture of the working life of policewomen' Walklate draws upon evidence from the mid 1980s and early 1990s to paint a bleak picture. She says that there is evidence that women are underrepresented in some specialist departments, and absent from others and that female officers are allocated work in low-status areas of the organisation because 43 per cent of those under 30 on station duty on Merseyside, UK, in 1985, were women (Walklate, 1995:116). As station duty is an area of police work which she describes as the 'least prestigious job', she is suggesting that gender is the controlling factor, but there may be other explanations. First, Walklate is comparing this statistic with the overall percentage of policewomen at the time (around 10 per cent), but does not mention that many of the women would be in the early stages of their careers, and therefore likely to be doing lower status duties. Many police forces now recruit a similar number of women as men, and so women could easily represent 50 per cent of the workforce at this position. Also, women who are pregnant are usually deployed in the station on light duties, and this can amount to a significant percentage of the workforce on some shifts. In her study of British and American women officers, mentioned earlier, Heidensohn (1995) claims that male officers seem to recognise that women can carry out unpleasant tasks, but still maintain there are certain areas in which they can be natural specialists. When members of the public they encountered on duty questioned the ability of women officers to 'change a wheel, or tow them home' male colleagues were reported to have supported their abilities, but in other cases the 'persistence of the "feminine" work-load on the shoulders of some British officers did lead to differences in reported reaction to them in situations where the gender agenda was being pursued' (1995:207). Earlier in her book Heidensohn explains that her aim is to give women in policing a voice, by using them to illustrate the role of women in social control and law enforcement. She concedes that no study of patrol work has been conducted in Britain, but she asserts that 'despite major legal and policy developments', there is no significant difference from their role in the past (ibid:64). She reviews the evidence and confirms Jones' claims about differential deployment, that integration is superficial, and women are still being confined to low-status work, such as administrative tasks, and kept away from detective or traffic work.

Another extensive study which considered the question of differential deployment linked working with women and children to losing the chance of promotion for women officers. Anderson *et al*. (1993) use extensive statistical data, collected using postal questionnaires, with a response rate of 69 per cent, with 1,810 female officers replying from an original target sample of 2,615. Respondents were asked: 'Compared with colleagues of the opposite gender how often are you asked to attend incidents involving the following?' They were then required to choose from 'Less, equally or more often', in respect of each of the categories 'victims of sex offences, young offenders and violent offenders'. When the data was collated it was discovered that a statistically significant number of women, representing 30 per cent of the total (428 respondents) indicated that they were being deployed with young offenders 'more frequently'. However, over double this number of the female respondents (970, or 69 per cent) said they were dealing equally with such cases (1993:62). The authors concluded that 'women officers were more likely than men to report being deployed on station duty; safer beats; accompanied patrol; dealing with victims of sexual offences and with young offenders' (ibid:61). In effect, however, almost 70 per cent said they were not being given duties associated with young offenders more often than their male colleagues.

Summary

It seems that the empirical evidence analysed here shows that the literature on differential deployment can be challenged. Indeed, although many previous studies assert that women are being coerced into dealing with children and young people, the evidence from this study differs from those findings significantly. Perhaps it is more convincing to write about women being discriminated against by reproducing some un-favourable impression of the work policewomen do, because as McLaughlin says, referring to a police ethnography, 'women are regarded as compassionate' (1996:78). In the study from which he takes this quotation, however, Brewer and Magee, (1991) say there were no examples of women being given cases to deal with children. In a similar way, Heidensohn relies upon a study by Jones (1986) and provides no primary evidence of women officers dealing with children more often than male colleagues, although in her interviews women officers say they do this type of work more than men. The study mentioned above, by Anderson et al. (1993), which Heidensohn quotes, also argues that women are differentially deployed because 30 per cent of the policewomen who replied to a questionnaire said they felt they dealt more with children than their male colleagues.

As noted at the beginning of this chapter, there is some evidence that women are working in specialisms linked particularly to child victims, but to what extent this is due to male structures is difficult to assess. It is argued here that there are numerous reasons women enter these specialist units, including being able to work office hours, which fits in with primary childcare; 'easier' physical work during pregnancy or following maternity leave and an interest in CID work thus using the child protection units as a route to gain investigative skills. Quite a large proportion of officers, both male and female, find their two-year pro-bationary period more than long enough to be in general uniformed patrol work and whilst men seem to be attracted to outdoor physical pursuits such as working with dogs, horses and specialist search and surveillance squads, women see themselves in 'clean' environments such as family protection. It is not really feasible to account for these differences using the explanation of paternalistic male structures in the police, as much wider questions about segregation in the workforce in society generally need to be addressed. However, from the evidence presented here it seems reasonable to assert that the small minority of women who are employed in the specialist departments, dealing with children, do not represent the majority of the work which is carried out with young people in general – this is simply the visible aspect. It could be argued that women are not being coerced to deal with children or to enter these departments any more than the men who apply for traditionally 'macho' specialties such as the CID are being 'controlled'.

Chapter 3

Sexual deployment: offences against decency

In the previous chapter it was concluded that beliefs about women officers being given work dealing with female survivors and child offenders and victims of abuse may be reliant upon their visible presence in specialist posts, rather than in terms of their general duties. In the first section of this chapter the differential deployment of women officers with regard to sexual offences will be examined, because it is generally believed that female officers have always dealt with the majority of these cases, as this type of work has been regarded as gendered (Brown and Campbell, 1991, Jones, 1986, McLaughlin, 1996, Walklate, 1995, Martin and Jurik, 1996). These findings are reinforced by Anderson *et al*, who found that 'Women constables were most likely to deal with victims of sex offences' (1993:62). In a more general discussion of the research that has been carried out on women in policing, Walklate (2001) explores two broad categories of investigation. The first, which has been termed the 'feminising' of policing and second, a debate about what constitutes 'proper' policing. In effect, she is citing these two areas as being at the heart of understanding the impact of equal opportunities policies and their effectiveness, drawn from Heidensohn's analysis of the situation (1995), which was discussed in the previous chapter.

This concept of 'feminisation' refers to the way published policies can be used by police forces to show that they are an 'equal opportunities' employer, so that posts which normally attract mostly female applicants, such as domestic violence units or child protection, can be openly advertised – and this involves a 'free choice' and self selection by women. Reasons behind these choices are therefore left unexplored by the force, as they have fulfilled their responsibility to be fair and equitable.

According to Walklate, however, 'cop culture' and a series of qualities which selectors may be seeking, such as being 'sympathetic, supportive, able to listen, able to communicate effectively etc' (Walklate, 2001:140) are often those skills women may see themselves as possessing. In effect, therefore, 'the resultant effect of these processes is that more women enter this specialist work and simultaneously a police force is able to defend its equal opportunities policy' because there are women working in specialisms. As noted earlier, an HMIC report in 1996 counted these women as being part of the general CID population, which points to the success of such policies nationally without really changing the position of women in the organisation.

To further this discussion, Walklate follows this description of the workings of 'feminisation' with arguments about what constitutes 'proper' policing. This, she suggests, is associated with core policing tasks and what are regarded as the main skills to do the job (2001:140). It is also linked to general notions about the ways in which women officers' qualities are best employed, mentioned above. Regarding the policing of the domestic arena, for example, she argues that police forces have been encouraged to take a more proactive stance – arresting the perpetrators and supporting survivors. This changing view of what the police are 'for' has an impact upon women officers because their role is also being redefined. Walklate offers two alternative views of the situation. The first is that as a result of the increasing prioritisation of domestic violence, women officers are moving into this reinvigorated area of policing, but are in fact just working in new version of the former, pre-integration, policewomen's departments. Some aspects of general police work are regarded as too dangerous for female officers, whilst 'problems' associated with women and children are their domain. This leaves the 'dirty work' to men and, as explained earlier, 'ghettoises' so-called women's issues such as the private sphere and women's ability to respond sympathetically to those subject to domestic violence, and yet allows the organisation to champion their women officers as specialists and for women officers to be convinced that they are working in the most effective way. Her second scenario is that equal opportunities policies are fully embraced and women and men can develop their careers equally in the police. Walklate provides less evidence and a less convincing argument for this latter scenario, stating that 'forces in the UK are a long way from achieving this goal' (ibid), but does suggest that it could be achieved with a fundamental reappraisal of what 'proper' policing is, by challenging male beliefs and assumptions.

These two categories of feminised policing and proper policing are based on Heidensohn's discussion of the types of research on women in the police. There are four, according to Heidensohn, in addition to the two described by Walklate, explored above. She begins with a category of police research on gender as 'keeping the law' (1995:102). This is fundamental to the 'Is it working?' aspect of research discussed here because it is about the way the law is used to prevent discrimination on the grounds of biological sex. In Britain the Sex Discrimination Act (1975) Section 6(2)(a) states that it is illegal to discriminate on the grounds of sex or marriage, except in a few nominated cases pertaining to decency and authenticity. Heidensohn argues that this is a relatively minor strand of some research in the UK and the US, but that a notable aspect of the area is the campaign for legal non-compliance with such legislation, by police officers, usually through their representatives, such as the Police Federation.

A second specific area of research category Heidensohn identifies is about achieving a 'representative bureaucracy' or public service approach (1995:102). This is a version of the police accountability and legitimacy debate, which has become more focused since the 1960s, especially in Britain and America, due to the rise of the civil rights and women's movements. The argument is about the extent to which the police should be representative of the policed, and how this should be achieved, if at all. The next category Heidensohn considers is the research which aims to bring innovation and change to policy, perhaps carried out by women inside the organisation, who, having chosen policing as a career might be expected to be concerned about the police service being modern and innovative in its treatment of all employees. In addition to the points already stated, about crimes such as domestic violence and rape becoming more politically sensitive, requiring more traditionally 'female' skills, Heidensohn also alleges that 'policewomen are seen to be the solution to the crisis in modern policing' (ibid:103) and are now viewed as a resource which the police need in ever greater numbers. Conversely, the implementation of equal opportunities is sometimes shown to be undermining police tradition or 'proper policing', as explained by Walklate in the discussion reported above. Heidensohn concedes that the scale and range of police research on policing and gender is confusing, and the researchers confused. Few studies report any primary empirical material, most seem to rehearse old arguments and some even contribute negatively to the *legitimacy of the idea of women in policing* (ibid:104 original emphasis).

Studies on attitudes towards certain aspects of police work have also been conducted in American law enforcement agencies since the beginning of the 1980s (see for example Golden, 1981; Wexler, 1985; Brooks, Piquero and Cronin, 1994). In the UK, similar work was carried out by Southgate in 1981, when it was found that policewomen 'could cope better with traditional cases such as child abuse' (Heidensohn, 1995:90). It is claimed that many officers regard sexual crimes involving children as emotionally demanding, unpleasant and to be avoided if possible. As such offences are considered to be 'literally or metaphorically unclean' by police officers, it is suggested that 'these sorts of incidents are particularly disliked by policemen, and are marginalised to policewomen, wherever staffing levels allow' (Brewer and Magee, 1991:60).

In Chapter 2 it was argued that there may be a complex range of explanations which underlie common assumptions about female officers being directed to the more familial, 'private' spheres of crime. This issue will be developed here by arguing that the situation is more complicated than has previously been suggested, especially in the field of sexual offences. Indeed, one of the more problematic aspects of this debate is the way the status of certain types of police work and attitudes towards gender and competence become confused. In some cases it is almost impossible to differentiate between organisational necessity and tradition; for instance, when allegations of rape or sexual assault are reported to the police, it could be suggested that women officers may be directed to deal with the case specifically as a result of their gender. On the other hand, the victims' rights to privacy, their preference and comfort, and evidential necessity may require the organisation to train women officers to be present at medical examinations. As a result it could appear that male officers can avoid dealing with matters connected with female bodies and physical assaults which require women to remove clothes. Even when the investigation is about the threat of sexual attack, requiring no physical intervention, it may be passed to female colleagues. Commentators such as Young (1991) and Heidensohn (1995) have claimed that this is simply one aspect of male police culture. As Fielding has argued, values commonly associated with this culture are 'an almost pure form of "hegemonic masculinity" ' (1994:47) and a part of the commonly accepted ways of working, which pervades all parts of the organisation. Connell has argued, however, that ' "hegemonic masculinity" is not a fixed character type, always and everywhere the same', although he does concede that 'the military and government provide a fairly convincing corporate display of masculinity, still very little shaken by feminist women or dissenting men' (1995:76–7). Before examining this in terms of the gender and police culture debate, it is useful to look at evidence on the deployment of women; to examine some statistics on sex crimes and to see whether there are reasons, other than traditional beliefs about their gendered competencies, for women to be confined and constrained within the organisation.

Abusing children

It is feasible to assume that work involving sexual offences in policing has become a more prominent issue because reported child abuse has increased dramatically over recent decades. Although it is difficult to ascertain whether the actual prevalence of these offences has increased, various authors and agencies have indicated that the amount of reported sexual abuse of children by adults is increasing so dramatically that there seem to be explanations other than a change in behaviour or patterns of offending. For example, this trend has been described by the National Society for the Prevention of Cruelty to Children (NSPCC) in the UK, using statistics collected between 1983 and 1987, which show that the number of cases they dealt with involving sexual abuse increased by 800 per cent. Another example comes from the UK Department of Health figures for 1991, which suggest that 5,900 children (0.55 per thousand) under 18 years were reported to have been abused (Browne, 1994:211). Furthermore, the Children Act Report (1993) found that the number of children placed on the Child Protection Register as a result of sexual abuse rose from 3,900 in 1991, to 8,300 in 1993 (Edwards, 1996:274).

These figures, indicating unprecedented increases in the number of cases coming to the attention of various agencies, have been described as the tip of a very large iceberg (Ghate and Spencer, 1995:2). Some authors have suggested that when an 'epidemic in the diagnosis of child sex abuse erupts', mass hysteria leads to a moral panic (Edwards and Soetenhorst-de Savornin Lohman, 1994:104–5). However, since the publicity arising from the Butler-Sloss Inquiry into Child Abuse in Cleveland, UK (1988), it has been recognised that measuring the pre-valence of child abuse is extremely difficult. Indeed, one of the recommendations of that inquiry was to investigate the extent of the problem, but it was not until 1994 that a feasibility study was com-missioned by the Department of Health. In due course, it was decided to investigate the possibility of conducting a national survey, and a year later, Ghate and Spencer presented the Home Office with their study (1995). As they note in that report, which aimed to clarify and define the problem and methodology, rather than measure any actual prevalence of abuse, previous studies have been discredited due to sampling problems. As a result, statistics which have been collected in the past have been disregarded as being unrepresentative (Nash and West, 1985, Kelly, 1991, and Baker and Duncan, 1985 are quoted as examples).

Another factor which makes it difficult to arrive at a reasonable estimate of the incidence of sexual abuse, even with 'official' statistics, is the way new directives are implemented by agencies such as the police and social services. One of the findings of the Butler-Sloss Inquiry, following the Cleveland sex abuse scandal, was that there should be closer cooperation between the police, medical practitioners and social services. Furthermore, these changes in procedures can blur the classification and recording of cases, because the new legal framework of the Children Act (1989) directed that 'for the most part, unless it can be proved otherwise, a child is best cared for in its own home by its own family … ' (Lyon and de Cruz, 1993:17). As the introduction of this more 'child-centred' approach to protection issues took effect, it gave rise to new legal questions and problems. For example, the inter-agency guidance document 'Working Together under the Children Act 1989', by the UK Department of Health (DOH) and Home Office (1991), created potential difficulties for agency workers, as it encouraged the rights of the accused to be balanced against the need to protect the child and the interests of justice. As the new rules require a court to be satisfied that the child would 'suffer significantly' by remaining at home, a care or supervision order would not be made unless 'it is satisfied that the child is suffering or likely to suffer "significant harm" ' (Section 31(2) of the Children Act, quoted in Lyon and de Cruz, 1993:15). As the 1989 Act does not define 'significant' but is simply used as a measure against some indication of normal child development, this represents a major change for all those involved with the legal protection of children. In turn, this may have affected the way cases are approached by other agencies such as police child protection officers, because of the need to raise the priority of the child's best interests and also the rights of the parents or carers. In addition, place of safety orders were replaced with emergency protection orders, which involve assessing whether a court would agree that a child was suffering, or was likely to suffer, significant harm. Due to these changes in the law, workers from all agencies have to be more aware of legal and 'natural' justice; parents are entitled to attend case conferences and to hear and refute any allegations which are made against them, perhaps leading to alternatives to prosecution (Liddle, 1995:333). In addition, the new Act was designed to give children in these cases more opportunities for having their views heard. Increasingly, multi-agency approaches emphasise that 'the welfare of the child is recognised as the overriding concern of all the professional agencies' according to the Home Office (Liddle, 1995:333). So it could be argued that these changes may have inflated the number of cases coming to the attention of the police, or, alternatively may have provided avenues for criminal law interventions to be avoided. In either case, it involves more work for officers, either in terms of prosecutions or paperwork, or attending meetings where the future of the child will be discussed. Due to these new interventions in practice and law, it is difficult to find any constant factors upon which to base an assessment of whether the incidence of child sexual abuse has increased. It also poses problems regarding the argument that the police caseload has increased significantly and that the status or prominence of child protection work has been affected. One fact which casts doubt upon the notion that police involvement has increased in recent years is that figures relating to cases requiring child protection are not always as the result of sexual abuse. As the 'Working Together' document indicates, 'significant harm' can include various types of sexual abuse, and it also specifies neglect, physical injury and emotional abuse in instructions to social services departments (DOH, 1991: 48). When considering whether a child should be placed on the Child Protection Register as the result of any of these types of abuse, police involvement may be sought if a crime is considered to have been committed, although other guidelines regarding the rights and needs of those involved may affect these decisions.

Another problem for the comparative analysis of statistics is the way other sexual crimes are amalgamated with child abuse by the police and the Home Office because they are regarded as being within the remit of the Child Protection Department. Data from one of the research forces showed that in 1992, a sexual crime was recorded every 11.5 hours (compared to every 1.1 hours for all categories of crime) and throughout that period, 239 women had used one of their confidential reporting centres. Only 1 per cent of these victims had declined police involvement in their case, according to the larger research force's Chief Constable's Report in 1992. However, the ages of these referrals are not recorded, so it is difficult to assess whether children were involved in the crimes. It is stated in the annual report for 1992 of the smaller research force, that they achieved a 100 per cent detection rate for 'some serious crimes', including attempted rape, of which there were three cases, and gross indecency with a child, totalling 39 cases in 1992. With the total number of recorded crimes for 1992 being 62,213 in the force area as a whole, there were 1,277 referrals of child abuse, which is an increase of 174 cases, or 16 per cent, on the previous year. In addition, staff from the Child Protection Department attended 804 case conferences, which was 9 per cent more than in 1991.

More recently, crime statistics for the whole of England and Wales reveal that the number of sexual offences recorded by the police is falling. Nationally, the overall incidence of offences fell by 5 per cent in 1995, to 30,300, which is the first reduction since 1990, although this has to be compared with a general lowering of recorded crime in this period of 3 per cent (Home Office, 1995:29–33). Over the past ten years, sexual crimes have generally increased at about the same rate as other offences, although around two thirds of the police forces in England and Wales recorded a decrease in 1995. Hence, despite an increase of over 10 per cent in notifiable rapes since 1985, the overall average percentage change has been an increase of 3.5 per cent for sexual offences (ibid: 33–37). So although there has been an overall increase over the past ten years, more recent statistics indicate a decline in the number of sexual offences coming to the attention of the police. In a similar way, there appears to have been a corresponding decrease in recorded notifiable sexual of-fences in the two research forces. In 1995 the number of notifiable sexual offences was recorded at 373 (or 61 per 100,000 of the population) in the smaller force, and 556 (or 39 per 100,000 of the population) in the larger force. This is a fall of 27 and 25 per cent respectively on the previous year. In 1995 the smaller research force cleared up 95 per cent of its notifiable sexual offences and the larger one 75 per cent of them (ibid: 40–45).

At the time the research was conducted for this study the smaller research force, which covers a largely rural, non-metropolitan area, had a significantly higher percentage rate of sexual offences per thousand population than the larger metropolitan force. This compares to a national average of 59 offences per 100,000 people. Clear-up rates for the metropolitan force (75 per cent) were near to the national average, which is 76 per cent for sexual offences, whereas the rural force, at 95 per cent, appeared to have a much higher than average success rate. These percentages may be related to the number of referrals received by the individual departments each year as a high volume could deplete the amount of time officers spend on individual cases. However, despite a difference in the size of each force mentioned, the units dealing with the offences connected to children appear to be about the same. This said, referrals, of which the smaller research force reports having 1,277, vastly outnumber the actual cases recorded, which represent an average of 75 cases for each officer per year.

Statistics such as these can be misleading because of inconsistencies in recording the data, variations in the willingness of victims to contact the police, increased recognition of the phenomenon of child sex abuse and the varying definitions of an 'offence'. As definitions from different sources illustrate, child sexual abuse usually involves dependent chil-dren or adolescents in sexual activities with an adult. In the course of the abuse the child may be used as a sexual object for the gratification of the older person, and the child is unable to give consent due to the unequal power in the relationship (Lancaster, 1996:131). Other definitions make reference to children taking part in sexual activities that they do not fully comprehend, or to which they are unable to give informed consent, leading to them being considered the victims of abuse. An alternative definition includes actions contrary to the social taboos of family life, or which are against the law. Some definitions are more explicit, referring to direct sexual contact such as sexual intercourse, masturbation or 'manual, oral or other manipulation of the genitals, breasts or anus, where the purpose of the interaction is the sexual gratification of one or more of the participants' (Liddle, 1995:315).

Legal definitions, however, which the police use, have to be extremely specific because they are open to the scrutiny of court processes such as cross examination. Sometimes the law is altered to take account of supposed changes in general social attitudes; examples include the recognition of male rape and rape within marriage and lowering the age of consent for homosexual sex. These changes are sometimes effected to clarify the legal definitions of crime and eliminate ambiguities. In comparison to the definitions of child abuse, above, the form of words police officers use in order to decide whether an offence has been committed, or to differentiate one crime from another, are specific and exact. A training manual for detectives reveals that the word 'indecent' has no legal definition, but its generally accepted as 'offensive to modesty, impure, obscene or unchaste behaviour in sexual matters' (Home Office, 1993:15). When words have no accepted legal meaning and are open to interpretation, the police must find some way of defining them in order to fit the evidence to the description of the offence. Another example is given in the section of the Indecency with Children Act (1960) which states that,

> Any person who commits an act of gross indecency with or towards a child under the age of fourteen, or who incites a child under that age to such an act with him or another, shall be liable on conviction on indictment for a term not exceeding two years, or on summary conviction to imprisonment for a term not exceeding six months, or a fine, or to both (Home Office, 1993:25).

Even this apparently unambiguous definition is fraught with difficulties for the police officers who need to provide evidence to prove the case in court. Several pages of the training manual are devoted to explaining how the word 'gross' should be interpreted and the difference in the meanings of 'with or towards' a child or 'inciting'. Police instruction manuals provide extensive lists of 'points to prove' in court and complex sets of legal rules about the circumstances in which children of different ages may be questioned about certain offences. So this need for intimate knowledge of definitions, legal rules and guidelines regarding sexual offences illustrates the complexity of the situation for the police and the apparently gendered nature of the specialist skills. Police officers who are trained in these areas have to provide evidence that certain behaviour and actions took place. Such behaviour is often described in ambiguous terms, are of an intimate nature and will probably have been carried out in private. Moreover, dealing with the issue of sexual acts and the limited understanding of children is thought to require even more specialised knowledge, which is why the set of guidelines, known as the 'Memorandum of Good Practice' (MoGP) (Home Office with the DOH 1992) was devised for use in England and Wales. This document recommends that in order to conduct interviews with sexually abused children, specialist skills are required and officers should undertake to become 'Memorandum trained'. One of the reasons for this perceived necessity for specialist skills was due to new regulations, introduced in the 1988 Criminal Justice Act, permitting children to give evidence from outside the courtroom using a television link. In the later Criminal Justice Act of 1991, it was decided to permit video evidence so that child victims and witnesses could have their statements pre-recorded and classed as evidence-in-chief, in order to minimise the distress they might suffer in court, although the child must still be available for live cross examination, possibly using a television link. Now they would not be required to repeat the main statement of their version of what happened in the witness box in open court.

Despite the good intentions of these rules, which were aimed at protecting young people in such distressing circumstances, they have created a number of difficulties for those involved in such cases because of two main legal problems: first, the admissibility of video interviews as evidence, and second, the reliability of such evidence (Lyon and de Cruz, 1993:19). In an attempt to standardise the interview and recording procedures and increase the evidential value of child witness statements, the Home Office, in collaboration with the UK Department of Health, produced the extensive set of guidelines, the MoGP mentioned above. Further problems arose, however, with the MoGP, because as a set of guidelines they are not embedded in law, and judges can exercise their discretion when deciding whether or not to permit activities such as video evidence. Court rules regarding the 'interests of justice' must be adhered to, concerning sound and picture clarity, hearsay, or 'inadequacies in testimony amounting to evidence insufficient to satisfy a criminal prosecution' (Lyon and de Cruz, 1992:279). In some cases the child may still have to appear in the witness box to be cross examined in open court, and police forces have guidelines reminding officers to keep this in mind, stating that,

> Nothing should be said to a child, parent/carer which will give them reason to believe that video evidence will automatically be admitted by the court instead of oral evidence, or that the use of a live television link or screen will be allowed. Application for such is required in each individual case, and whilst generally permission is granted, this should not be assumed as it is at the judge's discretion (Larger Research Force Training Manual, 1996:6).

As this short outline of the legal problems associated with child sex abuse cases illustrates, there are many problems associated with legal rules surrounding video evidence. In addition, the MoGP is an extensive document, covering extensive procedural instructions from child psychology to technical recording expertise. Within the Memorandum there are lists of clearly defined ages for different offences, certain conditions which must be fulfilled during the interview and extensive technical details regarding the way the videotape is recorded. In addition, interviewing principles are stipulated, such as the child being listened to, not questioned; the child must be allowed to freely recall significant events; careful notes must be made of timings, setting and persons present, and all interviews prior to the video recording must be recorded in writing. It is also stated that it is very important that coaching the child must be avoided. In terms of the location and planning of the video interview, the MoGP is also very specific: it should be conducted in a specially designated facility, if possible away from the police station. Even the equipment must be of a certain type, because some are not acceptable to the court. Preparation for the video interview is emphasised as being essential, with six pages of the document devoted to this issue. A further 13 are about conducting the interview, and five pages are about the legal constraints of using video evidence. Later, the Memorandum goes into details such as what to do after the interview, exact definitions of terms and legal Acts, age limits, and the points which need to be established for certain offences to be proved. In addition to the nationally agreed rules of the MoGP, individual force guidelines are often issued to officers being trained to conduct video interviews, which are available as a 'help screen' on the networked force computer system. Suitably trained officers in some forces are supplied with the 'Investigative Action Pack' which warns that 'the Memorandum of Good Practice is not mandatory', but strongly recommends that its guidance should be followed wherever practicable (Larger Research Force Training Manual, 1996:1). This research force's standing orders also inform officers that any 'recording not strictly complying with the MoGP will not automatically be ruled inadmissible but the MoGP should be followed when practicable to ensure acceptance'.

Sexual expertise

'Legal' warnings about procedures leading to a court case impinge upon the competence of officers because they require specialised knowledge of procedures and the ability to carry through the investigation. They illustrate how an aura of expertise can marginalise some aspects of police work. In cases of child abuse, this may be amplified because of the combination of children and sexuality and the taboo of incest. In addition, it is disturbing for officers to realise that those who would normally be expected to care for the child and in whom the child has placed trust, have abused them. It has been suggested that in the early 1900s, when incest was 'discovered', disbelief was replaced with horror, and a specific legal category was created (Bell, 1993:128). In 1903 Lord Davey stated that it was an 'offence not only against morality and decency but against every instinct of human nature' (ibid). One of the early pioneering police-women, writing in the 1950s, said that of all the work she had en-countered, 'the most repugnant was dealing with cases of incest' (Wyles, 1952:240). As Bell has argued, the specific wrong of incest and the taboo of intra familial sexuality has meant that legislation covering rape and other sexual assaults are not considered adequate to punish those crimes described as 'incestuous assaults' (Stanko, 1985:23). In his description of the marginalised role of women in the police, Young describes in-vestigating incest as not being regarded as 'real work for real polises'. He classes it as a 'care and welfare' issue, used to keep female officers away from the real work of thief taking. As women were officially segregated during his time in the CID in the late 1950s, the 'token woman' in the department took statements from the female rape or sexual assault victims (1991:221–2). As Table 2.1 shows, male officers now work in child protection departments, although many work in supervisory roles, as sergeants or inspectors. In addition to Memorandum training, there are sexual offences courses in some forces, which are open to all officers and compulsory for everyone entering the CID. However, due to the number of female victims, it seems to be accepted that it will be women officers who gain experience and expertise with children and sexual crimes. To what extent this is led by the preferences of victims, public demand, or a traditional belief in the 'natural' caring abilities of female officers, is difficult to quantify. In preparation for CID training, officers are told that it is necessary to develop '… the ability to handle victims and witnesses with compassion and understanding in cases of indecent assault' (Home Office, 1993:9). As these are 'feminine' skills, normally attributed to women, perhaps the prerequisite abilities which need to be displayed at selection interviews for posts dealing with sexual offences are also gendered. Indeed, it has been suggested that sexual abuse presents the police with peculiar difficulties, partly due to their inability to take responsibility for the problem of men hurting women and children, the police being overwhelmingly male, and partly because the private nature of the offence means that detection often relies upon the word of the victim (Campbell, 1988:69). In cases where the survivor is the sole witness and a child, beliefs about the unreliability of children, their speech, memory processes and lack of truthfulness may add to the problems of evidential credibility.

In Campbell's discussion of the UK Cleveland child abuse controversy, she uses evidence which was given to the subsequent Inquiry by police officers to support her assertion that they were unable to deal comfortably with offences concerning sexuality and injuries to genitalia. In addition, their evidence-gathering techniques were criticised for being incompetent, unsympathetic and 'confrontational' in the Inquiry findings (Butler-Sloss, 1988:245). One of the parents involved in the case reported that a woman officer who had been unable to get any information from a child victim was replaced by a male detective who said he had '... decided to try and browbeat a confession out of these recalcitrant kids' (Campbell, 1988:74). At a case conference, social workers and health professionals were shocked into silence when a detective announced he had 'told the boy he was a little so-and-so, that he'd pushed him until he cracked' (ibid:75). Another observation Campbell makes about the Cleveland case is the apparent discomfort police officers displayed during the Inquiry regarding the relationship between sexuality and childhood. Evidence of this was seized upon when a professional feud became public knowledge. It had developed in the course of the investigation between police, social services and the doctors, who had suggested that a large number of children were the victims of abuse. Relations between the various agencies had broken down when the police refused to allow their photographer to collect evidence of injuries to the children's genitals. When questioned at the Inquiry, the police officer in charge agreed that it was usual to take photographs of bruises '... in the immediate area' but the request to photograph the anus of a child was refused because '... it had no evidential value' (ibid:76). In the course of their enquiries, police officers '... were becoming increasingly embarrassed and reluctant to take these photographs' according to Edwards and Soetenhorst-de Savorin Lohman (1994:117).

After the Inquiry it was revealed that Cleveland Constabulary, where these officers were employed, had been one of the few UK police forces which had failed to implement Home Office recommendations contained in Circular 69/86 'Violence against Women'. In that directive, ten years earlier, it had been suggested that female victims should have the right to be interviewed by women officers (Campbell, 1988:70). There had been adverse publicity following the BBC programme *Police*, a television documentary series by Roger Graef, which showed male detectives inter-rogating a rape victim. In the press the next day, the officers on the film were described as subjecting the woman to a display of 'unmitigated toughness' and 'low-key brutality' (Scott and Dickens, 1989:81). The public outcry which followed was answered by several forces issuing statements about the treatment of women reporting rape, and new guidelines were issued by the Home Office, which acknowledged that '... *some* women might prefer to be interviewed or examined by another woman' (ibid, original emphasis). As Skinner explains, in addition to counselling being made available for survivors, 'the police developed examination suites ... training on rape issues for new recruits and some forces set up special women-only policing units to deal specifically with these crimes' (2000: 27). It is argued that change was effected in response to complaints by various feminist campaigners and those writing on sexual abuse, such as Stanko (1985), on 'intimate' violence and physical abuse (see Dobash and Dobash, 1992, Edwards, 1989). Various authors, published with Scott and Dickens in a collection by Dunhill (1989), were highly critical of the way so called 'women's problems' such as domestic violence and rape were dealt with by the police. In addition, publicised cases of sexual harassment and discrimination against women officers provided fuel for the press to confirm public suspicions about male power and misogyny in the police.

More specifically, Judge Butler-Sloss's recommendations, which were published as a result of the Cleveland Inquiry, said that especially in cases where teenagers have been sexually abused, 'Police, doctors and Social Services should have female staff ready to help children' (Butler-Sloss, 1988:10). Her clear reference to the need for women to be the specialists, not only in cases of unlawful sex, such as incest, but specifically to deal with children, appears to confirm popular beliefs and assumptions within the police. Although the case to which she refers is that of a teenager being embarrassed when examined by a male doctor, and there are inferences that her transitory stage of sexual maturity may have added to the discomfort, a very influential report has indicated that 'female staff' and sexually abused children are often associated with one another.

Women have 'the answer'

As a result of these criticisms of existing police practices, and the way women officers are perceived to be able to silence certain allegations of insensitivity, because of their 'compassionate nature' (McLaughlin, 1996:78), it has been suggested that women are regarded as 'the solution to the crises of modern policing' (Heidensohn, 1995:103). Indeed, these crises of confidence and levels of distrust were shown to exist by studies such as the Islington Crime Survey (Jones *et al*, 1986:205), particularly among groups such as the young and ethnic minorities, and led to recommendations regarding police training policies. As the Policy Studies Institute reported in 1983, the police in London were regarded favourably by the majority of the public until they had been in contact with the force. As a result of encounters with police officers, however, it was found that some officers were 'rude and bullying towards members of the public' (Heward, 1994:243). The police seem to have responded to these criticisms by attempting to improve their image on two fronts: first, by pacifying their critics regarding their interactions with the public, and second, through the transformation of their internal personnel affairs. They have attempted to control how they are perceived to be carrying out the task of policing and they claim to have been trying to replace a gender segregated workforce with an integrated service-style organisation.

As an example of this new image-conscious behaviour, it was reported that throughout the 1992 Chief Constables' National Conference delegates were aiming to find ways to regain public confidence by enhancing their image with 'new speak'. Phrases such as 'negative personal experiences' were used to describe being framed, assaulted or racially abused by the police. Miscarriages of justice, such as the case of the Birmingham Six, became known as 'high profile reversals'; and rather than the press being regaled by 'old fashioned coppers in braid' demanding more rubber bullets, the new breed of chief constables were now anxious to show their new sector policing, domestic violence or equal opportunities initiatives. 'Quality of service delivery' and 'performance indicators' are examples of this image management package, which Heward describes as being designed to 'empower consumers' (1994:242).

One of the difficulties which the police encountered in their drive to be seen as more publicly accountable was the reported treatment of their own female colleagues. Whilst the senior officers were engaged with changing the corporate identity of the police, a series of cases where officers alleged either racial or sexual harassment and discrimination came to light. As Halford's (1993) explanation of her treatment and subsequent resignation from Merseyside police illustrated, evidence of sexist behaviour within the organisation would not fit neatly with the new improved image of unproblematic gender and race relations in police encounters with the public. In response to allegations by a stream of women officers, (see Gregory and Lees, 1999), accusing the male hierarchy of everything from unequal deployment and denying them promotion to sexual assaults on duty, research defining 'best practice' initiatives, reports and Home Office inspections were conducted. Competitions were organised with awards made to individuals designing the most innovative solution to inequality in their particular police force; funds were provided for small research projects by the Home Office, ostensibly to encourage ideas leading to equality of opportunity, but in reality, as cynics might argue, aimed at getting more women and ethnic minority officers to be promoted or to apply for specialist posts.

In addition, there have been attempts by police managers to appear to be increasing the organisation's public accountability by responding to demands for the rights of victims or the 'injured party' (IP) to be recognised. As they became aware that it might be regarded as unacceptable for women to discuss the intimate details of a rape with a male detective, forces had to assess their methods of obtaining evidence in these cases. Aside from the political questions raised by feminist groups such as Women's Aid in the UK, there were also moral and ethical questions which the police had to negotiate. In the course of intimate examinations, privacy and decency became difficult issues because the policewomen's departments had been disbanded in the mid 1970s, and nothing had been done to replace the skills that were lost (see for example Campbell, 1989, Scott and Dickens, 1989, Stanko, 1985, Skinner, 2000). Male detectives, although trained in the theory and law of sexual offences, could not overcome the fixity of the gendered body to become female surrogates to attend examinations and were therefore distanced from the victim. As the evidence in the next part of this chapter will show, women are sometimes 'encouraged' to enter departments which deal with sexual matters, reconstituting the old policewomen's departments in all but name (Heidensohn, 1995). This results in men further excluding themselves, or being excluded, from such activities. This is an example of what Connell has described as a 'lumpy' period in gender history (1987:149), because as Morgan suggests, industries which become increasingly dependent upon female workers require not only a significant transformation of gender relations between men and women, but also between men (1991:182). The smaller research force had been making some attempts to equalise the opportunities for their female officers, who were in a very small minority, in terms of promotion. In response to some questions asked about the progression of women officers, their Career Development Officer explained that in order to encourage participation in sergeant's promotion examinations, he had,

> … written to every female officer in the force, personally, and really asked them if they would consider giving it serious consideration (male Superintendent, 1994).

He went on to describe how women could improve their promotion chances if they achieved a 'breadth of vision across the organisation' by gaining experience in 'specialist posts'. Asked whether this included traditional areas of specialisation for women officers such as Child and Family Protection Units, he replied,

> Difficult to comment – both the women who are in the present promotion stakes are in the CID; if more women were in the CID, dogs, traffic and so on, it would equip them, overall, with promotion prospects because it would give them a greater breadth of knowledge, it would enhance the prospects of female officers, definitely (male Superintendent, 1994).

As this suggests, he was ambivalent regarding the value of experience in the CPU as a positive career move, and the CID, traffic department and even the dog section seemed preferable. Later in this interview he outlined a system of 'highlighting' certain officers who appear to have potential to achieve promotion, assigning them a 'mentor'. Although he could not remember how the selection system to become one of these officers worked, he knew that of the 12 currently taking part in the scheme, three were women. In a similar way, the Career Development Officer's direct superior, a Chief Superintendent in charge of personnel, appeared to be anxious to make sure that women were treated 'more' than equally. He described how it is difficult to arrange formal attachments to the CID, which are necessary prior to an application to join the department, because of staffing shortages and 'rules'. Despite the fact that an individual sub-commander might want to 'develop' a particular officer, the 'Executive' or 'policy makers' would not agree to 'flex it a bit'. However, in one case, where an officer and their superior were in agreement that some experience in the CID would be appropriate, and could be accommodated within the department, he explained they *would* have made an exception,

It was, in fact, a woman who wanted to do it, but you've got to be very careful how you go about these things. To be quite honest, if I'd said it was for a female to do it, it would have been done like *that* (snaps fingers) ... but you've got to look at the situation and make it fair, or you could throw the organisation out of kilter (male Chief Superintendent, 1994).

As his reluctance to unleash a possible male backlash through what he described as a 'knee jerk reaction' illustrates, relationships between men in these situations appear to be paramount. In the other, larger force investigated for this study, it was found that senior officers were also concerned about the lack of women in their specialist departments. One of their internal memoranda, in 1995, stated that following a research project carried out by two officers in the force it was,

... identified (to no one's surprise) that female officers were under represented in Operational Support and, in line with the Equal Opportunities Policy within the force, positive action measures should be carried out to encourage female officers to apply.

As a result it was decided that for the next 12 months, women officers would be allowed to have a four-week attachment with a variety of specialisms, such as,

Motor Patrols, Dog Section, Tactical Support Group etc, ... to interested women officers which will provide a useful and worthwhile experience.

In the same force, at an Equal Opportunities Working Group meeting, attended as part of the research, the Assistant Chief Constable was reminded that Her Majesty's Inspector of Constabulary report in 1993 had highlighted the under representation of women officers at all levels. With the exception of the Child and Family Protection Units and the Community Relations departments, it was shown that few improvements had been made. An example that was cited was traffic, where just 2.4 per cent of the officers were female, compared to their overall level of 13 per cent in the force at the time (1995). In comparison, the smaller, more rural force researched had produced a booklet about equal opportunities entitled 'Guidelines for Managers' which included instructions about how the Sex Discrimination Act should be implemented. Supervisory officers were given the following instructions in an undated booklet.

1. Don't assume that all women are better at communication skills and dealing with children than men are. Some women are poor communicators and hopeless with children, and some men are very good.
2. Don't assume that all men will be better drivers and better shots than all women. Some men are poor drivers and hopeless shots while some women are very good.

In this document it was also pointed out that the Sex Discrimination Act (SDA) (1975) does allow employers to specify the sex of the person where there is a need for 'authenticity, decency or privacy or the provision of personal services promoting welfare' (S.8.7 of the SDA). Potential 'Genuine Occupational Qualifications' according to the guidelines could be,

a) Male officers searching male prisoners and women officers searching women prisoners in the interests of privacy and decency. This would have applied before PACE. (S.7{2}{b}{i})
b) Male officers being sent into all male clubs for surveillance purposes in the interests of authenticity. (S.7 {2}{a})
c) Women officers dealing with women victims of rape and other serious sexual offences where the victim prefers to speak to a woman and it is in the interests of her welfare. (S.7{2}{e})

Once again, the private/public dichotomy and the gendered division of labour can be seen in some of the assumptions underlying these examples. Men have clubs which may need to be 'infiltrated' by officers in secret and possibly dangerous circumstances. On the other hand, women victims are assumed to want to talk to a female officer as it may be 'in the interests of her welfare'. As these guidelines show, it is possible for the police to portray themselves as equal opportunities employers, as Walklate says (140:2001) and at the same time, improve their corporate identity by providing 'sympathetic' female officers to deal with women victims. It could also be regarded as being more cost effective, at a time when police budgets were being restricted, for a small group of officers to be trained as specialists. As female officers may be regarded as a more flexible resource, able to participate at all stages of a rape investigation, including medical examinations, and more capable of interviewing sympathetically, in addition to being 'politically' acceptable, it seems clear that they would be targeted for specialist training in sexual crimes.

Career choices

As part of the research it seemed essential to examine these assumptions about women officers and intimacy and decency and also to establish the needs and practices involved in the investigating of certain offences. One of the difficulties in this area is the notion of 'choice', both from the police officer's point of view, and the victim's. In a discussion with women officers who had been successfully promoted to high ranking jobs, there was evidence to suggest that their choice of career moves had been limited (see Westmarland, 1999). Senior male officers had viewed them as 'high fliers' and often, behind the scenes, suggested that they should be moved to areas which would help their promotion prospects. Another factor the top women police officers claimed had helped them was an element of luck, which seems to imply that something or someone may have been controlling their 'choices'. Similarly, officers working in Child and Family Protection departments seemed to fall into three categories. One group were aware that they had been 'required' to go into this type of work, a second group said they thought it may have been a good career move or liked the work, and a third group were more cynical, giving reasons such as biding their time until another job came along, or that they liked working office hours, fitting in with family commitments and so on. To examine the way 'natural' relationships between women and work with abused children have been defined, women officers were asked about the effects of these beliefs. As part of the study a series of group discussions were used to find out whether formal or informal measures or pressures had been used which would encourage women officers to accept this supposedly natural association. One of the ways this information was gleaned was by asking about their preferences for specialist posts and departments in a series of taped discussion groups. During these sessions with women officers, some of whom were working in child protection, they were asked about their motivation for becoming involved in specific areas of police work. One officer said she was awaiting a post in the CID, and another said she had just started a CID attachment. It was asked whether child protection could be regarded as a step towards the CID and, although they agreed it could be, the officer working there said she wanted to get out of the Child Protection Unit (CPU),

> … I'm not interested in the CPU full time, I'm half way through my sergeant's exam and it would hold me back, I wouldn't get any acting. I'm just filling in until I can get a place on the CID (female PC, 1994 Discussion Group 5).

Another female officer taking part in this discussion added that she was more interested in driving, at present working in a squad where car thieves were targeted. She claimed to like 'getting her ticks', or being measured by quantifiable markers of achievement, and that she was not interested in working in 'softer' areas such as child protection work. She said,

> I've always gone the other way. If anything comes in like child abuse, policewomen get sent to it anyway – without a doubt the policewoman gets sent (female PC, 1994 Discussion Group 5).

In other discussions on this subject, women compared their various experiences of gendered aspects of police work. In response to a question about whether male officers were becoming deskilled in cases involving child sex offences, as a result of women being regarded as 'the experts', one of the women said,

> Definitely – the men shy away from it, dealing with women and children, and yet they're the ones who are married with kids. I don't think there's any one of us here with children, yet we're expected to be able to go in there and deal with it. But, yes, definitely, the men don't get the skills (female PC, 1994 Discussion Group 5).

> Most of the (male) PCs put the barriers up, that's a woman's job, leave it to them we can't deal with that – kids, we are given them, but I don't know anything about them (female PC, 1994 Discussion Group 3)

Literature which has analysed the relationship between gender, occupational segregation and identity in other occupations suggests that a complex range of attitudes can be used to explain how 'doing gender' is an integral part of women's working lives. Hall suggests that 'women police officers are often seen as lacking the authoritative manner of men officers, whereas male flight attendants are described as giving less friendly service than female attendants' (Hall, 1993:452). In terms of a gendered organisation approach, as proposed by Acker, it is assumed that certain 'job evaluations, promotion procedures and job specifications' are embedded in an organisational 'logic' (1990 in Hall, 1993:453). Organisations also tend to justify and explain the creation of gendered distinctions which may have the effect of influencing the gender identity of employees (ibid:453–4). Gender, according to this perspective, is an integral part of the way firms and companies work, and as Acker suggests,

> ... advantage and disadvantage, exploitation and control, action and emotion, meaning and identity, are patterned through and in terms of a distinction between male and female, masculine and feminine (Acker, 1990:146).

Hence, the identity of a police officer who is able to be compassionate but detached, may not comfortably be equated with traditional views of the 'macho cop' image. This 'cop culture' is blamed by many writers for the gendering of certain jobs in the police. Walklate argues that fewer male officers are likely to apply for some jobs, perhaps because they evaluate themselves to have certain skills, as a result of what they regard as 'male' in the sense of 'what the police do'. Also, selection procedures might favour certain abilities such as displaying empathy, being good at listening and being supportive in distressing situations (1996:198). As the ability to deal with children and sexual abuse is perceived to require these specialist skills, but also certain 'natural' abilities, some women from the Child Protection Department were asked why they thought male officers might be viewed as unsuitable.

> ... they're frightened of the work, they get upset, the men – they want to kill the perpetrators (female PC, 1994 Discussion Group 2).

> Early in my service I was called to a cot death. It *was* distressing, the baby was dead, but the mother didn't want to give it to me, she wouldn't let go. I was only a few months into my service and I was alright afterwards, but the male sergeant with me was an absolute wreck (female PC, 1994 Discussion Group 2).

Another aspect of this discussion about the gendered identification of certain types of work within organisations has been examined by analysing the 'invisible' nature of some tasks. In her examination of the role of secretaries, Wichroski asserts that because women have been regarded as 'compliant, cheerful and non-competitive for male positions', in some service occupations, they were actively encouraged to regard this as their domain (Wichroski, 1994:33). As a result, the role of the secretary, which incorporated certain aspects which have traditionally been viewed as female, has become an occupation which is assumed to be carried out exclusively by women. Evidence of this supposed gendered conception of secretarial work was examined in a study of men crossing into 'women's' areas of work. It was discovered by Pringle (1993) that some men were able to avoid being labelled in ways that could damage the maintenance of their masculine image. She also found that gender alters the power relationship between boss and secretary, and states an incidence of a male 'marketing assistant' who replaced 'a girl who did a lot of typing'. As a result, his female boss referred to him as an 'assistant', 'offsider' or 'Phillip who runs round after me ... never as secretary' (Pringle, 1993:143). On the other hand, in another company,

> Raoul, unlike Phillip, is actually defined as a secretary and is thus placed at a cultural disadvantage, subject to ridicule. Yet he is able to develop strategies of asserting masculine power ... (as) he is not happy about being called a secretary, and goes out of his way to explain why the term is inappropriate. He says that when the job was first discussed, the term secretary was never mentioned (Pringle, 1993:145–146).

It has been argued that one of the reasons women fit more easily into occupations which involve servicing the needs of others is their ability to make their 'smile become the product' (Wichroski, 1994:34). Service-related jobs usually rely upon interaction, and because women are over represented in these occupations, the required skills have become associated with femininity. Although the actual tasks carried out by such workers are not defined as male or female, '... those professions that have been feminised have incorporated more fixed gender expectations, allowing the worker less leeway in negotiating a satisfying work role that integrates personal and work identities' (Wichroski, 1994:34). In addition, women who are involved in areas in the organisation that are hidden in some way, such as child protection, will be classed as carrying out 'emotional' rather than 'rational' labour. Rational labour, that which has an obvious production value – for example catching car thieves, burglars and drug pushers and thereby increasing the clear-up rates and per-formance indicators – is formally defined by the police. As rationality is therefore apparently valued more than emotionality, this has con-sequences for women, who are often, it is claimed by Nicholson, seen as emotional whereas men are regarded as rational. She goes on to argue that '... emotion is kept out of sight in the organisational world, and although some members are expected to exhibit emotion, they are the marginal, dispensable or inadequate staff' (1996:147).

As a consequence, the more feminine, private and 'emotional' aspects of policing, concerned with intimacies of sexual and familial violence, will not be afforded high priority in publicised strategic plans. In the 'war against crime', traditional policing targets include burglars and car thieves, but the 'softer' caring work is not made known in the same way. Even at an organisational level, the location of Child Protection Units, away from the general areas of police activities, means the work may not be recognised as being either of a high status or having fast turnover. On the other hand, many aspects of policing have been said to lack a coherent description, and as Cain has argued, studies of the police rarely define the object of their analysis (1992:3). In particular, Walklate suggests that this group of issues relating to 'women as police officers and women as police customers … has the potential to challenge fundamentally what counts as police work' (1996:199). However, attitudes towards the 'tea and sympathy' and 'nine to five' office job image in the Child Protection Units, as opposed to blue-uniformed, high-priority, 24 hours emergency work, may detract from this challenge. In general, the status of these departments appears lower than traditional crime fighting areas such as the CID, a point which seems to be conveyed by the following remarks:

> … there's a lack of criming in child and family protection (female PC, 1994 Discussion Group 2).

> A lot of the lads think it's a doddle in child abuse, that it's a cushy number. I've been in there since July, and it's harder than your CID attachment … the workload, you've 12 or 14 cases on the go at the same time; you're out there on your own – they don't know what's happening. Our results are never shown on the log, to show the amount of work. Nobody really sees what we have to do (female PC, 1994 Discussion Group 5).

It is significant that this woman compares the work in the CPU with the traditionally male specialism of crime fighting, the CID, because as Young (1991) has suggested, beliefs about the status of 'real' policing would place these two specialisms at the opposite end of the continuum of credibility. Conversely, in a report by the Home Office concerned with occupational segregation and equal opportunities (HMIC 1996), child protection officers are regarded as working within the CID. A more convincing view of the status of this department from those working in the organisation is that a 'move into clothes' (Hobbs, 1988:210) has always been regarded as a type of promotion. But despite the fact that the CPU is 'non-uniform' work, several of the women working in them who were consulted felt their capabilities were undervalued by the majority of their colleagues, although as one woman said,

> I think the women appreciate what we do, it's the men that don't know what goes on and don't appreciate it (female PC, 1994 Discussion Group 3).

Another woman in the group discussed the inability of her male colleagues to talk to each other about their emotions, stating that she thought they found the female officers more sympathetic,

> Men can let it out to women, although they call anyone in the CPU the 'social workers' of the office; they laugh when we use talk like 'mum and the children', and they say, 'It'll be different when you're in the CID, you'll have to stop talking like that' (female PC, 1994 Discussion Group 2).

So men are regarded as being able to show their feelings to women colleagues but, as the previous officers' quotes noted, are not regarded as capable of dealing with their emotions when investigating sexual offences against children. One of the ways this can be understood is by exploring the concept of 'emotion work' which has been developed to explain this phenomenon. It is suggested that in some highly charged situations it is necessary to suppress certain feelings in order to carry out tasks in the course of employment. Furthermore the 'caring' work which women sometimes have to do for men in the course of their occupation is sometimes compared to 'mothering'. Within organisations which demand high levels of rationality, competence and professionalism, Nicholson argues that men very rarely have the chance to 'expose and consider their vulnerabilities in a safe context … and even if the woman is their senior they are able to engage in an invisible emotional relationship' (Nicholson, 1996:148). It has been argued that this is one of the ways that women become the 'natural' carers in organisation, but also that the naturalised roles and identities they embrace become '… transformed into "non-work"' (Lawler, 1996:157). In the study of 'invisible work' mentioned earlier, it was found that although 'secretaries must know more than is acknowledged by the organisation', some work is unnamed and uncategorised (Wichroski, 1994:34) and their interactions at work, being service-based, became fused with their personal identity. Indeed, in some cases, it is apparent that women officers choose to work in areas such as child protection, perhaps believing that the 'product' they have to offer is their 'natural' or acquired ability to portray a caring persona, or 'service with a smile' as Wichroski describes this interactional style. As the following statement suggests, some people have a particular interest in this type of work, and do not feel that their gender has influenced the outcome of their application to the department.

> The only reason women are chosen at first is on an *ad hoc* basis. I personally put in for it (female PC, 1994 Discussion Group 3).

Another woman, a uniformed PC, was asked if there were any areas in which she would choose to specialise and she replied,

> Well, I'm on Communications at the moment, but I would like to do family protection. I applied for a Reserve (post), but another girl with more service got it (female PC, 1994 Discussion Group 4).

She went on to explain that she had worked for Social Services before joining the police and so had a special interest in this type of work. In many occupations there are areas which are considered to be specially reserved for men or women as they require certain attributes to carry out specific tasks. A study of the recruitment practices of a leisure park by Adkins, for example, revealed that applicants for seasonal work at 'Fun Land' were divided into operatives for 'fast' rides, supposedly requiring strength and therefore an 'essential maleness' (1995:99), the children's rides, allocated to women and older men over 36, and the catering department. A very high proportion of the catering assistants were young women, and Adkins found that '… the catering manager used a very particular set of criteria to assess the suitability of new catering assistants' (ibid:102). As might be expected in a service-related job, these criteria were based on physical appearance, and the manager who was interviewed in the study stated he was looking for 'brightness in their appearance' being 'attractive and looking fresh' (ibid). As Adkins' study suggests, women may be constructing a suitable image in order to enter segregated areas of work, such as the officer quoted above, who stated she was aiming to work in the child protection unit because she had experience of this type of work before joining the police. It is clear that the work at Fun Land is gendered, catering is seen as 'women's work', and that,

> … while the inherent maleness of the fast ride occupation and the criteria used to recruit fast ride operatives were both achieved by producing a link between the supposed occupational requirements and men (fast rides 'need' physical strength, and young men possess such strength), no such link was provided for the catering assistant occupation (Adkins, 1995:105).

In contrast with many studies which assume that work is gendered because male occupational power defines it as lower status, 'feminine' or emotion work, Adkins suggests an element of choice or agency is possible. She argues that although the recruitment manager has a specific set of criteria concerning 'facial display and appropriate clothing', rejecting women applicants he believes to look 'weird', 'too butch', 'too manly' or simply 'too ugly', she nevertheless argues that '… the criteria used derived from a particular construction of *workers themselves*, rather than a set of occupational "requirements"' (1995:105–6 original emphasis).

This concept of women taking part in the construction of their own gendered identity at work, either through physical appearance or a belief in their emotional and caring abilities, is also illustrated by a study of women surgeons in America. In an examination of attitudes towards gender status and competence, Cassell (1996) found that women had to attend to the image they portrayed in front of colleagues. One of the female surgeons she was observing confided that she had been instructed by her male senior that she should always wear lipstick in order to deflect the assumption that she was a lesbian. In the middle of the night the author saw two of the women medics waking up and borrowing each other's cosmetics before rushing to the emergency room to attend to a gunshot victim (Cassell, 1996:44). In other areas of health care, there are similarly gendered specialties and it has been suggested that rather than having a negative or discriminatory effect, this leads to '… a non-competitive, complementary aspect … in the form of non-competing gender groups'. Kazanjian argues that 'complementarity rather than competition governs the placement of men and women in different fields of work and creates a labour market for predominantly male or female occupations' (1993:151). As the majority of nursing staff are female, it has been suggested that work relations between these women mean that there is a feminised culture and female sociability in evidence that could make men 'strangers in a female world' (Halford *et al*, 1997:236). Rather than a negative environment in which to work, it is suggested that these single-sex workgroups are friendly and open, although male nurses were sometimes regarded with suspicion. Men had to refute suspicions about their motives for wanting to work in a 'female' occupation by 'negotiating non-hegemonic and more acceptable forms of masculinity' as they were regarded as 'strangers in a female world'. 'Unacceptable' forms of masculinity on the ward included sexist or harassing behaviour, but they could refute the suspicions and become accommodated by carrying out considerable amounts of 'relational work' (ibid:237).

In some ways the women officers working in child protection tend to justify their role as being engaged in both rational and emotional labour. In order to refute the 'social worker' image, they need either to show particular interest in this type of work, or to claim to have a credible reason for applying, such as the officer who said she had worked for Social Services previously. Another strategy is to show that the work is undervalued in terms of crime, workload, or some other vague but specialist knowledge. In order to counteract the masculinist categorisation of child protection work as private, female and therefore of low status, the women seem to feel they need to enhance or explain their position. As Cockburn has suggested, men dominate the workplace because organisations 'are not just of casual interest to men … they are crucial to the production and reproduction of power' (1991: 221). One of the ways power is perpetuated is by changing the way some work is defined and 'loaded with gender symbolism. Generally, masculinity is associated with higher positions, while assisting work is not just subordinate but also regarded as feminine' (Alvesson and Due Billing, 1997:95). As a result of masculine ideologies informing competencies and the status of 'male' knowledge, it is suggested that when women appear to be replacing men very often the job has been redesigned and devalued in some way (McNeil, 1987:192). This is the opposite of the phenomenon described above by Wichroski, where male secretaries redefined themselves as 'personal assistants' and so on, although it could be argued that a man would not want his 'masculinity' diminished by being called a secretary.

This point was illustrated during a discussion group attended by male officers. They were talking about public order training, firearms squads and women being on the Public Order Unit, and two of them agreed that it was 'not a place for a woman'. On the other hand, when asked whether they thought that their female colleagues had particular skills, one of them replied,

> I think so. The emphasis is on understanding a woman who's just been raped or a child who's just been molested. I think a woman can come across, whether it's a boy or a girl that she's interviewing, a damn sight better than a fella can. A woman is naturally less intimidating to a child (male PC, 1994 Discussion Group 2).

In response to this statement it was asked why he held this opinion when so few policewomen have children of their own, and one of his colleagues interrupted with,

I was going to say, I disagree with that. I could speak to a child a hell of a lot better than a policewoman who hasn't had children. I've got three children of my own (male PC, 1994 Discussion Group 2).

As the group discussion progressed, one of the officers pointed out that the CPU in his own subdivision had two women working in it and he asked, 'Whose choice is that?' inferring that some women were able to obtain special advantages in the selection process and that it was an easy posting. In effect, childless women are separated from those with personal experience, with the second officer, above, arguing that he could be better at interviewing a child than a woman who was not a mother. As Rich (1977) has argued, women are often defined in this way, in terms of mother or non-mothers, and Lawler develops this point by saying that 'not all women stand in the same relationship to maternity … as childbearing is socially approved only for certain groups of women' (1996:155). Furthermore, when the officer who was arguing in favour of the inclusion of men in the departments pointed out that one of the subdivisions had a man on the CPU, the other retorted,

Yes, but would you take *your* car to a mechanic who doesn't own one himself? (male PC, 1994 Discussion Group 2).

This remark echoes Oakley's discussion (1993:21) that men view the body in terms of a machine, which can be 'faulty' and need repair, which is discussed in the concluding chapter of this book.

'Real' police work

Discussions about the status of work in the CPU compared to the 'real' task of crime fighting and 'rational' quantifiable success, leads to distinctions between that which is typically regarded as a 'male' specialism in the police and other work. Departments such as the CPU, seen to be carrying out the softer, feminine work, are judged by male 'standards', such as the CID. In quite a few cases when women were asked about their preferences and the CPU they compared the status of the work with the CID. As an example, a woman who explained that she was a Reserve Officer on the CPU, which means that she was trained, and would be called upon when needed, but normally worked in the CID, was asked about differences between the two departments and whether there were any specific problems for women in the latter. She replied in a manner which seemed to be accepting of the situation, remarking that there was always 'a bit of a laugh and carry on in the CID; get in there and make the coffee and wash the dishes' from her male colleagues, but she went on to assert that,

> You get that in any job, but if you can't take the criticism or the jokes they direct at you, you shouldn't be in the job (female PC, 1994 Discussion Group 4).

When asked about the actual tasks she had to carry out in the course of her work, and whether any particular difficulties arose for her as a woman in a specialist crime department, she remarked,

> That depends on the individual and your status – whether you're married or have children. CID can be quite demanding, if you're single and you've got no commitments then you can work the hours; if you've got children or a husband to feed, you can't always put the job first (female DC, 1994 Discussion Group 4).

However, contradicting some of the earlier comparisons between CID and CPU working hours, one of the other women officers from the Unit said,

> In child protection you don't know what time you're going to finish (female PC, 1994 Discussion Group 2).

Another woman talked about specialist posts and problems for women as a minority working in a high-status crime squad, saying that as the only woman in that department, she found it quite predictable that as her period of tenure was coming to an end in a few weeks' time, another woman had been brought in as a replacement. At the moment however, there was a short overlap, because the incoming female officer was brought in as a male officer had just vacated a post. When asked whether this system of apparent tokenism caused any problems in terms of operational procedures for the squads, and she replied,

> I think we should have more women on them, because obviously, if we do follow people, a man and a woman sitting in a car is much less obvious than two men, and yet when Pam came on, it was in fact my partner who left, and Pam should have come and worked with me, but there's no way they would put two women working together; in fact, in all my service I have never ever worked with another policewoman (female DC, 1994 Discussion Group 4).

To explore this suggestion of tokenism or the exclusivity of high-status posts such as Crime Squads, another group of women officers were asked whether they had experienced any problems getting accepted into departments of their choice. One remarked that she had transferred from a force in the south of the UK and had always wanted to 'drive fast cars *fast*'. She said that when she had expressed an interest in the traffic department she found that,

> There was only one girl on traffic when I came up, and the head of the personnel department targeted me (female PC, 1994 Discussion Group 3).

As a result, she felt she had been moved into her chosen speciality quite swiftly, and this perception also seemed to be reflected in the following remarks which were made in response to a question about how easy it is for women to join the CID.

> It's just the same I think. An attachment and then on a list. Same as everybody else (female PC, 1994 Discussion Group 5).

> Yes, it's just the same (female PC, 1994 Discussion Group 5).

They were asked if there was an absence of sexual discrimination in general, or whether localised attempts to recruit women into specialist posts were taking place. One officer who was present said there had been difficulties, over the years, but now 'It's easier' (female PC, 1994 Discussion Group 3). Another remarked,

> In the last two or three years we're getting treated better. Before, it was a real bad attitude towards women (female PC, 1994 Discussion Group 5).

> With the younger, newer policemen and their attitude is; there's a lot more women, plus the Career Development Officer, there's someone up at Headquarters, who seems to be taking an interest. I mean, we had a questionnaire last year and they seem to be more interested (female PC, 1994 Discussion Group 5).

However, this was still causing problems in some areas, as one woman recounted,

Well, I've applied for the CID, but in all the seven years I've been here, no woman has been interested in putting in for the CID. You weren't – you couldn't get them to apply for it. It's a boys' club sort of thing. One did apply, they weren't keen on taking her, but because she's a woman, and there were six men, they had to (female PC, 1994 Discussion Group 3).

Given these experiences, which are presumably repeated in other forces throughout the country, in a study by Martin (1996) women officers were asked whether they thought their force's equal opportunities policy could help them. Few respondents had heard of it and yet felt they had been offered every chance to train and undertake aideships. Exceptions to this were some specialised units such as the then Regional Crime Squads and Special Operations. On the other hand, the women officers described difficulties when returning to work after having children. As Martin points out, equal opportunities policies aim to prevent unfair discrimination whilst working within the organisation 'but do not even consider the most indirect forms of institutionalised discrimination which effectively require women to make a choice between their career and a family' (1996:521). Male officers who were interviewed also expressed the belief that although career prospects for their women colleagues were equal to their own, 'family life and child rearing' were considered to be the greatest barriers to women's advancement in the career rank structure, which policies were not addressing (ibid:525). In summary, Martin argues that prejudice against women police officers is still evident and that problems surrounding childcare and maternity leave were 'having the most serious ramifications for the career structures of women police officers' (ibid:526). She argues that the force's equal opportunities policy appeared to have removed certain barriers to some specialist posts, but women were still 'choosing' to work in the 'traditional' roles associated with sexual offences and child abuse. There was also some evidence of sexual harassment within a macho and sexist working environment, which may have dampened women's ambitions to gain promotion, and policies seemed fairly incapable of preventing this.

Returning to the problem of whether women are choosing to go into specialisms such as the CPU however, this woman had also worked with the only male CPU officer and she complained that,

… in the majority of the cases, a man just wouldn't be suitable to talk to that little girl, and they found that the two women were carrying the vast majority of the work (female PC, 1994 Discussion Group 3).

Another officer, talking about the 'maleness' of certain specialties and the lack of prospects for women, when asked about her career aspirations, said,

> I applied for traffic six years ago, and every year since and I have been intimidated so much I almost came out of the service. I also applied for the CID and drugs squad. I'd like to do the CID but there's a long waiting list and one woman only on each one (female PC, 1994 Discussion Group 3).

On the other hand, another woman had encountered difficulties of a different type.

> … when I was working at (local subdivision), about a year ago a Chief Inspector came along and said, 'How do you fancy going on CID?' I just said, 'Yeah, that's what I want to do', and then the DI came in and said 'Right then, we've got to have a woman on the CID because we've had the Home Office inspectors round and you're going to be *it*' (female PC, 1994 Discussion Group 2).

However, when this young officer pointed out that she had not had the requisite preliminary training period, another woman who did have such experience got the job. Indeed, one of the problems that managers sometimes draw attention to is the lack of women who apply or are suitably qualified for specialist posts in the police. A Home Office thematic study in 1992 (HMIC) suggested that female officers were less ambitious than their otherwise equivalent male colleagues. Furthermore, because women tend to be less qualified by experience in years' service and exams, there is a disproportionately large number of relatively inexperienced women officers grouped at the bottom of the rank structure. In effect, this causes problems for the organisation when responding to calls for internal fairness and sympathetic service delivery in terms of sexual offences.

Gender and sexual assaults

As discussed in this section so far, certain aspects of police work concerning sexual offences are regarded as specialised and complex, and therefore structural constraints, in the form of decisions about who is trained, create barriers. As a result, sexual matters and crimes which have an element of 'indecency' seem to be regarded with particular caution by male police officers who regard themselves as relatively untrained and non-specialist. Even in ordinary, routine encounters, rules regarding organisational image, legal processes and decency are kept in mind by police officers, who are always conscious of complaints which could be made against them. Male officers are only allowed to feel into the pockets of outer garments such as coats and jackets of females, and look at pockets which are turned out on other clothing. Normal 'patting down' searches are not allowed by officers of the opposite gender, and custody officers, both male and female, have expressed concerns about possible allegations regarding taking prisoners to the lavatory. A male custody officer explained,

> If there's anything requiring the removal of clothes, I get a woman officer in to watch over the prisoner (male Inspector, 1996).

In other words, to protect himself, as the only officer with access to the cells in a locked custody suite, if a woman he was 'guarding' needed to use the toilet, have a shower or be searched, he would request a woman officer to carry out the necessary supervision. On another occasion during the fieldwork, a female custody sergeant was being observed when a male prisoner pressed the buzzer to be let out of his cell. She went over to his door, unlocked the cell and opened the toilet door for him. Asked whether she felt there were any problems about decency or possible allegations being made against her in this situation she replied,

> Well, no, not with you standing there, but if I was on my own I would call for another officer to be present (female Sergeant, 1995).

So in normal everyday police work, not only sex, but also gender seem to cause problems on two fronts: first, with regard to rules about decency and allegations of sexual harassment of prisoners and the public, and second regarding rules about legal processes such as collection of intimate samples as evidence. In addition, there are structural issues which overlap into cultural areas, because they create a distance between skills, competencies and gender. Some female officers complained about investigating sexual offences being classed as 'their' work simply because they were women. Instances were observed of female officers being told to go to other sub-divisions where none were on duty to interview women alleging sexual assault, often returning to report that it 'was nothing' and a male officer could have taken the case. It is understandable that they feel resentful at travelling large distances and being taken away from their duties for the sake of a few basic questions which could have been asked by someone else. In another case a female officer was asked to attend a rape case at the opposite end of the sub-division, which meant a journey of about an hour. When the officer arrived she found the statement had already been taken by a male CID officer, and as a result she said she felt 'useless',

> We just sat in this room and stared at each other, and I thought, 'What am *I* supposed to do?' (female PC, 1994).

Another officer who was accompanied during the fieldwork complained that she was called back to the police station on two of the three evenings she was on duty that week because women had called at the enquiry desk asking to 'speak to a female officer'. She said that in each case it was 'nothing' and they could have given the details to a male officer, or to the female administrative assistant who was working on the public enquiries desk. This officer was asked whether this type of thing was a frequent occurrence and she said,

> Oh yes, all the time, but they're (male officers) frightened and they won't ask what it is (female PC, 1995).

Again, there are certain cultural explanations which have been offered for behaviour such as this, i.e. men refusing to get involved in unproductive, frustrating work, or sexual and familial matters being regarded as 'natural' tasks for women. During field observations another example of this apparent lack of willingness by the male officers to pry into intimate 'female matters' was witnessed when a woman was brought into the police station by traffic officers. She reported having had her handbag stolen, but when it emerged that she had been hitch-hiking and had escaped from the car following a sexual assault, a female officer was called in from patrol to take her statement. It seemed a rather futile exercise, because the victim had no idea of the make or registration number of the car her attacker had been driving, and he would be well away from the area by now as the incident took place on the motorway. Shortly after the woman got into a car the driver started touching her leg and requesting sex in payment for the lift. She had told him to stop the car, but in her attempt to get out quickly she had turned back to reach for her handbag, and he had driven off with the door still open, throwing her to the ground. As a result her shoulder was twisted awkwardly, and the police officer who had been called to the scene had taken her to the hospital, where she had her arm strapped up. Although there were no physical injuries to look at and the details of the sexual assault were relatively innocuous, in terms of intimacy – the victim said he had placed his hand on her thigh and referred to the area between her legs as 'the promised land' – because there was some reference to sexual activity it was felt to be more suitable for a woman officer to take the statement. In the literature on police culture, this would be regarded as an example of a reluctance to get involved in the domain of women. As most previous studies suggest, female officers seem to be dealing with more sex crimes than their male colleagues. It is argued that this is due to various aspects of male power and beliefs about men's lack of 'female' skills and expertise. Consequently, men control the definition of 'real' police work, and sexual offences, in particular 'supporting' the victim, are activities of less worth. As explained at the beginning of this chapter, it is almost impossible to separate structural from cultural influences, and it must be accepted that there will be an element of the latter, which will be explored fully in the next chapter. However, it is argued here that this situation is due to structural constraints as much as cultural ones because male officers lack expertise, and as a result they feel unqualified to ask even the most basic questions.

Parallels are evident within the literature on women and children which was discussed earlier. Women are trained to deal with the victims of sex crimes, the 'injured parties' are usually women and children, and when rape or sexual offences are reported, in most cases, the 'Officer in Charge' will be a male CID officer. Due to the lack of women in these departments, female officers serving in the CID will probably be the ones who are Memorandum trained, and will therefore be the obvious person to take the victim's statement. In order to discover whether there is a structural element to the situation it is useful to think about two questions. First, to what extent is it necessary, in terms of the legal processes or organisational rules about 'decency' to have a female officer interviewing the victim? Second, is there a circular process of training and experience due to structure which confuses the issues of preference and need regarding gender and sexual offences?

In order to attempt an analysis of the way occupational structures may be affecting the work women do in connection with sexual offences, it is necessary to separate the type of tasks women do, and to look at whether they appear to be doing these simply because of their gender and to what extent structure plays a part. From one point of view, it is plain that if a woman has been raped it is in the interests of everyone if the same officer is the main contact for the woman throughout the whole process. Officers who work on cases such as these complain about the distress caused to the victim if she has to repeat her story several times to various officers. It is also clear that if an intimate medical examination is to take place, and a police officer must be present to receive and verify the samples as they are collected by the doctor, then in terms of decency and comfort, this should be a woman, even though female doctors are not always available. Health professionals of the opposite sex are accepted in intimate examinations, but it is not considered decent, appropriate or within the rules for male police officers to be present in such circumstances. With this concern about continuity being important, the officer's presence at the medical examination being vital, and relevant training only being offered to women, it becomes clear that there are issues other than men controlling the immediate working environment. As illustrated in the earlier discussion on training for interviewing sexually abused children, it is very important to the eventual outcome of the case that each stage of the investigation is carried out meticulously according to the rules of evidence. It is obvious, therefore, that a very complicated process – and one where mistakes can have disastrous consequences – must be closely monitored. It seems to make sense to those managing the training and planning to make sure that only these officers who they believe can carry through the whole process competently should use and develop their specialist skills.

In some ways, however, this belief in the power and authority of sexual offences training seems to have reached over into the normal 'decency' part of the organisational rules. In some instances it was noticed that even the naming of body parts appeared to make male police officers uncomfortable. In the example given previously, of the male inspector who was concerned about women removing their clothes in the custody suite, he seemed defensive and embarrassed as he explained his reservations about looking after female prisoners. He had simply been asked, 'What happens if you get a woman in the cells?' In response he had explained about bodies, lack of clothes, and how he would protect himself from possible allegations. Perhaps, as Young suggests, as a closed institution, the police need to neutralise women, creating a 'universe where the body is subjugated and unsexed' in order to maintain control (1991:211). Another illustration of this took place during a police training seminar, in the larger research force, where search procedures during drug raids were explained. As this was a seminar for general patrol officers, a drugs squad officer was giving instructions on how to conduct a 'strip search' of someone believed to be concealing drugs. First, he explained how meticulous they should be about working 'top down', beginning with the outer clothing of the upper body, working down to the socks, turning them inside out and looking between the toes of the suspect. He became embarrassed when referring to the genital area, which he described as 'the naughty bits', and then explained that an 'intimate' search would only be carried out if the trafficking of Class A drugs was suspected, such as several ounces of heroin. He also said that in terms of those conducting a straightforward strip search,

> ... two males with a male is ideal, and two females with a female, but that's not always possible ... there's a limit to what I'd do. Just get them to drop their drawers, and squat up and down a few times, and if anything drops out ... (male Detective Inspector, 1995).

His words were then drowned by laughter from the audience, but he finished his presentation with a warning about being careful to wear rubber gloves, saying,

> ... and just remember, these are *horrible* people with all manner of horrible diseases (male Detective Inspector, 1995).

Once again, a specialist was giving the general police population a small and incomplete version of his expertise, but his juvenile lack of vocabulary and embarrassment are simply a source of amusement. Policing is an occupation based upon experientially gained expertise and officers often have a high regard for almost anyone who can display knowledge based upon experience. This officer's knowledge of drugs was evident as he had just given a comprehensive outline of what each type of substance looks like, who uses it and how. This was easily accepted by the audience in exchange for any lack of linguistic finesse. As with other forms of expertise, comfortable and confident use of terms describing sexual activities and the 'correct' names for intimate parts of the body come with training and experience. One of the women in the Child Protection Unit explained she was worried that she was so blasé about such matters that she had to be careful in her personal relationships not to seem strangely pedantic or over-experienced. However, because most people find talking about sex quite difficult, this female officer said that women can use their expertise and their supposed lack of sexual 'know how' in interview situations, remarking,

> A colleague was interviewing a man who was accused of abusing his daughter, and he wasn't having it, but I looked straight at him and said 'Can you tell me if you have any unusual marks on your penis Mr Smith?' and he didn't like *that* (female Sergeant, 1995).

On the other hand, another man who later confessed to having sex with his daughter, aged eight, refused to talk to a female officer, because she was a woman, and he found describing acts and parts of the body impossible. The reluctance of male officers to deal with victims of sex offences is discussed in greater detail in Chapter 5. When the study by Anderson *et al* (1993), quoted earlier, asked male and female officers who was more likely to deal with the victims of sex offences, of the women officers who were questioned, 90 per cent, representing 1,252 of the 1,810 officers who returned the questionnaires, replied that they thought they were dealing with these cases 'more often' than their male colleagues. The remaining 10 per cent said they thought it was equal, and the findings recorded as '0 per cent' those women who thought it was 'less often'. Male officers seemed to agree with these results; approximately two thirds (64 per cent) said that they were dealing with sex victims less often, a third equally, (33 per cent) and only 3 per cent thought they were dealing with these cases more often than their female colleagues.

In the previous chapter Anderson *et al*'s study was criticised for the findings regarding differential deployment of policewomen, as assertions were based upon a minority (30 per cent) of the women questioned, who felt they were being sent to cases concerning young offenders more often than men. On the basis of the fieldwork analysed here, it was argued that observations contradicted these findings. Other findings, however, that 'Women constables were most likely to deal with victims of sex offences' (Anderson *et al*, 1993:62) is supported by the research for this book. But it should be noted that the study did not ask questions about how these women became involved with this work and why they were so extensively deployed in this area. Indeed, as explained earlier, it is difficult to separate cultural and structural constraints in organisational studies and it is tempting to assume that all phenomena concerning women in the police and their apparent differential deployment are due to culture, and more especially to a 'cult of masculinity' (Smith and Gray, 1983:91). Specialist expertise, particularly the knowledge gained through the complicated and extensive Memorandum training, creates a certain distance from general policing. Hence, women become experts at sexual language and interview techniques and a sort of 'feminine mystique' appears to have been created. From varying perspectives this may be seen as an advantage in terms of occupational prospects for either men or women, and at the same time either an organisational constraint or an enabler.

Tight financial constraints on police training always seem to exist and, as resources are finite, it would appear wasteful to train a large number of male officers in dealing with sexual offences, especially as they are largely redundant in terms of collecting statements and intimate samples. However, as with all other financial 'reasons' or 'excuses', it is important to examine their validity in order to assess whether this is simply masking, or contributing to, the situation. It may be simply more convenient for police managers to insist that this is the case. Although it has not been possible to provide a definitive answer to this question here, it has been shown that women are dealing with most of the sexual offences which are reported, and in some cases this is because their male colleagues are leaving this work to them. As the trained experts, women are perceived to be the 'safest' officers to cope with the often complicated and distressing aspects of sexual assaults. In some situations, it seems that male officers could quite adequately deal with the victim or complainant, but feel that they should not begin a case they would not be able to continue with because of the necessity for intimate examinations, or a lack of expertise.

Summary

The intention here was to provide an account of factors affecting the way women are deployed in the police. Throughout the evaluation there has been an attempt to determine whether women are confined to certain 'traditional' aspects of police work, and to assess whether this is a result of certain organisational structures; perhaps an example of what Young calls 'prestige structures' (1991:191), those beliefs which influence the way things are, and shall remain, due to male power and preference. It was shown that where sexual offences are concerned, there does seem to be a specifically gendered division of labour. In some cases, this seems to be due to structure, training, resources, and legal and evidential requirements. In general patrol work situations, however, involving standard statements which may have a minor sexual offences element, it seems that some officers are reluctant to take on cases because they regard this as 'women's work'.

This chapter, this is partly due to certain training being restricted to women, leading to a belief in their specialist knowledge on sexual matters, and to the cloistered domain of sexual offences becoming, or possibly remaining, female. This may have influenced previous perceptions of differential deployment. Women officers are seen in certain high-priority areas, dealing with notable cases which become public knowledge, and the categories 'sexual, domestic and children' become mixed together. Skills associated with sexual matters are assumed to be linked to children and domesticity, but this is not necessarily the case, and it does not result in women officers dealing with all three types of case as a primary part of their role. There are certain reasons for these beliefs, and in the following chapter some of the cultural aspects of this debate will be examined.

Chapter 4

Gender arrests: men and women on patrol

In a study of women on patrol in the US, the experiences and 'dynamics associated with their occupational mobility within the structure of police departments' were explored (Wersch, 1998:23). She asked male and female officers whether they thought the jobs they were given were gender specific – whether women were given domestic assault and sexual violence and male officers received more 'assaults in progress' and 'perpetrator with gun' calls (ibid:31). Wersch found that women who became associated with 'suspect' specialisms were said to lose their credibility as a 'real cop' and become known as a worker in 'warm, fuzzy policing' or the 'pink ghetto' (ibid:35). Another American study of women and men on patrol compares the 'Hard Charger' with the 'Station Queen', illustrating that 'expressions of masculism in police culture are numerous and varied' (Herbert, 2001:57). He argues that some officers describe 'the everyday reality of peacekeeping' and community policing roles as 'chicken shit' whilst 'sprinting out to dangerous calls to preserve their warrior image' (ibid:66–7). Hence, to describe the 'role' of the police officer as gendered raises a number of fundamantal questions. It could be argued that even to suggest that female officers may have some different 'place' in an 'equal' organisation is to say that they are not full members of it. Further, to assign a certain 'role' to one group of workers and not others is to demarcate them as being 'suitable' for certain tasks and duties, whilst others are not. On a wider, more conceptual basis, however, the roles people play in society, at work, within families and so on, has been argued to be better understood from a 'multiple roles' approach. In effect, this view of the way people behave in society tends to suggest that roles are fluid, changeable and can sometimes be chosen by the individual. In other words, the role that women play in the police is not necessarily assigned to them by others, the organisational hierarchy or society itself, but rather, is the result of negotiation between these social forces and the officers themselves.

Two other US studies analyse this aspect of roles and the police. The first is a study of women in the criminal justice system in America, with a chapter discussing women in law enforcement by Martin and Jurik (1996). They argue that officers have to strike a complicated balance between 'traditional feminine stereotypes' and an oppositional stance which emphasises physical courage, being willing to use force and 'using humor to develop camaraderie and thwart unwelcome advances' (Martin and Jurik, 1996:98). Similarly, in a more recent study, also in the US, Miller describes the role of community policing and its relationship to gender. Her analysis makes some pertinent observations of officers working as 'neighborhood police officers' (NPOs), and the way the role is seen as 'softer' and more 'service' orientated, and hence, often 'female'. The author spent time observing conventional patrol officers and NPOs, and concluded that women officers were not only more comfortable with the 'image of social work, the "touchy-feely" type of tasks it involved', but were also better at the job. Community policing, she argues, represents the opposite of the masculine values of police culture, which were 'interrupted only when patrol officers had participated with NPOs in joint activities or when a well-respected, macho officer bid for an NPO position in a tough neighborhood' (Miller, 1999:170).

In practical terms, however, very often members of an organisation do not feel they have a choice about their role. Women officers in Heidensohn's study said that they were very often assigned duties because of their gender and felt that however hard they 'tried to be just "one of the boys" all had to face questions about their role and status' (1995:129). Heidensohn argues that being a 'distinguishable minority' in any organisation is difficult, but due to the special 'cohesiveness' of group dynamics and an 'insistently masculinist culture' these effects are multiplied (ibid). In terms of law enforcement Heidensohn is making a transatlantic comparison of whether women are, or can ever be, 'in control'. One of the problems, she argues, is that in the Anglo-American systems women were always an afterthought – separate from the main body of the police, and often resented, accepted only due to their useful-ness in certain roles, such as dealing with women offenders and abused children. She asks, *'Are women now in control?'* and answers that this depends on how the question is asked, saying that although they are more widely deployed in state agencies of social control, they are 'not in charge of formal control agencies' (1995:237).

In a later book Heidensohn wrote with Brown, where international comparisons are drawn regarding women's role in policing in other countries, it is argued that the contemporary picture shows that women officers are still subject to control that 'results in deprofessionalisation and/or defeminisation' (2000:76). Processes by which this was achieved included the use of 'rhetorical devices, such as scurrilous humour, satire and appeals to "nature" ' (ibid), which were being used to 'prove' that policing is an unsuitable occupation for women. More subtle ways of reinforcing this were also reported to Brown and Heidensohn in their survey of Anglo-American and European policing, where women were told that their duties 'to do with women and children and controlling sexual behaviour of other women' were praiseworthy, leading to the justification of their segregation and restriction of role, whilst 'informal comment, cartoons and official discourses serve to keep women in their place by sexualising them' (Brown and Heidensohn, 1995:76). Their results show that the discriminatory treatment women reported in Britain and America regarding their perceived 'role' is replicated throughout Europe. Indeed, the authors conclude, stereotypes and caricatures of women officers as 'oversexualised or butch and terrifying' throughout the history of the integration of policing throughout the twentieth century reflect 'concerns about the changing roles of women in society' (Brown and Heidensohn, 2000:150). Further, as the authors suggest that female officers were originally employed to police other women, it follows that when they demand parity – to be promoted for example, they may be seen as competitors or troublemakers and therefore 'must be put in her place and the power differential preserved' (2000:155). So in terms of women's roles and comparative research, they argue that despite claims that police culture is harmless (see Waddington, 1999), female officers' health and well-being 'can be undermined'(ibid). They also claim that discrimination and harassment have not, as predicted by some commentators such as Moss Kanter (1977) been 'bureaucratised out' (ibid:156).

Indeed, throughout their work Brown and Heidensohn conclude that women officers are still being subjected to discrimination and harassment, partly due to traditional 'male' police culture which is very difficult to change. This debate is taken up by Gregory and Lees (1999), arguing that sexual assault and harassment are also part of the 'danger zone' for women, which is a symptom of male-dominated cultures in organisations. In an extensive catalogue of assaults upon policewomen by their colleagues which were not properly investigated or simply dismissed, they ague that the 'lip service paid to equal opportunities in the higher echelons of the police' (1999: 29) has done nothing to dispel the 'strong male culture' (ibid:27). They argue that women officers must either suffer in silence, collude by becoming 'one of the boys' and no longer be seen as 'women', accept the 'feminine role as defined for them by the occupational culture' and attract more sexual harassment or be unable to do their job adequately to achieve promotion (ibid: 28). A similar picture emerges from Brown's discussion of women in policing in Europe and the problems they report in being accepted due to the dominance of masculine values (1996b:6). She compares the acceptance of policewomen by their male colleagues in Eastern Europe, Western Europe and Britain, revealing that they were accepted by 'all' policemen in only 17 per cent of cases in Britain, compared with 28 per cent in Eastern Europe. In the 'accepted by most policemen' category, Britain and eastern Europe were comparable, with 59 per cent and 57 per cent respectively. Western Europe, at 72 per cent, was shown as the most accepting of policewomen (Brown, 1996:2).

In order to test some of these hypotheses, the remainder of this chapter uses empirical evidence to consider the argument that policing tasks and duties are classified and often allocated by considerations associated with gender. Analysis of the types of calls officers attend and the arrests they make is conducted, leading to a discussion of beliefs about the appropriateness of men and women being involved with certain activities. Various aspects of the status afforded to some types of call, their outcome and the resultant conferring of competency upon certain officers will be explored. This will lead to an analysis of the actions and behaviour upon which police officers are judged and the credibility afforded to officers who make specific types of arrest. Finally, there will be an evaluation of the way some types of police activities are assumed to be 'real' or 'proper' police work, whilst others are 'rubbish' and to what extent these values and assumptions are informed and perpetuated by beliefs about masculinity and femininity.

One of the reasons these fairly complicated discussions of status and competency are necessary is because throughout the world, uniformed patrol work is the starting point for every officer's career, and as such it is natural that it should often be regarded as a low-status activity. Even potential 'high flyers' begin their working lives as probationers, with at least two years learning the basic occupational skills. Some officers then leave for specialist posts or departments, others take promotion exams and become supervisors, whilst many simply carry on for the remainder of their careers as constables. Within this lowest rank order, therefore, it is inevitable that there will be a wide range of experience and abilities leading to certain tasks being allocated to particular officers. In addition, organisational objectives that are devised by chief officers and implemented by line managers can affect the status of certain types of police work. In his discussion of the status of 'beat work' for example, Holdaway suggests that uniformed patrol officers who chose to carry out this work were often demeaned by their 'promotion conscious peers'. In addition, he argues, senior managers in the organisation did not recognise general patrol work as having 'a measurable criteria of effectiveness' (1983:173).

The work of patrolling the streets will be examined in the first part of this chapter. By reflecting upon the influence of a supposedly masculinist police culture, the relationship between gender and occupational cultural identities in the police will be discussed. This will analyse an area of police work that, it has been argued, places women officers on a disadvantaged path for the remainder of their service, as they fail to achieve the full range of experience of male colleagues. This will be examined empirically through evidence collected during participant observation.

On the beat

Patrol or 'beat' work, as the task of the vast majority of uniformed officers, is not only difficult to define due to its many diverse forms, but also lacks acceptable measures of success. Public reassurance through their visible presence, and the daily grind of statement taking, missing children and domestic disputes, are often believed to pass without recognition of the effort needed to carry out these tasks. At the same time, these general duties attract a certain 'street level' status, which is slightly higher than 'soft cop' specialisms such as community liaison or crime prevention. As a male detective, who was dismissive of such posts as not being 'proper' police work, remarked cynically,

> Crime Prevention Officer, now that's a really dangerous job – you might trap your finger in a door (male Detective Sergeant, 1994).

Another male officer described a woman colleague, working in the Schools' Liaison Department, as being on a 'cushy number',

> No cold Saturday nights working the town and lots of school holidays – what does she do when the kids are off? (male PC, 1994)

As the status of every aspect of police work seems to be open to scrutiny in this way, and by association, each officer, it seems likely that the 'working personality' (Skolnick, 1975:42) or occupational 'style' an officer adopts may be influenced by encounters with those of more experience. When new probationers join a shift, most of the existing members of the group seem entitled to continually 'give them the benefit' of their experience; a tutor constable explaining how he always starts off his relationship with a new recruit by saying,

> Right, you've had your time at training school, now we're going to show you how to do it *our way* (male PC, 1995).

Probationers are expected to make the tea for their colleagues at break times as 'junior man' without being asked, and their acceptance of this without question is regarded as a sign of their acknowledgement of inferiority or 'fitting in'. On one occasion during the fieldwork observations for this study an inspector was in the process of setting the cups out on the parade table as officers were coming on duty, and one of them asked,

> Why is the boss brewing up?
> Well, Mark and Bob are off, so we've just worked it out and we've all got more years than him (male PC, 1995).

As a young, newly promoted inspector, it was still regarded as proper that he should make the tea, which he accepted because he had least service, despite his rank. Jokes and remarks were made at parade time about the quality of the product and the service, lack of sugar and so on, to lighten the effect of having the 'boss' make their drinks. In addition to keeping 'young' officers in their symbolic place, another function of the other officers on the shift is to monitor the probationers, to keep them in line with the 'informal' rules and interpretation of the more formal, institutional rules. One evening a new female recruit was having trouble getting her protective jacket fastened and having pulled it on over her head had made her hair untidy. A more experienced women officer came over in a friendly way to help her pull the jacket straight at the back and she asked,

> Do you want me to stick your hair back under your hat at the back? (female PC, 1995)

Seeming anxious about force 'regulations', the probationer asked,

Is it too scruffy like this?

No, it'll be OK, they can't say anything, you've got it fastened up.

It's at the in-between stage. Once it grows a bit more you'll be able to keep it in better (female PC, 1995).

It could be argued that status is linked to gender as one of the ways it is attributed to officers such as police constables, who are all effectively the same rank, is through the transmission of cultural 'glue'. Reiner has claimed that it is these shared 'values, norms, perspectives, and craft rules' which lead to the perpetuation and survival of group identities because of a 'psychological fit with the demands of the rank-and-file cop condition' (2000:87). Despite the fact that much of the work is carried out alone, it has been argued that as a member of an occupational group which carries out a function such as policing, there must be some 'acceptance of the rank-and-file definition' of the way it is conducted (Holdaway, 1996:158). On the other hand, Reiner argues that although what he describes as 'cop culture' is not monolithic, 'it reflects and perpetuates the power differences within the social structure it polices' and is generally based upon danger, authority, including the potential for force, and the need to produce results (2000:88–9). Here Reiner is acknowledging the difficulty of defining and explaining what Fielding describes as 'several variants of culture' in the police, which are generally dominated by masculine values, as there is 'little evidence of a female occupational culture among British police' (1994:52). A certain 'masculine ethos' of the occupation combines with 'old-fashioned machismo', argues Reiner (2000:97) which, amongst other factors, is linked to danger and authority, as 'interdependent elements in the police world, to cope with those pressures cop culture develops a set of adaptive rules, recipes rhetoric, and rites' (ibid:88).

Similarly, this issue of rules, authority and masculinities is considered by Smith and Gray (1983) in their study of police attitudes and behaviour. One of the criteria they discuss regarding the likelihood of organisational policies or controls having an effect on behaviour was dependence upon the interaction with the shared norms and objectives of the rank and file. They concur with Reiner when they say that the 'central meaning for most police officers is the exercise of authority and *force* is the main symbol of authority and power' (1983:87, original emphasis). As they maintain that the police service resembles an all-male institution such as a 'rugby club or boys' school', they outline the attitudes and norms that illustrate the alleged 'cult of masculinity' – which are evident, they suggest, in certain behaviour and espoused beliefs. These are: remaining dominant in any encounter and not losing face; placing an emphasis on masculine solidarity and on backing up other men in the group, especially when they are in the wrong; the stress on drinking as a test of manliness and a basis for good fellowship; the importance given to physical courage; and the glamour attached to violence (Smith and Gray, 1983:91).

Further, from their observations Smith and Gray suggest that force, strength and physical violence, in combination with excessive drinking, seem to reinforce common assumptions about exclusively male attitudes and behaviour. They provide evidence, throughout the discussion of their field observations, of the difficulties experienced by men and women working as close colleagues. Women are denigrated by 'what still remains essentially a group of men' (1983:92–93), whilst the female officers reported that the men are 'rude and physical' and avoid them as partners, often regarding them as 'dumb sex objects' (ibid:96–7). Given such evidence it seems reasonable to assume that the complex picture which emerges regarding the deployment of officers by status and gender appears to have some basis within the early years of the careers of police officers. It is clearly much too simplistic, however, to argue that women are being assigned certain tasks because 'male power' is operating in some conspiratorial way to constrain them. In certain situations, gendered role expectations seem to be sharply defined and endlessly re-emphasised in the occupational culture of the police. For example, departments traditionally regarded as female enclaves, such as those concerned with child, family and sexual offences, are staffed by women but supervised by male officers. Officers' beliefs about the reasons they were working in these departments was that they were encouraged, assigned or simply chose to do this type of specialist work.

One of the ways task differentiation, on the basis of gendered status, has been alleged to operate in the past is through the actions of the first line supervision – usually male sergeants or inspectors – who were allocating 'quiet beats' to women. In addition, formal and informal restrictions reportedly prevent access to 'male' specialisms such as traffic, firearms and plain clothes departments (Jones, 1986:65). It has been argued that women are in the Child and Family Protection units rather than the CID because they have failed to impress the selectors for such posts due to their lack of access to 'real' police work in the same volume as men. As a result, it is suggested, women do not achieve promotion because their work records are less impressive than their male colleagues. In addition, it has been suggested by Jones (ibid:64) that women regard making arrests as a less important part of their work than men, who would rank it first in a list of general police duties. By contrast, in Jones' sample, women officers cited 'interviewing suspects' as their most 'interesting assignment' (ibid). Studies of this type therefore raise a series of important questions about an assumed causal relationship between assignment of duties, interest in certain aspects of police work and access to promotion and specialist departments. It is also important to reflect upon the evidence which supports the argument that women are deployed in a differential manner by their supervisors. Perhaps the most significant aspect is that this may be seriously detrimental to their career prospects. Several studies have reported that female officers regard themselves to be carrying out different, less force- and 'crime-'orientated tasks than men (see for example Heidensohn, 1995, Walklate, 2001, Anderson *et al*, 1993, HMIC, 1996). However, these assertions have not been analysed in terms of outcome previously – either in terms of wide experience leading to promotion or the lack of it being linked to a lower percentage of arrests for certain offences or categories of suspect. In addition, it is not clear which elements of general police duties women need to take part in to gain experience for supervisory roles and 'macho' departments such as those connected with cars, guns and horses.

Managing to be equal

It is possible that structural constraints may be leading to certain types of gendered deployment in the police. In 1992 an HMIC Thematic Report argued that most officers are highly sceptical of management policies on this topic. One solution, suggested by the authors of the report, is the engendering of confidence in a commitment to equality by senior managers, so that eventually officers' disbelief in the system will be overcome as 'the evidence gained by routine monitoring proves without doubt that members of the service are treated fairly and rewarded on merit' (HMIC, 1992:16). The Inspectorate acknowledges the pervasive effects of 'white male values' (ibid:15) and states that although '… women are not institutionally barred from opportunities … their expectations may be restricted by the existing culture' (ibid:16). Home Office findings such as these were supported by a study of sex discrimination quoted earlier, which concluded that,

> Whatever the rank of the woman officers they were equally likely to indicate that their skills were only sometimes utilised, or that they were restricted in duties due to physical strength (Anderson *et al*, 1993:67).

In addition to the specialist roles where female officers were located in departments dealing with women and children, these findings seem to indicate that patrol officers were being deployed in certain ways due to what is described as their 'strength', which is presumably physical power. Women officers surveyed by Anderson *et al* found that across all ranks of women officers, over 60 per cent felt they were restricted by supervisors due to this aspect of their capabilities (1993:68). In other discussions of police work and gender, studies such as these, which attempt to account for the effects of male domination in organisations, have been criticised for concentrating on the issue of coercion and force. For example, Heidensohn uses Bittner's discussion of the way 'force *may have to be used*' to illustrate the way policing has been singled out from other occupations as one which requires the use of such powers (Bittner, 1990 in Heidensohn, 1995:73). She goes on to argue that the violence of police work has been overemphasised, and that most writers on the subject agree on the 'relative absence of glamour, drama or violence' (ibid:74). On the other hand, studies such as the investigation conducted into the Police Complaints Procedure in Scotland, suggest that the potential for violence is constantly in the minds of many patrol officers (Uildriks and van Mastrigt, 1991:161). It was also argued by these authors that physical remedies were more commonly used by officers than statistics suggest, due to the under-reporting of complaints by the public and the group loyalties of the police (ibid:131). In addition they found that officers usually felt the need to 'act tough' (ibid:161) in a great deal of their patrol activities. To what extent this applies to female patrol officers is not explored in that study, although Jones has suggested that women seem to be concerned with more service-orientated activities, rather than the 'real' work of '… the "control" notion embodied in the "thief taking" or "good capture" ' (1986:62–3).

Powerful bodies

'Force', 'strength' and control therefore tend to be regarded as synonymous in the literature that has analysed the specifics of gendered policing. Such concepts are intimately bound to notions of physical capabilities, authority and power, in terms of aggression or assertiveness, measured on an apparently masculine scale. As a more recent HMIC report observed, fitness tests for recruits are based '… on assumptions about the ways in which large males deploy their strength' (HMIC, 1996:22). On the other hand, it is possible to subdivide the different types of tasks carried out by men and women on patrol into those involving 'force', which includes coercion, assertiveness, and beliefs about the role of women in activities normally associated with male power and dominance, and 'strength', which does not necessarily involve an element of 'control'. An example which illustrates this distinction is the difference between a heavy, aggressive drunk and an unconscious one. If the 'body' is awake, an arrest involves mental as well as physical powers of persuasion, whereas the sleeping drunk requires only the latter. One of the reasons this debate is so difficult to differentiate however, is that a continuum of force, beginning with simply asking someone to do something, ending with a full scale deployment of physical compulsion, including firearms is within the remit of the police. As McKenzie reports, American police officers are taught a model of escalating 'force options' which are used to protect them against civil liability claims (1996:140). One of the 'force continua' he quotes as an example, from Fort Worth Police Department, begins with 'officer presence' – simply existing in the marked police vehicle or uniform and insignia which may deter certain behaviour. In the following five levels of force identified along the continuum, the use of warnings and unarmed bodily acts is supplemented by aids such as handcuffs and batons, culminating in the instruction that '... the officer must shoot the actor or strike the suspect with an instrument in a manner that is likely to cause death or great bodily harm' (Fort Worth Police Department in McKenzie, 1996:141).

Several problems are apparent with this description of the use of a measured escalation of permissible force by police officers. Clearly, in real life encounters the behaviour of the actors does not move along a smooth path of increasing violence or aggression. In addition, levels of force are difficult to measure, and the Fort Worth 'force continua' mentioned above, seems to take no account of the strength or projected authority of the officer being associated with gender. In terms of this discussion about the deployment of female officers, therefore, it is necessary to separate bodily strength from some other notions of authority and 'force', in order to identify to what extent each may be regarded as more or less dependent upon gender. It is clear that in occupations other than policing, there are examples of people of either gender supposedly doing the same job, but because of a perceived lack of physical strength, women being allocated tasks which are subservient or secondary, rather than 'core' tasks. In a study of the taboo surrounding death and dying, for example, it was revealed that women were considered to be suitable for counselling the bereaved, but the caring for the corpse, described as the 'difficult heavy work', was reserved for men (Cline, 1996). In discussions with female funeral directors, Cline provides evidence of the difficulties women experience when they attempt to move from secretarial, clerical or reception duties to train for the more skilled work of preparation of the body, helping clients to decide upon arrangements and conducting funerals. Women were considered to be unsuitable as pall bearers and even qualified funeral directors were rejected as 'a bit of a girl' by relatives who demanded to deal with a man (ibid:126). In addition, regarding the physical aspect of lifting the bodies, the women Cline interviewed described how police officers and those present at the death would offer to move the corpse or place it in the coffin, whilst they were advised to 'go and talk to the family' (ibid:125). One of the interviewees explained that,

> Women are almost never allowed to conduct funerals, so they earn less than men. They won't willingly let me go on removals either. They say women aren't built the same as men! If you hurt yourself it would be the firm's fault so they try to stop you (Cline, 1996:125).

As a result of these restrictions, several of the women undertakers stated that they had joined small family firms and made themselves in-dispensable, and almost 'ungendered', although one of the trained embalmers remarked that the men would not leave her alone with bodies of children or babies. However, in general, the women seemed to report that they had worked their way through the system by gradually pushing back the barriers of acceptable gender roles, or failing this, had started their own businesses in order to find suitable work in the trade for which they were qualified.

Differential status

In general, studies of occupations and gender usually concede that it is difficult to find methods of analysis that can separate the experience of work from the effects of home and family, societal expectations and personal choice. For example, in a study of work and female sexuality, Dunne describes the way one of her respondents complained that she encountered male hostility when she was working as a stage assistant in a theatre. 'Lifting scenery' was considered to be a threat to 'areas that men have traditionally been able to call their own' (1997:149). In her study, however, Dunne found it difficult to separate these 'traditional' sexist attitudes from the 'interrelationship between employment opportunity and the lesbian lifestyle' (Dunne, 1997:166). Just as it is difficult to show that women are being discriminated against because they are lesbians, it is difficult to argue convincingly that one group of workers, carrying out a series of apparently random functions within a certain area of the organisation, such as patrol work, are being deployed differentially. One of the main problems, aside from deciding what is masculine or men's work and what is feminine or women's work, is finding a way of recording, classifying and analysing the actions of individuals. A similar problem has beset the Home Office in their various attempts to study the activities of police officers in order to find ways to maximise their duty time. In calculations of 'undirected' patrol time, it has been revealed that patrol officers have quite large amounts of time on duty alone and in groups when they are able to control their own activities. One such study, which was a Home Office activity analysis conducted in two London divisions in 1988 reported that,

> … officers in (study area divisions) do have substantial amounts of uncommitted time available to them: conservatively estimated at about 35 per cent of their total duty time (Burrows and Lewis, 1988:37).

In their discussion of these findings the authors suggest that this percentage is 'sizeable', more likely to occur on night shifts, when few constables were seen by supervisory officers, and most spent '… significant amounts of their time patrolling *alone*' (Burrows and Lewis, 1988:37 original emphasis). As the authors acknowledge, methodological problems arose because officers were required to keep a diary or 'activity report' of how long they had spent doing an individual task, and 'there is no guarantee that they will complete their updates honestly' (ibid:48).

Due to these problems of monitoring, recording and defining the nature of the individual tasks, studies of patrol work have either tended to be activity pattern analyses which ignore gender, or have focused on the deployment of women officers in terms of their specialist roles or rank. One of the problems with this method, as Jones suggests, is that the classifications are so broad (traffic, CID, uniform patrol work, office duties) that data often give very little idea of particular duties (1986:56). She goes further than this and says that even where women were employed in specialist activities and squads, they were not involved in the 'law enforcement function' but were 'in the majority in juvenile liaison' (ibid:59).

Similarly, in other occupations there are examples of men and women being employed in the same position, but who may be carrying out different tasks of subtly differing status. The example previously given of the male secretary who became a 'personal assistant', replacing a 'girl who did the typing', illustrates the emphasis on certain tasks that can change within the same job description (Pringle, 1993). Also, the importance of an occupational title in the maintenance of certain gendered identities at work is revealed. By contrast, police constables are supposedly gender neutral in name, and the multitude of working activities they encounter, often alone, make differentiation and classification of tasks extremely vague. As the policewomen in Jones' study seemed to be in more service-orientated activities, rather than the 'real' work of '... the "control" notion' (Jones, 1986:62–63), she asked them which aspects of their duties they found most interesting. In her sample she found that the women and men had a similar interest in the value-enhanced law-enforcement activities

> ... Nevertheless, women *do* find some 'service' type aspects of policing more interesting than do policemen, especially when they coincide with their 'traditional', feminine gender role (ibid:63 original emphasis).

In an attempt to assess their job satisfaction and the 'male perogative to power in the organisation and its use (and misuse)' (ibid:65), Jones discusses the 'quality of male and female assignments within nominally the same role' (ibid:69). Her findings, she argues, indicate a 'substantial difference' in this 'quality' of deployment experiences, which are particularly evident in uniform foot patrol officers. As the following examples of 'front line supervisory practices in the deployment of women officers' shows, Jones claims that she has ample evidence that there are 'substantial qualitative differences in the way in which policemen and policewomen are deployed' (Jones, 1986:79), such as the 'frequent use of women patrol officers on general routine police station duties; allocation of women to less busy beats, "pairing up" of women officers with male colleagues on "panda" and foot patrol duties, allocation of women to different types of incident; and deployment of women on "traditional" activities concerned with women victims, offenders, children and juveniles' (ibid:69).

Women on patrol

As explained in the introduction to this book, since the implementation in the 1970s of the sexual equality legislation in Britain, this debate about the gendered nature of police work has been conducted in many arenas. A large part of the discussion about deployment has been based on the notion that female officers have been restricted by their supervisors not allocating them certain types of tasks. As explained above, little empirical observation has been conducted to test this thesis. In order to attempt to rectify this lack of data, extensive periods of fieldwork took place, which inform the findings of this book. One particular subdivision was the focus of the analysis on women and arrests, but three different command areas from this force were observed in total. To gain an overview of the general types of calls and offences which come to the attention of the police the two other sub-divisional command areas which were studied are discussed as a comparison.

One of the two research forces studied had 15 'command areas', and three were identified, in consultation with a liaison officer, as having particular elements of interest that could be investigated to discover possible contrasts. It is these areas which are now concentrated upon, to analyse the daily activities of patrol officers before moving to a more in-depth examination of one of the subdivisions. In each case, data were collected which consisted of the daily computer log, selected at random, and compared for the number and types of calls. Approximately 100 recorded incidents from each command area were compared in terms of number of calls and where possible placed in general categories such as burglary, assault or car crime. In each of the three command areas, around 15 to 20 per cent of the calls can be categorised into recognisable collections of incidents, such as burglary, assaults of some type, or car crime. The area which was finally chosen for more in-depth analysis, 'West' command area, differed from the other two due to a very low number of 'miscellaneous' calls. In other words, the calls which were received in this time period in that subdivision were more likely to fall within a smaller number of classifications. Only 13 of the incidents were unable to be grouped with other similar events, compared with 34 and 31 respectively in the 'Central' and 'South' areas. Hence, in each command area certain types of incidents were significantly more frequent than others, although there were certain similarities, and due to the diverse nature of the 'patch' the miscellaneous incidents were quite diverse. Where incidents occurred more than five times in one of the areas, they were counted as a category. To contextualise the frequency of these individual categories it is important to note the methods used to construct them in terms of crime classification. As incidents are coded by control room staff, often working some distance from the location of the incident, reliance is placed upon the officer attending the scene to describe the type of crime which has occurred. In some cases communications staff rely upon calls from the public in order to decide what sort of response is required, and 'the codification of type of incident' is often carried out 'on the basis of a crude account' (Ackroyd *et al*, 1992:94).

Problems arise from these attempts to categorise crimes because of various practical and cultural anomalies and ambiguities. Codification relies upon an 'established cultural context of policing' which defines 'real' police work and encourages officers to view the recording of incidents in terms of arrest rates and their promotion prospects (Ackroyd *et al*, 1992:97). Furthermore, considerable discretion is necessary in order to assimilate a wide variety of tasks and the needs of a 'complex organisation, with many different subdivisions and consequent problems of liaison, communication' (Shapland and Hobbs, 1987:67). Computer dispatch systems (CADs), which are used by the police to record their daily activities, tend to rely upon fairly traditional categories, based on black letter definitions of crime and notifiable offences which can be collated by Home Office statisticians. As a result, incidents have to be judged, recorded and coded in 'legally relevant ways' although policing often 'defies categorisations in ways that can be effectively indexed by the requirements of many current IT systems' (Ackroyd *et al*, 1992:100–101). In each of the three command areas, specific problems for the police appear to be connected to geography, types of buildings, environment, locale and social circumstances. For example, in the 'West' command area there was a high level of burglary, due to a mixture of local authority and privately owned, densely packed housing, unemployment and inner city disintegration. In the 'Central' command area, a large city centre with shops, offices and entertainment venues, shoplifting and incidents connected to public order and drinking were more common; by way of comparison, this area had no recorded instances of burglary of dwellings. Finally, in 'South' command area, a conurbation approximately five miles from 'Central' city centre, a mixture of housing and amenity areas, including several large local authority housing estates, has led to it being given the title 'Domestic City'.

Wild West

As these comparisons suggest, it is possible to gain a preliminary picture of the area and situation by analysing the types of calls the police receive. The 'West' command area will now be used to look at the types of incident in more depth. One of the reasons is that this area is regarded as a busy 'promotion' station, where levels of 'core' crime such as burglary, drug offences and car-related incidents are high. Officers who patrol this area achieve many diverse and valuable experiences in a short period of time. Working in the 'West' command area also confers a certain amount of occupational credibility, as one of the inspectors explained on the first night of fieldwork with his shift,

> Welcome to West Beirut–if you can hack it here you can manage anywhere (male Inspector, 1995).

His remarks are supported by figures from the force database, which categorises various crimes and compares them by command area. The statistics show a higher than average annual level of burglaries, at 1,721 per officer, compared with the force average of 1,127 and the average per officer in the Central area of only 130. Theft of motor vehicles in the West command area was 911, slightly lower than the force average of 968, perhaps explained by the low car-owning population, as evidence from census data shows. Racial incidents were standing at 80 in the West, compared with an average of 21 across other command areas and only 3 in Central. In addition to the remark from the Inspector quoted above, officers who were accompanied on patrol constantly reminded each other that this was a 'dangerous' area. Although the subdivision is quite compact, there are problems with radio communications perhaps due to the geography of the sloping site, close to the river, with a high density of buildings. As all the personal communications systems had recently been encrypted, which means they are 'scrambled' to prevent scanners intercepting police messages, officers claimed the situation had worsened. Problems would occur at least once or twice on each shift, and more regularly if weather conditions were adverse. Some difficulties were simply examples of speech 'breaking up', but often patrol officers would receive a totally indecipherable message, sounding similar to taped speech played backwards at speed. In these instances, officers would regularly remark upon the irony of being in an especially dangerous locality, without means of calling for help. A young male probationer with about two years' service explained,

> It was a real shock for me when I first came here – I'd only been at work a week when me and another cop came round the corner to find two blokes fighting in the road. We stopped, tried to separate them, and the whole street came out and joined in. We were calling all the time on the radios, but they couldn't get the street name, and we got a pasting (male probationer, 1995).

As might be expected, 'street cops' blame some vague aspect of the management organisation or officers at 'Headquarters' for this lack of reliable equipment.

> Oh, they'll have gone for the cheapest, crap, out-of-date system – it's not their necks, is it? (male PC, 1995).

> What I can't understand is, if they can speak to people on the moon, how come I can't get through to the control room from bloody Boxwell? (male PC, 1995).

On one occasion, an officer became frustrated at the lack of response from the staff at the control room, although he felt they could hear him calling them a few times, and said over the air 'Thunderbird One to International Rescue. Come in please' (male PC, 1996). Throughout the West command area, in addition to danger associated with lack of instant communications, other small details of personal safety affected by the spacial environment and the local 'anti-police' population would be remarked upon. On a warm summer evening the personnel carrier was being used in place of a patrol car, as extra officers were on duty. It was parked at the end of a street looking across to a terrace of shops which had been the subject of some racial taunts and attacks. When it was time to move on, however, the van refused to start and it was proposed that we should walk back to the police station as it was nearly time for a meal break. As the officer who was driving, and therefore responsible for the vehicle, remarked, however,

> We can't leave it *here*, by the time we get back with the jump leads the scrotes will have it in a million little pieces (male PC, 1995).

On another occasion, I was on patrol with two officers who arrested a couple of young lads for stealing a car, and they needed all the space in the panda car to take them back to the station. As we were only about half a mile from the station, it seemed sensible to offer to walk back and meet them there, but they said,

> No. No way, you're not going out along the West Road on your own. I'm not being funny, but anyone might have seen you out with us earlier on tonight (male PC, 1995).

This was reinforced by a chief inspector who had arranged the fieldwork access a couple of months earlier. When I met him in the corridor of the police station one evening, he said,

Oh, hello, are you still here? You haven't been going out on your own have you? (male Chief Inspector, 1995).

One of the results of this general distrust of the local community was that a much higher level of 'internal solidarity' seemed to exist than in other command areas studied. This was tangible, not only in terms of police and non-police distinctions, but also by the way each shift seemed to need to have an image or identity which made it distinct from the others working in the same subdivision. By chance, the shift with which most of time was spent in this command area had dubbed themselves the 'Wildebeest', and it was explained that they had gained a reputation for going to potentially dangerous calls *en masse.* Members of other shifts called them 'cliquey', although this was an accusation levelled at the others by the Wildebeest themselves. One of the women on the shift explained how this title had originated,

> Oh, we just have a reputation for looking after each other, we all turn out if something sounds a bit dodgy – they don't like it, the bosses, they say there's no need for more than one car to go, but they don't know what it's like out here (female PC, 1995).

One of the reasons the resident population were regarded as dangerous was perhaps the living arrangements of the officers themselves. Unlike the other command areas, which have residential areas the police officers consider 'suitable', in this area most officers lived outside the locality they were policing. In general they had not grown up in the area and, as one of them explained,

> You couldn't be a cop and *live* here, too many prigs – people get followed home and all sorts of things. You just come in, do your shift and drive out again as quick as you can (female PC, 1996).

A male PC also had mixed feelings about the area.

> It's a great place to work, but a shit place to live; most of the blokes are comic book characters – straight out of *Viz,* and the women are the 'Fat Slags' (male PC, 1996).

It has been argued that the attitudes of the police reflect those of the community they serve and therefore the specific nature of the way these officers operate on the streets may be related to the social environment. The following census data from 1991, supplied by the research force, show a series of indicators of the demography of the locality. In each case the West command area is compared with the other two command areas where fieldwork was conducted (Central and South), and then with the force average. Force statistics show that all the indicators of social deprivation and involvement in crime are high in the West command area. So for example, unemployment is 23 per cent, compared with the force average of 13 per cent. There is a slightly higher than average rate of young people aged between 16 and 24, at 15 per cent, compared with the force average of 12 per cent. Households without a car make up 67 per cent, compared with the force average of 47 per cent. In addition, although the neighbouring Central area has a higher percentage of the population within the 16–24 age group, this is artificially inflated because two universities have their halls of residence there. Compared with force averages unemployment is high and car ownership is relatively low in the West command area.

One of the main reasons for the high levels of what this force describes as 'core crime' in the West command area seems to be burglary statistics; in the 24-hour period being analysed here, there were 15 examples of house breaking and entering and 13 alarms activated, although some were false alarms. The next five most common kinds of incidents, except for 'youths/children in street' were all cases which involve car crime in some way – another priority for this research force. In the next significant block of incidents, those which have been recorded at least five times, theft, violence and again burglary are all recorded. A miscellaneous list of other incidents shows that there were also a large number of 'non-core' activity events which were recorded on the daily computer log for information only. Most of these were not necessarily related to any crime, and included 'youths/children in the street' 'fire in a skip', 'missing from home' or 'concern for an occupant'.

Some incidents cannot be fitted into general categories. Very few of these miscellaneous calls suggest that the commission of a 'crime', and hence an arrest, is likely. Some of the incidents seem to have a very tenuous connection to traditional notions of police work. On the other hand, burglaries, intruders and other reports of ongoing events are perhaps the categories most likely to result in a high-status arrest – and therefore, arguably 'real' or 'proper police work. Indeed, it has been suggested that one of the ways status is allocated to calls is by considering the possibility of an arrest, especially where chases, excitement or violence are anticipated. During the fieldwork, the way in which calls were observed being unconsciously classified by patrol officers was noted. 'Information only' calls involving intelligence that may be used later, or crimes which would be handed to another agency such as the drugs squad, were low priority. Similarly, calls which may help with improving the image of the police or simply alleviate boredom were also given low status. Next, calls suggesting a good possibility of a 'result', such as an arrest, or where the victim was considered to be especially vulnerable, or a potential arrest conformed to a policy initiative such as domestic violence, would be regarded as medium status. High-status calls involved crimes which may attract a long sentence, and/or the perpetrator is known to the police, and a 'score' is to be made even. High-status calls also included those involving high-adrenalin chases, specialist cunning or force and crimes which offend officers' sense of decency, such as child abuse and drug dealing.

The categories defined above equate to Fielding's 'hegemonic masculinity' thesis, discussed earlier, which suggests that police culture is based upon aggressive and competitive physical action, overtly heterosexual displays, misogynist attitudes and 'in-group out-group' distinctions (1994:47). He outlines the existence of a 'pecking order among arrests; a good crime arrest, for instance, a domestic burglary, is better than arresting a drunk' (ibid:56) and the importance of a 'portfolio of good arrests' for 'promotion' to departments such as the CID. Fielding argues that, because of values typically associated with femininity and masculinity, women officers are prevented from gaining such arrests. They are disadvantaged because, although 'WPCs certainly walk the beat, they do so less than their male counterparts, because women are thought to be better at clerical and administrative work and are more often deployed in the station' (ibid:57).

As discussed at the beginning of this chapter, it has been argued that women not achieving promotion in the police and not being involved in 'macho' departments such as CID and traffic, can be traced back to patrol work. It has been suggested that this discrimination begins at the earliest stage in an officer's career, on uniformed duties. Even in similar patrol situations, Heidensohn has argued, women are expected to play a part in the 'soft cop' policing approach. In a wider view of the organisation she argues that the more 'feminine' approaches, such as communication skills, community involvement and 'attention to incivilities' are seen as a solution to various policing crises (1995:151). As a consequence of differential deployment, it seems obvious to assume, new female recruits fail to gain the experience which is necessary to achieve credibility, which in turn makes it difficult for them to get into the CID, be promoted, or attain high-status or specialist posts such as crime teams. One of the explanations for this is linked to various discussions of 'what the police do' and the way this could be carried out. Manning (1977) has argued that arrests are regarded by the police as their most important function. He states that the 'product' of policing is 'variously defined as "justice", "law and order", crime prevention and law enforcement, and often glossed by criminal statistics bearing on crime known to police, substantiated crime, and cleared crime' (1977:211). As he has defined what they are aiming to 'produce', Manning proceeds to describe how the police measure their rates of success, one of the methods being their response times to calls from the public. A principal concern, however, he suggests, is 'solving a crime – or at least producing an arrest' (ibid:214).

To show how vital this is to police officers, most can usually describe their first 'lock up' in detail, in addition to being able to recount the circumstances of their first attendance at a sudden or gruesome death. Both are regarded as important practical experiences – turning theory into practice, but more significantly a symbolic a rite of passage. So new recruits who fail to 'find a body' (alive or dead) in a reasonably short amount of time are often put under pressure by their peers and managers. Depending upon the group dynamics of the shift and the status of their tutor constable, they may be told, 'Not to worry, after your first one they'll start coming' or be teased about 'never having come across an angry man' as a signal of their 'virginity'. A young male probationer, described by his female tutor constable as 'useless', was advised that he should use the forthcoming Christmas and New Year's celebrations period to commence this process.

> We were doing lates on New Year's eve, so I told him: 'Right, tonight, the first person who tells you to fuck off – arrest them'. Later on, after everything quietened down, we'd had plenty of push and shove, but he still hadn't managed to nick anyone. I asked him 'What happened?' He said, 'But Sue, you were the only person to tell me to fuck off all night' (female PC, 1994).

As this young male officer was acutely aware, his personal credibility was dependent upon being able to carry out a core function of his occupational group. Indeed, if Reiner's argument about the occupational culture of the police being created and perpetuated by the functions with which they are engaged as 'the nature of police work does seem to generate a recognisably related culture in all forces which have been studied' (Reiner, 2000:106), it would seem that arrest becomes an essential part of their 'working personality'. Another probationer who was observed during the fieldwork, when he had about 12 months' service, was said to have a very low 'work rate' or arrest record, at his annual review. He was moved to a busier area of the subdivision where it was thought he would have a better chance of catching up with his peers. He was still doing 'badly' compared to others at his stage in the probationary period, so after another month or two he was put on report. This involves close monitoring of performance and indicates the probationer is in danger of not becoming a fully-fledged officer. In a supposed attempt to help, his inspector told him to stand by a traffic light and stop and charge anyone who went through on red. As the probationer retorted later, in response to this instruction,

> How the hell was I supposed to catch them, standing there on foot patrol? (male probationer PC, 1996).

A need to produce results, which often means arrests or at least reasonable 'clear-up' rates, has caused pressure to be exerted on police officers to a greater or lesser degree throughout their careers. Various authors have described this element of police life and show how 'crime-fighting', in which the evidence of success is the arrest of a suspect, has been elevated to a higher status than can realistically be maintained without bending the rules (see for example Skolnick, 1966:42 in Reiner, 2000:88). To what extent gender can be introduced to this debate about status, arrests and the 'product' of policing will be examined in the forthcoming discussion. Indeed, although Reiner goes on to discuss his policing 'ideal types' in terms of this crime fighting aspect of the work, not really thinking gender is an issue, as the crux of his argument is that 'the culture of the police depends not on individual attributes but on elements of the police function itself' (2000:103). He does, however, agree with Walklate's (1996) argument that more women in the police 'might alter the masculine ethos' (ibid), supporting Fielding's argument that the relationship between 'culture and action' in the police needs to be investigated (1994:47). Conversely, some studies of other occupations have shown that lack of representation in terms of numbers does not necessarily disadvantage minority groups. A study of trade union executives, for example, found that women were just as likely to be appointed as officials, although their general participation was much lower than their male colleagues (Lawrence, 1996:33). Nursing and teaching are also examples where the (male) minority is over represented in supervisory positions in percentage terms, as explained by Witz (1992).

Another question which will be examined in the following discussions about differential deployment, linked to credibility and the 'good pinch', is one which Walklate has raised in her discussion of gender and police work. She suggests that we need to debate everything from 'what counts as the central policing task to what counts as the central skills to be associated with police officers' (Walklate, 2001:140). This is indeed a crucial point and will be incorporated in the following discussion about the extent to which women take part in processes of arrest during their patrol duties, and whether their arrest patterns differ from men in terms of volume and status. In order to address these questions this section will begin with an analysis of the arrest records for one month in the West command area. As mentioned earlier, it is regarded as a young, competitive, and dangerous policing area. The number of men and women on the shifts, how many arrests they make per month, who they are arresting, (men, women or juveniles), and for which crimes will all be examined and compared. In a subsequent section some of these arrests for selected offences will be looked at to see whether this pattern is continued over a longer period of time.

West End streets

To put the discussion in context there follows a description of the geographical area concerned and an outlinine of the shift patterns, composition and gender profiles of the officers who work in the subdivision. It is a densely-populated area, with closely-packed housing and an apparently high, yet evenly distributed incidence of reported crime, according to the research force's analysis of calls. There are five 'reliefs' or shifts working in this subdivision, which is a part of the larger West command area. Each area is divided into 'beats' (given names such as such as alpha, bravo, charlie, for ease of identification). Hence, officers are directed to certain designated patrol areas, but in busy subdivisions, as there is very little undirected time, officers have jobs or duties assigned to them which may not correspond to their beat or 'patch'. In effect, officers will simply be allocated the next job 'on the screen' by the control room staff if they are coded as available. In this command area there were 123 officers working over the five shifts, providing 24 hour cover with some overlap periods. Of these, there were 97 male officers (79 per cent) and 26 females (21 per cent), which includes, overall, 31 probationers.

Hence, there was an approximate 80:20 ratio (men to women) in the subdivision, which represents a higher than average percentage for women, compared to the national average at the time of the study (12.3 per cent of officers nationwide were women in 1992 rising to 13.71 per cent in 1994), and the force average of 10.8 per cent in 1992 rising to 12.3 per cent in 1995, or 14.2 per cent including probationers. Of the 26 female officers described here, 11 were probationers, and 10 had less than six months' service. It is significant that over 35 per cent of the probationers in the subdivision were female. Of the total 31 new recruits, 20 were men and 11 women. This reflects the research force's female recruitment rate, which was rising rapidly around this period, with 39 women officers joining in 1992 and the recruitment rate for women rising to 28.3 per cent in 1995. One of the factors which needs to be kept in mind regarding these probationer women constables who form a large percentage of the work-force is that, in common with all new recruits, their arrest rates may be lower than average. Over 90 per cent of the women probationers in this subdivision had less than six months' service. The majority were under the supervision of a tutor, who may or may not pass arrests to them. Some of the new probationers may have been on the streets for only weeks or days and consequently have been excluded from the calculations of arrest rates that follows. Indeed, although the number of probationers of each gender with less than six months' service was equal – ten males and ten females – half of the male probationers had less than six months' experience; but 91 per cent of the women probationers had less than six months' service. Overall, as a percentage of all serving constables in this subdivision, female officers with less than six months' service represent 38 per cent of all female officers, whilst only 10 per cent of all male officers have this limited amount of experience.

So excluding these very new officers, in this subdivision there were 102 officers, spread over five reliefs, with between 19 and 22 officers in each. There were 83 men and 19 women, and the number of women on each shift ranged between two and five. There were between 14 and 19 male officers on each shift. These 102 officers, with their approximate 80:20 representation, will be used in the following section to compare the percentages of male and female officers with the numbers of arrests over a period of one month in the command area. In order to draw some pre-liminary conclusions about arrest rates and gender, the type of arrestee will be analysed, comparing this with the gender of the arresting officer. As a result it will be possible to see whether women officers are more or less likely to be engaged in the allegedly 'mainstream' work of arresting male offenders, or if they seem to be dealing mostly with women or juveniles. Another aspect that will become apparent is the type of offence for which women officers are making arrests in this subdivision. The statistics will be discussed in terms of 'real' police work, and in the next section a selection of supposedly 'macho' arrests will be considered to see whether women are equally involved in this work.

To begin with some statistics relating to arrests from the command area, the total number of arrests recorded for one month in 1994 was 527 and of these, 457 or 87 per cent were male suspects and 70 or 13 per cent were female suspects. Of these arrestees there were 122 male juveniles (27 per cent) and 22 young women arrested (31 per cent of the female arrestees). It is to be expected that women represent a much smaller percentage of total arrests than men, and also that within these groups a slightly higher percentage of the females arrested are juveniles. Studies examining the peak offending ages of each gender reflect these patterns, as the peak age for offending is 18 years for males and 15 for females (Tarling, 1993:15). When the gender of the arresting officer is taken into account it is found that male officers arrested 102 or 84 per cent of the male juvenile suspects and 18 or 82 per cent of the females. Women officers arrested 20 (16 per cent) of the male suspects and four (18 per cent) of the females. In total, 122 juveniles were arrested by males and 22 by female officers. As this suggests, male juveniles were slightly more likely to be arrested by male officers when the 80:20 ratio of officers' gender is taken into account. In a similar way, a small difference is re-produced when the figures for female juvenile arrests are analysed. However, this is not a significant statistical difference. From a total of 48 women arrested 36 (75 per cent), were arrested by male officers and 12 (25 per cent) by female officers. It is possible to conclude that female officers are slightly more likely to be involved in the arrest of a woman. If the 80:20 staffing ratio is used as a baseline, a five per cent movement from the expected norm is detected. Again, however, considering the small numbers and the limited time frame involved, this is not a finding from which generalisations can be made.

In contrast, adult male suspects were arrested by male officers in 90 per cent of cases (301) and female suspects in 10 per cent of cases (34) from a total of 335 arrests in total. There now begins to be a divergence from the figures for juveniles. It seems from these statistics that male offenders are more likely to be arrested by officers of the same gender. In addition, as Table 4.1 suggests, women in this subdivision, for the year as a whole, seem to have a lower overall arrest average than their male colleagues. It should be noted that the following table represents figures for the whole year, to contextualise the monthly figures, above.

Tables 4.1 and 4.2 suggest that the women in this subdivision have a lower average arrest rate than the men for this particular year. One of the explanations could be related to the point above, that female officers were less likely to be involved in the arrest of male offenders. It is possible that this could be because, with a larger target group available (male of-fenders) it might be relatively more likely that an arrest could be effected. However, these figures are still rather inconclusive, and to move this analysis forward it is necessary to look at the type of offences for which male and female officers are making arrests. In Table 4.3 offences are listed according to classifications of crimes and 'non crimes' recorded in this subdivision for one month in 1995.

Table 4.1: Yearly average arrest rates by shift and gender

		Number of officers	Total arrests by shift	Individual average
A RELIEF	Male Officers	16	702	44
	Female Officers	4	166	42
B RELIEF	Male Officers	14	630	45
	Female Officers	5	193	39
C RELIEF	Male Officers	19	1,007	53
	Female Officers	2	96	48
D RELIEF	Male Officers	19	744	39
	Female Officers	3	96	32
E RELIEF	Male Officers	15	489	33
	Female Officers	5	160	32
TOTALS		102	4,283	42
	Male Officers	83 (81%)		
	Female Officers	19 (19%)		

Table 4.2: Yearly arrest rates by gender of officer

MALE OFFICERS	
Total Arrests by Male Officers	3,572
(Number of Officers)	83
AVERAGE (Yearly) ARREST RATE FOR MALE OFFICERS	43
FEMALE OFFICERS	
Total Arrests by Female Officers	711
(Number of Officers)	19
AVERAGE (Yearly) ARREST RATE FOR FEMALE OFFICERS	37

By comparing Tables 4.3 and 4.4 a further divergence can be seen between the male and female arrest rates for various offences. Although the arrests by men and women for categories classed as 'crime' show male and female officers having different arrest rates within the various types of crimes, when added together their overall percentage is almost identical to their staffing ratio of 80:20. In the case of their 'non-crime' categories, however, the women officers have a much lower arrest rate, which could explain their lower average illustrated in Table 4.2. It seems

Table 4.3: Number of crime arrests by offence and gender

	Female Officer ARRESTS (%)		Male Officer ARRESTS (%)		TOTAL ARRESTS
CRIME					
Assault	7	(28%)	18	(72%)	25
Burglary Dwelling	5	(9%)	49	(91%)	54
Burglary OTD*	1	(7%)	13	(93%)	14
Theft from Motor Vehicle	1	(17%)	5	(83%)	6
Theft/TWOC**	7	(24%)	22	(76%)	29
Criminal Damage	7	(21%)	27	(79%)	34
Deception	2	(11%)	16	(89%)	18
Robbery	3	(60%)	2	(40%)	5
Handling	1	(33%)	2	(67%)	3
Shoplifting	5	(29%)	12	(71%)	17
Other Theft	2	(5%)	35	(95%)	37
Going Equipped	0	(0%)	4	(100%)	4
Sexual Offences	5	(62.5%)	3	(37.5%)	8
Drugs	0	(0%)	12	(100%)	12
Murder	0	(0%)	3	(100%)	3
Other crime	2	(12.5%)	14	(87.5%)	16
TOTALS	48	(20%)	237	(80%)	285

* OTD = other than a dwelling
** TWOC = taking without owner's consent

that women are making less of the 'non crime' type arrests, which may be lowering their overall average, but their 'crime arrests' correspond to their percentage of the workforce. In the following section a more detailed analysis of arrest figures for a small number of crimes will be conducted. To complete the analysis of the quantitative data there is a discussion of the arrests by male and female officers in the command area for one year. A fuller picture of some supposedly high-adrenalin calls can be seen, in order to conclude the discussion about what men and women do on patrol. Crimes focused upon in this section were chosen to illustrate some supposedly 'macho' areas of policing.

Arresting by type

Car crime is often associated with male values of fast driving, pride in vehicle ownership, and competitiveness. In Anglo-American culture men

Table 4.4: Non-crime arrests by offence and gender

	Female Officer ARRESTS (%)	Male Officer ARRESTS (%)	TOTAL ARRESTS
Section 25 PACE	0 (0%)	9 (100%)	9
Drunkenness	5 (22%)	18 (78%)	23
Public Order Offences	5 (11%)	42 (89%)	47
Breath Test	0 (0%)	12 (100%)	12
Disqualified Driver	1 (10%)	9 (90%)	10
Warrant	7 (7.5%)	86 (92.5%)	93
Absconders	0 (0%)	5 (100%)	5
Other non-crime	4 (13%)	27 (87%)	31
TOTALS	22 (8%)	208 (92%)	230

are the 'natural' drivers, and the chasing and hunting aspect of certain types of these crimes has been said to attract male officers to traffic departments. Another 'male' crime fighting incident is burglary, with the possibility of catching a criminal who will spend a significant amount of time in prison if caught, but who also may be preying upon innocent and especially vulnerable victims. It is often regarded as a force-wide priority and combatting burglary becomes the ideal vehicle for police officers to display their crime fighting, heroic masculinity. In addition, burglary involves the encroachment of personal space or territory and may involve close hand-to-hand fighting in cases of 'intruders suspected', 'alarm activated' or 'burglary in progress'. Similarly, calls to attend cases of assault may involve physical action and the protection of the vulnerable, as the injured person may be regarded as weaker than the attacker, especially in domestic scenarios. As calls to assaults have the possibility of turning into life-threatening events, with officers becoming the targets of violence, it is plain that these calls may be regarded with anything from trepidation to eager anticipation. Wherever the feelings can be placed along this emotional continuum, however, the result will be an adrenalin 'rush', which has tended to suffuse this type of call with a certain masculine status. To what extent this may be supported empirically can be shown by comparing the annual arrest rates for assaults by gender of the officer. For assaults known as 'Section 47', for instance, from a sample of 244 cases, arrests by male officers equalled 200 and by female officers 44 (22 per cent). For 'Assault Section 20' there were 23 arrests by male officers and 5 (22 per cent) by female officers. For arrests for 'Assault Section 18' there were 48 cases, with 45 of these being made by male officers and 3 (6.7 per cent) by female officers.

These figures suggest that women officers are more likely to be arresting people for Section 47 assaults than the more serious and violent offences. In other words, in cases of actual bodily harm (ABH), which is a Section 47 assault, women are making 22 per cent of the arrests, which is higher than their employment ratio of 20:80. On the other hand, although this is maintained for Section 20 assaults (wounding without intent), with female officers making 22 per cent of the arrests, when the figures for Section 18 assaults are analysed the picture changes. Arrests for grievous bodily harm (GBH) and wounding with intent are being dealt with, in the vast majority, by male officers, with only 6.7 per cent of the arrests being made by women. This pattern changes, however, when the annual figures for various categories of burglary are compared, where the more violent and potentially dangerous arrests are made by female officers. Here burglaries are divided into 'non dwelling' including factories, shops and business premises; dwellings and a further category of 'aggravated' burglary. In this third category some factor has made the offence more serious or violent, such as the use of a weapon or breaking in when it is known that the occupants are inside the building. In the command area there were 49 cases of burglary 'Other Than a Dwelling' (OTD), with 43 arrests by male officers and 6 by female officers (14 per cent). For burglary of a dwelling, there were 358 cases with 303 arrests by male officers and 55 (18.2 per cent) by women officers. For the most potentially violent cases, burglary of a dwelling with some aggravated feature, there were 11 cases with nine arrests by male officers and two (22 per cent) by female officers. In this third category, female officers are again exceeding their employment ratio by two per cent. It is interesting that figures for this potentially violent crime show an inverse relationship to the figures on arrests for the most violent assault classification, although again, the sample is small.

Similarly, when various types of vehicle-related crime are examined, such as 'Theft from a Motor Vehicle', of 133 cases, 117 arrests were made by men and 16 (13.7 per cent) by women officers. In the category of 'Taking Without Owner's Consent' (TWOC) there were 127 cases, with 112 arrests by male officers and 15 (11.8 per cent) by women. In the aggravated cases, involving injury, damage, or driving dangerously, of 53 cases, 43 were arrests made by male officers and 10 (23 per cent) by women. Finally, in the aggravated vehicle taking, causing death, there was one arrest, by a male officer. In the first two categories of car crime however, involvement by female officers is lower than might be expected, at 13.7 and 11.8 per cent respectively. In the first aggravated category, however, excluding the one 'cause death' incident, they are again exceeding their predicted percentage rate by making 23 per cent of the arrests.

In summary, therefore, as many women as men arrest suspects involved in the more violent and potentially dangerous cases of burglarary and car crime. This appears to contradict the belief that because women seem to lag behind in terms of promotion in the police, often leave at an earlier stage in their careers, and are not involved in 'macho' departments such as CID and Traffic, they must also be differentially deployed on patrol. A causal relationship is assumed which suggests that this process begins at the beginning of an officer's career, on uniformed patrol. As a consequence of differential deployment, it seems obvious to assume, new female recruits fail to gain the experience which is necessary to achieve credibility, which in turn makes it difficult for them to get into the CID, be promoted, or attain high-status specialist posts such as those in crime teams. However, these assertions raise at least two questions which were highlighted in the introduction to this chapter. The first is whether it is possible to establish a causal link between promotion, specialisation and general deployment patterns. In other words, how essential is the traditional, 'real police work' arrest portfolio for promotion and lateral movement into certain areas of specialism? A second question which was raised in the introduction, about differential deployment, is linked to credibility and 'proper' police work; namely, to what extent are women excluded from certain arrests, and how do their arrest patterns differ from men in terms of amounts and types?

This chapter began by examining arrest rates for a month, in West subdivision, and it was clear that in some categories, significant differences could be shown to exist. An example of this pattern was the overall arrest rate, which was slightly lower for women, at 38 per cent compared to 43 per cent for the men, although when certain offender classifications were examined it was revealed that there was very little difference in arrests of female or juvenile suspects. On the other hand, when it came to detaining men, male officers were carrying out 90 per cent of these arrests. If the arrests for various crime categories are then added into the picture it is possible to gain a clearer view of the type of arrests that women and men are making. For example, in order of frequency, sexual offences (62.5 per cent), robberies (60 per cent), handling stolen goods (33 per cent) and shoplifting (29 per cent) are the crimes for which female officers were more likely than men to make an arrest. Murder, drugs, going equipped and burglary were the top four arrests where men are more likely than women officers to be involved. It could be argued that this is confirmation of a very stereotypical pattern of gendered policing, but the figures in Table 4.4 show that arrests for offences classified as 'non-crime', which might be regarded as the 'softer' aspects of the service, are dominated by male officers. Over 90 per cent of the arrests in this category were by men.

Moving on to the analysis of yearly arrests in the subdivision, statistics for assault, burglary and car crime are investigated. The way most violent assaults, such as wounding with intent (Section 18), are dealt with by male officers was highlighted here. As this type of crime is commonly male – with national statistics at the time showing that there were 26,400 males convicted of violence against the person as opposed to 2,800 females in 1995 (Home Office, 1995:109), it is clear that men are much more likely to be found committing these offences than women. As 90 per cent of male suspects in the West command area are arrested by male officers, and this is an offence more commonly committed by men, it could be expected that these officers would make more arrests for Section 18 offences. Women committing violent offences amount to only about 10 per cent of the total male incidence of similar crimes nationally, which equates to the arrest rates for violence made by female officers in the West command area. Hence, men committing the general violent assaults are shown to be more likely to be arrested by male officers, and violent women by female officers. What is harder to explain is the inverse relationship between gender and the more serious and potentially violent arrests for burglary and car crime described above. In both of these categories, aggravating factors connected to the offence lead to a higher percentage involvement by female officers; women making arrests for aggravated burglary represent 22 per cent of the total and for aggravated TWOCs, 23 per cent. Again, an inverse relationship seems to be apparent when these figures are compared with 'normal' burglary (female arrests 14 per cent OTD, and 18 per cent dwelling). As this is repeated for car crime, with arrests by women standing at 13.7 per cent (Theft from a Motor Vehicle) and 11.8 per cent (TWOC), which are much lower than their rates for aggravated crimes, more questions about differential deployment seem to arise.

Working technologies

One factor which needs to be taken into consideration is the effect of computer aided dispatch (CAD) and personal communications systems upon deployment practices. In a study of the impact of such technological innovations, it was argued that 'mechanised policing', has encouraged supervisors, since the 1960s, to use systems such as control rooms as 'managerial centres' (Ackroyd et al, 1992:73). New technologies, such as computer aided dispatch and systems recording the day-to-day activities of officers, were introduced in anticipation of 'facilitating a more operationally expeditious match between police services and resources, but also providing police management with information about operational performance for both long and short term planning' (ibid:79).

In addition to the widespread use of patrol cars, new technologies including personal radios and computer systems which are described as 'command and control' by Ackroyd *et al* (rather than simply for general personnel use or information storage) have been introduced by the majority of police forces in the UK. Ackroyd *et al* note that over 90 per cent of the 43 forces possess such systems, and the increasingly pervasive role of computers in the daily working lives of police officers is discussed. As a result of introducing this type of mechanisation, various conflicts have arisen between 'practical' operational officers and those holding an 'ivory tower' (ibid:84) view of policing. Some of the problems include the system being viewed as 'an unjustified interference in patrol officers' ability to determine when and how the work should be performed', altering the relationship between 'patrol officers and their superiors, as well as provoking conflict between those line managers who wish to maintain a custodial style' (ibid:85) and data input being regarded as time wasting compared to 'real police work' (ibid:109).

One of the positive results of improved access to police vehicles, however, is the speed at which officers can travel to incidents. As Holdaway has observed, 'cars allow PCs to concentrate on "getting work", which generally means arrests'. He argues that another result of this transport revolution has been that,

> Cars can also create and sustain the action and excitement that PCs expect from their work. When a patrol car reports over the personal or force radio that it is chasing a stolen vehicle it is quite usual for other drivers to join in even though they are formally prohibited from doing so and will probably make what is a fairly dangerous situation even more precarious (1983:135).

Over the past 20 years the integration of women into the mainstream of policing, and the role of information and communications technology have become increasingly important. Neither of these changes seem to have taken place systematically, however, as throughout the course of the research for this book, 'old' and more modern systems were both observed. In the former type, a civilian dispatcher sits behind a desk in 'Comms', often a room with telephones and a Police National Computer (PNC) terminal, answers the phone, and calls officers via their radios and directs them to jobs. This relatively 'user friendly' system involves the caller speaking to the person who will match the officer to the call, often overseen by the shift supervisor, either the sergeant or more likely the inspector. An inspector working this 'old style' system explained,

> I can listen to everything that's going on, and if I hear someone dealing with a job in a shoddy way – for example a domestic or something – well then I can speak to them or more usually go out to see to them myself (male Inspector, 1993).

In one of the police stations visited during the fieldwork, a red telephone which was reserved for emergency calls was sitting on an elevated platform beside the operator. It was explained that members of the public ringing 'three nines' would be automatically diverted to the 'Bat phone', and it would be answered as a priority. When asked what would happen if more than one person called the emergency number at the same time, as the population it covered was approximately 90,000 people, it was explained that '… they would just have to wait' (male PC, 1994). By way of contrast, in the other force studied, as the subdivision focused upon for this chapter was regarded as a very busy, 'dangerous' area, any new computer, vehicular or protection technology was considered essential to efficiency. At one stage during the fieldwork it was announced that a new type of more comfortable and protective body armour (flak jacket) was to be purchased 'for every officer'. At around the same time it was publicised that the force would be one of the testing areas for the intro-duction of CS spray canisters. However, a PC from one of the other command areas remarked,

> Oh yes, but it'll be, "Let's try them out in West (command area) first, then the others can have them" (male PC, 1996).

In contrast to the red 'Bat phone' dispatch system mentioned above, the West command area had installed computer systems in most of their panda cars: behind the sun visor a small screen could be revealed and a keyboard opened out of the dashboard. From this mobile terminal the Police National Computer, the local electoral register, and the force's own mainframe could be accessed directly. All of the calls to officers regarding requests from members of the public would be routed through a central dialling system which automatically sent calls to one of three control rooms. In these centres, operators used a computerised system to record details of calls and view the officers who were available to be sent in response. As noted earlier, Ackroyd *et al* (1992) have suggested that in some situations the computer aided dispatch system is regarded as another hurdle to be negotiated by officers in their achievement of 'proper policing'. At other times it was seen as a valuable source of useful information – in some cases this distinction was dependent upon the status and competence of the control room operator. Certain operators were regarded as incompetent and given 'outsider' status by being referred to as 'civvie telephonists' with little under-standing of the operational difficulties and dangers of officers on the 'front line'.

In principle, however, at least from a managerial perspective, it seems clear that computerised dispatch systems are designed to match re-sources, such as police officers and vehicles, with calls requiring attention in order of priority. Control room staff need to be aware of the officers they have available when calls come in, and so at the beginning of each shift officers are required to 'book on' with the operators. As they leave the police station, following the parade briefing, officers call the control room by radio, telling them they are 'State Zero', meaning available for direction to incoming calls. Other 'states' include attending to paper-work, carrying out enquiries from previous shifts and 'State 4', which means unavailable for work due to a meal break. As calls come to the control room from the public they are usually answered by civilian staff, although they are supervised by a police officer of sergeant or inspector rank, and entered on a computer screen. Next, messages are sent to the subdivisions by calling up individual officers by their collar number, and directions are issued via personal radios. As they reach the incident to which they have been directed it is announced to the radio operator that they are 'on scene' so that their response time can be noted. Upon the resolution of a job, officers radio the control staff to tell them the result of the incident, or sometimes they wait until returning to the police station and use an internal extension to speak to them by telephone.

As a result of this computer dispatching system, a 'daily log' is pro-duced. In each command area, computers located in various police stations receive a continuous printout of details of calls which have been allocated to officers in their own subdivision. Each morning, at the beginning of the day shift, it is usual for an inspector to check the record of the activities of officers in the preceding 24 hours. Sometimes he or she will review incidents which seem to be unresolved or unclear from the details recorded, but generally it is used as a localised overview of the officers' activities. It is also used to identify crime patterns and it may lead to a decision to carry out a 'special operation', as a female PC explained,

> Upstairs they've noticed from the log that we just missed that burglar last night and so we're setting up a special operation next weekend to watch the streets around the one that was done over, and I'm going to be coordinating it because it was my intelligence (female PC, 1996).

As this example suggests, knowledge of events and management involvement in deployment, as a result of computer dispatch systems, tends to be after the event. In the incident mentioned in the quote above, the female PC was being observed for the study as she followed a man who was crossing the main road near the police station with something hidden under his jacket. As we drove by the PC had noticed a lead with a plug attached hanging down by his side, so she made a quick 'U' turn down a side street, but he had disappeared. She parked the car and walked around, looking over walls and in gateways, and found a video recorder, portable CD player, and small 'jemmy' hidden behind a low wall. As she was unwilling to allow me to stand on guard with the loot in case he came back for it, and we were in a deserted street, with the panda car in a back lane about 50 yards away, I was sent to retrieve the car so that we could quickly and quietly put the evidence in the boot and tour the streets in the direction of his house to see if we could catch him.

In this case the officer's involvement was self-directed; she could have chosen to simply drive down the road she saw the suspect take, and upon his disappearance, decide that there was no point pursuing the matter. In the course of my fieldwork there were examples of officers, both male and female, deciding for various reasons that they should ignore certain events which may have led to solving a crime or arresting a suspect. To concentrate first on the way officers are directed by others, however, the issue of assignment to calls by the CAD system will be re-examined, and deployment by supervisors will be considered subsequently.

Computers are used by control room operators as an aid to decision making, and the dispatchers are located away from the general activity of the police station. Thus CAD has had the effect of de-personalising the relationship between police officers and those taking the calls. On the other hand, a certain amount of 'emotion' work is carried out by both sides of the communications link to endeavour to maintain some sort of rapport. Examples of this were overt 'sexual' remarks between male police officers and female operators, asking about each other's appearance, saying they have a nice voice, and general flirting during telephone conversations. On a couple of occasions control room staff were asked to leavers' or Christmas parties, and a series of exclamations of surprise took place as people who had talked but not seen each other were introduced.

In terms of deployment, however, there seems to be a certain amount of discretion involved in the way operators decide to whom they will assign calls. For example, a frequent complaint by some officers with easily recognisable numbers was that they were more obvious as targets, and they predicted that they would be called more regularly. Another complaint was that sometimes the control room staff would take revenge on certain officers for any unpleasantness in the past, by calling them during meal breaks to provide them with 'updates'. One of the control room staff was known for being lax in his conveyance of important intelligence prior to the officers' arrival. As one officer complained,

> That Fred, I asked him, on the way there, is there any relevant intelligence on this guy I'm going to arrest, and he says, 'Yes, 12 pages'. So I says, well if it's not too much *trouble*, could you look to see if he's likely to have a gun? (male PC, 1995).

On another occasion the operator had given some instructions about the direction in which two gunmen had run off down a disused railway line, and at the end of the message, over the air, had added,

> Oh, and Paul, be careful out there. (Control room operator, 1996).

As the people listening to this message were already wound up and extremely wary of the situation, having just arrived at the scene of a shooting, it was regarded as a highly patronising remark. However, despite minor gripes about directions, the number of calls they are given in quick succession and some decisions about the priority of calls, in general the system appears to be unaffected by gender. During the periods of observation there were no calls which were specifically directed towards women or men or allocated on the basis of size or strength. In any case, it would be unlikely that the control room staff would know the physical attributes of any individual officer. In addition, they have so many calls waiting for attention on their screens that they simply need an officer, regardless of gender.

In respect of the directions that are given personally by supervisors such as inspectors or sergeants, some cases do provide the potential for discrimination on the basis of an officer's gender or supposed physical strength. In certain instances members of the public telephone the station directly and may report some incident they think needs police attention.

To deal with these calls the inspector or sergeant will generally catch someone as they are coming in for a refreshment break and ask them to deal with it before they book back on with the control room. He or she may simply ask if they are 'busy' and if not, could they 'fix something up' for them. In other cases the supervisor might ask an assembled group of officers if anyone is willing to take on a certain task. In most cases someone will volunteer, as in the following example of a request which was made during the parade at the beginning of the shift.

> Inspector: I've got a repeat arson in the cells, disturbed woman, boyfriend's left her, she's done it before – basically she's tried to kill herself.
>
> Female PC: Oh, poor thing, I'll do it – we'll do it, won't we? (turns to her female partner who nods).

Later, when the volunteer was asked why she had offered to take on a very low-status, difficult case which would probably result in the woman being committed to some sort of secure mental institution rather than being charged. She explained,

> Oh, well, it's just that I feel sorry for them, I'm known for being too soft. Josie and me, we like that part of the job – being nice to the punters (female PC, 1995).

In a similar way, large, male police officers who like the 'street fighting' part of the job will often 'volunteer' themselves by responding to certain messages,

> Inspector: (coming into refreshment room with a piece of paper in his hand) I've got a bloke in Forsyth Street says he won't leave his girlfriend's house.
>
> 2 male PCs: (In unison, getting up and putting on their jackets) *Oh yes he will!*

In the course of the fieldwork there was little evidence of women officers being directed to jobs on the basis of their gender, due to the combination of the CAD system and the lack of 'spare' officers. Supervisors have very few women on the shift and as human resources seem to be scarce, there is little room for discrimination. Some male officers, however, appear to be uncomfortable around female colleagues, as one officer explained,

Your research, it's about women in the police, isn't it? Well you're in the right place here because the inspector, he *hates* women (female PC, 1995).

This issue is taken up in more depth in the next chapter, but of course much of the work which concerns the 'action' or arrest is enacted away from the supervisor's gaze, and in some cases without discussion, so a 'natural' gendered division of labour seems to occur. In group situations or where couples are involved in disputes, women officers seem to allocate themselves the girlfriend or partner, whilst the male officers deal with the men. As it is more usual for males to be arrested for violent acts, as described in the discussion earlier, this may explain the large percentage of arrests by male officers for violent crimes. In the few cases where women were observed being arrested, and female officers were on the scene, they took charge in a seeming unwritten and unspoken agreement. One of these arrests was quite violent, as a young woman was taken in a neck hold by a female officer to get her into the van. A couple had come to the attention of the police as they were having a screaming row in the street, and originally the van stopped to simply check whether the woman needed assistance and to tell them to be quiet. However, despite the police presence, she kept screaming, started shouting at the woman officer, was warned, and then arrested. Upon arrival at the charge desk she refused to give her name; the woman officer who had arrested her got hold of her round the neck again and she agreed to cooperate, saying,

I'm gonna knack ye (fights, then submits). Just get her off me, right? (female suspect, 1995).

Later the female officer who made the arrest was teased by her colleagues, and as she had been the subject of attention at parade time for having just had her hair curled that day, they used this as additional ammunition.

Male PC: Did you see Emma lose her rag with that woman she arrested?
Act.Sarge: Yes, well that's what happens if you have one of those curly perms.
Act.Insp: Have you checked with the CCTV operator in case they caught that arrest on video Emma? You'd better get them to 'lose' it if they have.

When the acting inspector was asked later about this arrest he said that it was fairly rare for women to be detained by force like that but he was 'very relieved' that Emma had done it, as he explained,

Act.Insp:	I don't like arresting women, don't like it at all.
LW:	Why not?
Act.Insp:	It's the handling of them, I don't like laying my hands on women in an arrest.
LW:	Are you worried about them making an allegation?
Act.Insp:	Partly, but it just doesn't seem right somehow (male Acting Inspector, 1995).

At another incident which began as a report of prowlers in the rear yard of a house, practically the whole shift arrived in a small back lane behind some terraced houses. One of the local residents was annoyed that the police were there, in such large numbers, at 2 a.m. This was a fairly common complaint by members of the public in this area if too many officers appeared in a group. Remarks such as 'Where were you when we were burgled last week?' and 'I bet you don't hassle other people like this' are common. On this occasion, the householder was being a little too aggressive in his proclamations of the uselessness of the police, and he was arrested for breach of the peace. At this point his partner ran out into the street, tried to intervene, kicked the door of the police car, and was arrested. By some unspoken agreement the only woman officer, a young probationer, stepped forward and carried out the cautioning and hand-cuffing of the woman suspect. However, the female arrestee was quite violent and the officer was scratched and punched. Half an hour later the officer was still in the women's toilets at the station, shaken and upset. Both of her ears had been scratched and were bleeding but she couldn't tell whether the pierced part of her lobe had been damaged. She was gulping back tears as we cleaned up the cuts and rubbed some scuff marks off her uniform, saying,

I hate this part of the job. I always seem to catch it (female PC, 1995).

Violence and women's bodies

It has been suggested by other studies of police behaviour that male officers do not like dealing with women as suspects. In his description of female lawbreakers as 'disarmers' Holdaway describes how they were afforded 'soft' treatment (Holdaway, 1983:77) and Smith and Gray report that male officers only used force to arrest women under extreme circumstances (1983:88). Holdaway also documents the belief amongst his colleagues that 'women should not normally be prosecuted for motoring offences' (1983:78); and as the following quotation from a uniformed patrol PC suggests, this belief still exists.

> I've been a cop now for over 10 years, but I've never done a woman for a traffic offence. They always say the right things like 'What did I do?' and 'Well! Was I?' when you tell them what they did. They don't argue like men do, they just say 'Well, I'm really sorry and I won't do it again', so what can you do? (male PC, 1995).

On the other hand a female traffic officer, talking about some women drivers she has stopped, said,

> When you pull them over they look in the mirror as you get out of the car, and you can see them thinking 'Oh no, it's a woman', and they know they won't get away with it. I had one try it on; she sat in the back of the car and she said her husband will kill her when he finds out and starts crying. My partner, Bill, was sat in the front and I could tell he thinks we should let her off, and if I wasn't there, I bet he would have done (female Traffic Patrol Officer, 1994).

Further, most of the shifts observed had at least two or three male officers who regarded themselves as 'fit', able to 'handle' themselves, experts at the 'unofficial' holds, and willing to pursue and catch 'runners' to get an arrest. These officers would 'self-select' themselves from a group at an arrest, because they would be left to run after the suspects whilst everyone else jumped into cars to head off the chase. During the fieldwork it was not unusual to have to jump into a car or van quickly as the pursuit of one or more suspects was undertaken in support of officers chasing on foot. Sometimes officers need to find the direction their partners have taken and so they ask the control room to locate them. As the following interchange between an officer and the control room illustrates, however, in the heat of the chase things can get confused.

> Control room: Calling 659 – for your information – pursuit on foot in progress in the Smithfield Estate.
> Male Officer: (breathless) 659 replying – I know, I'm running after him. (male PC, 1995)

On another occasion two youths had walked past the police station and kicked the window-mounted extractor fan, which was at ground level, and it fell into the administration office where several officers were sitting doing paperwork. One of them jumped up and ran out of the building, and after a short chase returned with both the offenders, to tumultuous congratulations. Later, he was proudly recounting the tale to some officers from another shift, and making them laugh by saying,

> I was dead chuffed at first – I haven't caught someone younger than myself for years, but when we booked them in, they both said they had asthma! (male PC, 1995)

One of his colleagues, commenting on how this differs from his usual work rate, retorted sarcastically,

> What – *two whole arrests*, in one day – that's a record for you isn't it Mike? (male PC, 1995).

However, the first officer was ready for this comment, replying,

> Well actually, it's three, because I had a lock up at the leisure centre earlier this morning. (Smirks.) Can you do better? (male PC, 1995)

At another burglary, panda cars arrived at the scene to find an officer in his thirties, known to be an athletics club runner, proudly holding up a video recorder by the cable. His female partner, a probationer, was sitting in the car with the suspect. His sergeant asked,

> Sergeant: Did you catch him actually running out of the flat?
> PC: Yes, Sarge.
> Sergeant: How far did he get?
> PC: About 250 yards.
> Sergeant: Well done, a really good result (male Sergeant, 1995).

So we can see that some officers 'select' themselves for certain types of arrest rather than being 'deployed'. In this latter case, burglary charges would probably be aggravated by a 'resisting arrest' element, making it a significant 'catch' for the officer's work record. Furthermore, as arrests are counted by the 'first touch' principle, where they are attributed to the officer who makes physical contact first, young, fit and apparently more usually male officers can apprehend their adversaries more regularly. As the following example shows, however, where other police skills such as observation and shrewdness are required, physical attributes may not be so important. In the following case a female officer had just arrested an 18-year-old male suspected of burglary. As he was led to the cells she explained,

> He's mine, we had a call from the neighbours that they'd just seen someone crawling into the house through a hole in the patio doors, and we drove along the road, and I said, 'Hang on – he doesn't look right' – it was this bright pink jacket he had on. So we stopped the van and he started to run and I got first touch (female PC, 1995).

Supervising gender

In conversation with supervisors about their feelings regarding the deployment of women, they are obviously unlikely to confess to being overtly discriminatory. A male inspector was quite frank about his fears regarding women and danger, however, saying,

> On my shift they're all my kids, my children, and the girls – I worry about them on their own; I'm always listening on the radio if they're out on their own (male Inspector, 1995).

Another sergeant, well known for his tenacious manner, yet small stature, placed more emphasis on physical size and presence than gender, when asked about women and arrests,

> Take me for instance – if I go into a pub and tell someone to leave, they might turn round and say, 'Ye's not gonna make me', but I always say, 'No, but *he* will (points to a large member of the shift) and if that's not enough, there's plenty more of our mates back at the nick'. Another thing, it's not just your size, but your attitude; it's always best to get the first punch in – don't let them wind you at the start (male Sergeant, 1995).

Another day there was an example of this when a young drug user was carried into the back of the police station and forcibly taken into a cell by four uniformed officers, who intended to search him. Once they managed to get him through the doorway, he refused to take his clothes off and so the Sergeant, quoted above, smashed the door back on its hinges, and, pulling on a pair of rubber gloves, made him comply by shouting at the prisoner, army style,

> Right, you're gonna get your fucking kit off, *now!* (male Sergeant, 1995).

As the door was closed behind him there were no further sounds of resistance and the body search was completed.

Culture and strength

It has been discussed in the past that occupational status in the police is dependent upon the ability to run, catch and restrain the prime targets of the 'fight against crime'. As these 'core' criminals are usually young, male and 'tough' burglars and car thieves who are prepared to use violence to escape, it is argued that the police must be able and willing to retaliate if necessary. As writers on police culture in the past have suggested, occupational myth and that which Holdaway describes as a 'good yarn' or 'rich mixture of narrative' (1983:138) play an important part in the perpetuation of shared values and beliefs. Smith and Gray regard 'stories of fighting and violence' and 'sexual conquests and feats of drinking', as essential to the maintenance of male officers' standing in the group as 'good policemen who made "good arrests" '(1983:87).

Fieldwork observations suggest that part of what has been described as the 'toughness code' seems to be the ability to recount tales of feminine frailties, designating women colleagues as 'nice in their place, but not up to the job'. In their study of police violence in Glasgow, mentioned earlier, Ulidriks and van Mastrigt observed that recruits may already have 'traditional' values concerning physical prowess and a willingness to fight as measures of manly worth (1991 :160) and these are reinforced in an occupation such as policing. Indeed, as Hobbs has suggested, with the exception of criminal entrepreneurship, there are few job opportunities remaining in the traditional trades which 'have been crucial in defining and shaping images of masculinity' (Hobbs, 1994:119). However, as police officers come from 'traditionally working class backgrounds', according to Uildriks and van Mastrigt, 'in certain police circles, "acting tough" ' may be one way for an officer to acquire the reputation for being a 'good' police officer (1991:160).

In order to sustain this belief, however, 'challengers' who can 'offer a threat to the secrecy and interdependence of policing' (Holdaway, 1983:81) such as women must be continually viewed within the 'homologous binaries' of police culture (Young, 1991:209). Male officers encountered during the fieldwork were keen to praise female colleagues, saying 'She gets stuck in' (fights) or 'precise and thorough' (with her paperwork). However, a male PC said he drew the line at a female supervisor.

> What you don't need is someone who is supposed to be in charge of a firearms incident, way out of her depth, not knowing what to do, her voice going higher and higher, about to burst into tears – it's putting everyone at risk (male PC, 1994).

Another female colleague was regarded as lacking in credibility due to her body size, as one of her colleagues explained,

> I mean she is fat, bordering on the obese. She's regarded as a joke – she's got no operational capability in terms of uniform work (male Inspector, 1995).

Conversely, lack of body weight was often commented upon by male officers when they described their worries about the capabilities of female officers. One story, which seemed to be part of police urban mythology, was retold by a male traffic officer.

> During the miners' strike, a female officer, eight and a half stone in her nylons, arrested an 18-stone picket, and she handcuffed him. He just let her, and then he picked her up and walked off with her – nothing she could do (male PC, 1995)

Another story which an officer recounted was the result of a 'manly confidence' between him and a male prisoner.

> One day there was a woman custody sergeant and a female PC working as her gaoler, and I was in the suite doing an interview, and my prisoner said, 'If you weren't here, if it was just those two – I'd get out'. Personally, I think he would have tried it (male PC, 1995).

Stories concerning women making arrests which required physical courage were rare, and never told by male officers. General conceptions of female strength do not seem to have been influenced by what Heidensohn (1995) and Walklate (2001) have called the feminisation of the police, the move from 'force' to service and women as the answer to the crisis in policing, mentioned earlier in this book. Capabilities at 'street level' seem to be controlled by maleness and reinforced by events, colleagues, members of the public and even those who are arrested. As an ethnographer during the fieldwork, even taking the researcher's non-police status into account, gender was undoubtedly a factor which influenced some of the activities with which it was 'permitted' to be involved. One evening, following a fight outside a nightclub, two of the officers said they'd been worried that,

> ... you were a bit too close. I can't help it – I feel protective (male PC, 1994)

This was despite the fact that there were several officers around the arrestees. On another occasion, another two male officers were trying to arrest a fairly volatile young man who was becoming excited and anxious, so I went out into the hallway to give them more space, and they said afterwards,

> That was useful, you'd have blocked him if he'd made a run for it but we wouldn't have let him get you (male PC, 1995).

Upon arriving at speed to calls with potentially violent situations, officers would warn 'don't get involved'. At an incident where the landlord of a notoriously 'rough' public house had reported being threatened with a shotgun, despite my having spent almost six months with various officers from this subdivision, the officer being observed said,

> Now, can I make a suggestion – that you wait outside when we get there? (male PC, 1995).

At another incident, inside a custody suite, I was watching a young burglary suspect being charged. He was told that because he had been arrested 32 times in the past year, the police would be opposing any further bail applications. He was to be held in custody for court on Monday morning and it was only Saturday evening now. As he had expected to simply walk from the cells after an hour or so, he was shocked and upset, and a group of five officers, including the woman who had arrested him, watched as he struggled to maintain his composure. Without warning, however, he suddenly lurched forward, broke from the group of officers, made a run for the door, where I was standing, and attempted to push me aside. As I instinctively jumped in his path and grabbed his arm the whole group sprung into action and fell upon him. He was pushed to the ground and then carried away bodily, with an officer at the end of each arm and leg. As they got him round the corner he was thrown into a cell, and had his belt, shoes and personal property removed from him forcibly and without regard for his complaints of pain. As he was struggling and being restrained I could hear what sounded like several blows and remarks being made such as 'You don't go for women, laddie' and 'She's not even one of us', as my gender and outsider status somehow made his escape attempt more unacceptable in their eyes. After the situation had calmed down everyone was very apologetic, the custody sergeant asking if I was alright, and the female officer in whose control the suspect had been said,

> I'm really sorry about that, he was my responsibility. I should have been watching, and realise he might try it on (female PC, 1995).

This incident provides, like many other daily examples of stories about violence, danger and excitement, a way to reinforce the beliefs and internal solidarity of the police. This is reinforced by other 'folk narratives', as one of the officers explained at a social evening later in the year.

> Here, I heard you stopped one of the toe rags legging it out of the back of the West End. I hope your university pays danger money (male PC, 1995).

Due to this constant telling and retelling of these so called 'rich narratives', cultural values can be reinforced and tested; as Holdaway says, when the practice of 'verballing' is rehearsed, 'trust is tested, secrecy reinforced and teamwork strengthened' (1983:118). In this way, policing offers, particularly to men, what Hobbs has suggested is in decline – 'viable gendered careers for men' (Hobbs, 1994:119). Just as the criminal entrepreneur uses the ability to physically threaten weaker individuals, so with the exercising of power and exclusion of women, he goes on to argue, violence is an essential tool in structuring male identities (ibid:119–120). The following chapter will explore the way masculine identities are maintained and recreated for each generation of recruits, both male and female, by analysing some of the ways 'being a man' is enacted in the police. This theme of masculine identities will be explored by looking at the meanings behind the behaviour, beliefs and actions described here. In essence, reasons for the apparently indefatigable 'cult of masculinity', which appears to be alive and well in the modern police, will be sought.

Chapter 5

Cars, guns and horses: masculinities in control

In this chapter the observed activities and behaviour of police officers on patrol and in specialist posts usually occupied by men will be used to illustrate the enactment of 'masculinity', masculinities or simply 'being a man' in the police. We have seen that, despite management policies and directives on equal opportunities for women, certain underlying attitudes towards the gendered nature of police work are still pervasive and influential. It seems that for arrests where physical force is required, men are considered to have the necessary skills, whilst their female colleagues, despite evidence that they take part in what might be regarded as the more violent and dangerous incidents, are thought to be in need of protection, or considered simply 'unsuitable' for these tasks. Although male and female officers appeared to be equally involved when violent or physical arrests were made, several officers commented that they regarded this to be inadvisable.

Studies of police behaviour concerned with promotion or transfer into departments traditionally regarded as 'macho' include one Heidensohn conducted in 1994. She reviewed the ability of women to 'handle' physical, street policing and the attitudes of male colleagues towards their supposed helplessness and physical inability. Women officers in the US that Heidensohn interviewed claimed that they could 'handle it out here' (1994:293) and did not need constant surveillance and over-enthusiastic back-up by male colleagues at fights and public order incidents. At the same time women officers from both Britain and the US said that they were aware of the way they would be perceived by the public as less authoritative in some instances, particularly those concerning public order. This is described as 'police presence' by

Heidensohn and she reports that women she interviewed had developed 'a variety of psychological techniques and tricks' to compensate for a 'lack of physique' (ibid:299). Firearms departments, who have traditionally been nearly all male, have also been investigated. In 1995 Brown and Sargent found that only 2.6 per cent of authorised firearms officers were women, with 5 per cent of forces having none, and 42 per cent having only one or two women (1995:3).

In a continuation of their discussion about policewomen and firearms, Brown and Sargent (1995) explore the motivation of women to join these departments. They suggest that from a sample of about 700 officers '3 out of 10 women compared with 1 in 10 men thought they were not strong enough' (ibid:7), although twice as many women as men said that they thought a day training might make them change their mind. In terms of being interested in the job, there was not much difference between men and women, with five out of ten men and four out of ten women stating they might apply. As might be expected, regarding the roles women see themselves fulfilling, the reasons they stated for wanting to become firearms trained showed a difference in motivation between men and women. The biggest reported differences in women and men's motivations was that women thought it would give them more 'variety' (37 per cent compared to 13 per cent), whilst men wanted to join because they saw it as a valuable public service (13 per cent compared to 5 per cent) which would enable them to learn new skills (again 13 per cent compared to 5 per cent). Teamwork was also more important for men in their reasons for wanting to join. When male officers serving in the firearms departments were asked, for example, whether they thought women were suitable for their department, one remarked that 'most women being slight in build and light in stature would understandably struggle under the weight of body armour' if they were required to rescue a colleague as 'We depend on our fellows to get us out if we are hurt. I doubt if most women could manage with a fully equipment clad male officer if he were hurt' (Brown and Sargent, 1995:11). The authors conclude that rather than the women not being motivated to join such departments, or less motivated than their male colleagues, results from their study suggest that it is 'more likely to be aspects of police culture and embedded individual and organisational attitudes which inhibit women from becoming firearms officers' (ibid:13).

Other reasons for women being supposedly 'unsuitable' for jobs involving firearms or responsibility for promotion, ranged from the physiological, mentioned above, to the biological (premenstrual syndrome, for example) and the psychological. Women were thought to lack the 'aggression' or 'ability to kill' in a life and death situation, or they could be too 'weak' to withstand the mental stress of isolation if they held promoted posts, especially where most of the people they would manage, and may have to discipline, would be male. Another study by Brown, with Grover in this case (1998), looks at the levels of stress reported by male and female sergeants. They argue that when women officers are injured on duty, media responses are often much stronger than for similar incidents involving men. They suggest that the reasons for this are the 'protective, paternalistic attitudes that women officers still invoke from colleagues and supervisors and latent assumptions about the appropriateness of women being put at risk' (Brown and Grover, 1998:47). As they point out, research in the field of health studies shows that women are more likely to report psychological problems and so it might be assumed that this would be the case in policing, but their results showed 'no statistically significant differences between the men and women in terms of their emotional responses to stressful policing tasks' (ibid:50).

In public order situations, as Heidensohn argues, women are seen to be vulnerable because of their weight and size. She says that the 'nature' of women's physical and psychological characteristics and the 'nature of policing – involving danger, and macho camaraderie' are seen as incompatible (Heidensohn, 1996:174). She argues that, as the history of women in the police showed them having a caring and protective role, and looking after women offenders, their role in physically restraining disorder 'is, in short, an unsuitable job for women' (ibid:173). Regarding their 'natural characteristics' or femininity, these 'are perceived in terms of *deficits*: lack of physical presence, of tough physique, above all of masculinity' (ibid:176 original emphasis). The concept of law and order as a 'male preserve', she argues, prevents women from fully penetrating this arena despite a series of scandals and disasters which have been the result of unbridled masculinity and the inability of the police to 'accept and work with gender' (ibid:181).

It is perhaps understandable that for some officers the use of physical violence or force is a masculine preserve. Indeed, the belief that 'fighting' and physical expressions of aggression are purely masculine attributes, which men have the right to 'use' as they are essentially male, can be observed throughout general society. However, this 'right' becomes further internalised through police cultural values, as a 'core characteristic' (Reiner, 2000:87), apparently becoming closely aligned to their occupational identity. To employ Messerchmidt's definition, there is an idealised version of masculinity which is 'culturally honored, glorified and extolled' (1993:82) which may be amalgamated with general police cultural values, leading to mutual reinforcement. As a result, despite efforts to feminise the police machine through training, policies and senior officers' orders to reduce the use of force as a strategy, tension may be created. Male officers being told not to act in ways they traditionally associate with 'being a man' and a police officer, is perhaps equated with being asked not to behave as men. In addition, officers on patrol are being required to resist and deny that which they regard as a practical necessity – actions through which they can defend and reinforce their masculinity, creating dilemmas and difficulties for themselves, colleagues and the organisation as a whole.

One of the ways this can be illustrated is through Brittan's suggestion that, despite certain fluctuations in men's behaviour over time, 'masculism' remains a dominant ideology and 'provides the under-pinnings for a particular way of organising gender relations' (1989:15). As suggested earlier, policing and masculinity seem to be intimately connected. Fielding argues that certain cultural values and behaviour are responsible for producing 'an almost pure form of hegemonic masculinity' (1994:47). Similarly, Connell has suggested that hegemonic masculinity is constructed in relation to women, with force and the threat of it being used to maintain certain power structures (Connell, 1995). Gendered power relations and the working of occupational ideologies have also been described by Smith and Gray throughout their discussion of a 'cult of masculinity' in the Metropolitan Police. In their study they observed that women officers were being excluded from bonding and initiation rituals (Smith and Gray, 1983:83), most of which involved excessive drinking. Female officers, working as 'equal' colleagues by demonstrating that they are willing to take part in the violent physicality of policing, may, as Messerchmidt observes in a discussion about women shop floor workers, be challenging the practice of 'accomplishing masculinity' (1993:132). On the other hand, as Heidensohn has pointed out, cultural beliefs and values which lead to such behaviour might not be held by a majority of officers, but become apparent due to a number of 'subcultural guardians' who express their opinions vocally (1995:216). In addition, she observes, policing has never been analysed from a 'men's perspective' and although 'macho cop culture' has been written about extensively, its existence has been *'justified* rather than properly *explained'* (ibid:13, original emphasis).

These issues will be examined throughout this chapter using evidence from two main areas of fieldwork. First, the analysis will draw upon observations of the specialist departments which seem to attract very few female officers, such as those concerned with firearms, cars and horses. Next, these 'rarified' male specialisms will be compared with general, uniformed policing by examining certain aspects of traditionally 'male' behaviour. Four areas of interest, which illustrate the problem of maintaining an image which is sufficiently 'male', will be included. The first is professionalism – the ability to maintain a 'macho cop' image when things go wrong whilst being observed by a public, 'outsider' audience. Second is competence – appearing to be a sufficiently valid member of the shift, despite challenges to traditional 'masculine' values by critical 'insiders' or colleagues. Third is sexuality: displaying clearly heterosexual desire at appropriate times, yet managing to be credible and sympathetic with victims of sex crimes. Finally, there is heroism – acting as the protector of women and avenger of the weak, whilst remaining emotionally strong, particularly in tragic and disturbing situations.

Masculine status

As argued in the previous chapter, occupational competence in the police appears to be largely dependent upon high-status arrests which involve physicality, danger and competition. This supposition will now be examined with reference to police culture and masculinity. Throughout this chapter some basic observations will be made about the way men act 'as men', how some officers 'appropriate' or resist certain behaviour and how variations of masculinity are enacted in given situations. 'Doing gender' and acting as 'real men' is shown to be more difficult than it might appear by examining various tasks associated with policing. This will be carried out by constructing a series of explanations for certain attitudes and beliefs, including looking at instances where maintaining a front of masculinity is problematic. The discussion will include some of the police's 'huntin' and shootin'' activities, but also their performance as caring public servants. Evidence will include examples of officers 'being men' with varying degrees of success. In essence, by examining issues of power, sexuality and identity, Fielding's suggestion that 'police forces are sites for competing ways of being a man and expressing masculinity', of which 'stereotypical machismo' (Fielding, 1994:56) is only one example, will be tested.

Physical courage in the face of danger and the capability to use strength in situations requiring force, control and coercion, are typical examples which are used to explain the 'macho cop' behaviour which is alleged to be part of the working approach of the police. It is part of the performance of assertiveness, dominance and appearing to win the war, at least against disorder, if not crime, which is demanded by managers, politicians and increasingly by members of the public. A significant number of situations seem to require the resolution of problems through means which tend to involve at least the threat of force. It has been argued, for example, that in the course of their careers all police officers will encounter situations which they feel are dangerous and perhaps life-threatening. As Reiner has suggested, this is a result of facing 'sudden attack from another person' as explained earlier (Reiner, 2000:88) – one of the unique aspects of police work.

As the excitement and status which are attached to physical violence are enhanced when an incident turns into a possible encounter with firearms, the following scenario illustrates the way 'death defying' bravado can be displayed. An inspector was instructing the shift of officers who were assembled outside a house where a woman had been threatened by her partner with a shotgun.

> Right, two of you, get over there down behind that car, but keep out of the line of fire as you go across the road. You two, round the back of the house, find some trees to get behind for protection. When the ARV gets here, we'll loud hail the house and hopefully they'll decide to give themselves up. If anyone comes running out, keep your heads down (male Inspector, 1995).

In the ordinary daily working lives of police officers the 'stake out' of a house, as described above, is not considered a common occurrence. In the course of a period of fieldwork lasting 12 months, only two such incidents were encountered. Although many officers regard gun incidents as becoming more prevalent, it is clear that, compared to the mundane regularity of some tasks, jobs involving guns are exciting, potentially hazardous and therefore remarkable. One of the notable aspects of these events is the way a series of specialists become deployed in the process of extracting people from premises when firearms are believed to be present. As the 'incoming' experts, firearms officers, or those with other rarified skills, especially those linked to certain 'male' pursuits such as driving and shooting, are regarded with some animosity by their uniformed colleagues, but also with respect. As they are taking over the 'patch' from an existing group of officers, proprietoriality is an issue, but the way the firearms teams take a unique responsibility for their actions and face death more regularly than 'ordinary' officers inspires respect and reverence from the others. As police guidelines for the use of firearms emphasise, these officers are warned that they may have to justify their use of lethal force in court. To be responsible for the death of another and then face legal proceedings as a result of 'doing the job', is considered an onerous and largely unfair responsibility by police officers. It is impressed upon gun squad members on each occasion prior to the entry of any premises using weapons that the force will not take the blame for mistakes made by individual officers. Legal reminders are given in each case, as a superintendent has to authorise the deployment of the firearms team. Prior to the operation going ahead, he or she must read the text of the guidelines aloud to the squad, checking they understand it and agree to accept the consequences of their actions.

As this chapter is about various ways of 'being a man' in the police, the way the concept of 'masculism' operates to 'naturalise male domination' (Brittan, 1989:17) is important here. This idea is the key to Brittan's thesis on masculinity and power in which he examines various ways of explaining male sex roles and criticises the assumption that 'masculinity is timeless and universal' (1989:1). In order to provide empirical evidence to analyse the validity of these theories, certain areas of special expertise in the police will be examined in depth. Some specialist departments, it could be argued, allow officers to 'contract out' of general patrol work, and possibly out of the need to work with women as equals. In particular an analysis will be conducted of the occupational ethos of some of these specialist units, in which very few women are employed or seem to aspire to join.

Avoiding women

As Smith and Gray observe, the police force is very similar to the army in terms of masculine occupational values and attitudes, except that in the police the male majority are obliged to work alongside women as colleagues (1983:91). On the other hand it seems that some departments seem to operate as self-contained groups within the wider and more general policing machine. In this way they allow officers to distance themselves from female colleagues and to a certain extent from 'service' or 'softer' activities. During the fieldwork officers from various departments were observed, including a Central Traffic Task Force, the Mounted Branch, the Marine Unit, several versions of a Territorial Support Group and the Dedicated Firearms Team. In each of these cases very small percentages of the overall workforce were female, when compared with the force average for women officers. So for example, in the Mounted Branch, known as the 'Horses', there were ten male officers and one woman. In the Central Traffic Task Force, known as the 'Cruisers', 180 male officers had three female colleagues. In the Marine Unit, known as the 'Boats', the ratio was 14:1 and the Firearms Team, (the 'Guns') had 12 male officers and one woman. Finally, in the Territorial Support Group, known simply as the 'Group', 27 men and one woman comprised the total strength.

More revealing than these statistics, however, is the working environment and atmosphere of these departments, which could be a controlling factor when women officers decide to apply for postings. In the course of the fieldwork one of the Mounted Branch officers was asked why he thought his department seemed so unpopular with women officers, considering the image of horse riding with the general population being a 'women's' sport or recreation. He replied,

> Oh, yes, but this isn't like riding out on a Sunday afternoon you know. People get a very mistaken image of the work of the Branch. They think we're just out trotting about in the nice weather, but they come to us for a two week attachment, get wet and cold and mucky, and they realise this is a *hard, physical job* (male PC, 1996).

Although he did not specifically refer to women as being unsuitable for this type of activity, his inference was that anyone lacking traditionally 'male' characteristics would not choose to be put through the hardship and discomfort involved. In response to this enquiry, however, he proudly showed the temporary building which had been installed as a changing and toilet suite for the female grooms and the solitary female officer currently serving with the department. When he was asked again, in view of having such good facilities, why he thought there were so few women on the team, he retorted in quite a defensive way,

> I've really no idea why it is, although one thing that might put them off is that you have to pass your HGV licence so that you can drive the horsebox, and that's not everyone's cup of tea – a ten ton, articulated trailer to reverse out of the football club's car park every week (male PC, 1996).

It was asked whether competition for places in the branch was very strong, adding to the exclusion of women applicants. As he had explained that much of their work was concerned with crowd control at matches, I wondered if one of the attractions for male officers might be the opportunity to watch premiership football every week, but he replied,

> Well, no, not really, because we box the horses up whilst the match is on, and we have our meal break, so we never see the football (male PC, 1996).

Upon accompanying the mounted officers to the match the following Saturday, this explanation was shown to be accurate. After the fans had been shepherded safely into the ground they were monitored by officers on foot inside the stadium. Personnel from city centre shifts were deployed for the duration of the match; quite a few of these officers did seem to have chosen to work this duty period, as I was standing with an officer on overtime, who remarked several times that some of the officers he could see should have finished their shift at 3pm, before the match started. Indeed, at one point the whole of one seating area rose to their feet to complain about a player being sent off and the Chief Inspector, who should have finished his shift, stepped forward, pointing at the crowd to indicate they should sit down. As they took no notice of him, but merely retrieved their seats when the matter on the pitch had been resolved, the officer I was standing with remarked sarcastically,

> See? Even *they* know he's off duty. Great supervisor that – I'd follow him to the ends of the earth – if only to find out what happened (male PC, 1996).

By way of contrast to the 'Horses', the next specialist department visited was the Central Task Force, which was formed to operate as what appeared to be an elite traffic department. At the operations centre several high performance cars in the yard at the back of the police station and their engine capacities and gearing systems were proudly displayed as a precursor to the day's activities. One of the drivers explained that they had changed from high speed saloon cars with 'racing chips', to more suitable, if slightly slower ones because the ground clearance of the latter was superior. He conceded that,

> Of course, in this department we do a lot of off-road chasing and the scrotes had learnt that any rough ground with bricks or rubble would mean we couldn't follow them in the old vehicles – they knew that the sump was too low, so they would go for rough terrain on purpose. Now we've got these new cars though, it's a whole new ball game (male PC, 1996).

He proceeded to explain the technicalities of ground clearance in centimetres and then, having filled the windscreen washer system with water, we got into the car to drive to a local roundabout to watch the morning rush hour traffic. Sitting at the junction of two dual carriageways watching for speeding motorists and monitoring the radio for accidents, the officer explained the impressive range of controls, from fingertip operated radio controls which could be used in 'hands free' mode to the sophisticated, 'on board' speed trap system. In addition, he showed his personal expertise by casually reading vehicle excise licence expiry dates as cars came towards us at speed. At one point a report of a road accident which had happened reasonably near to where we were waiting came over the radio. However, it was not considered serious enough for us to attend, as he explained,

> No, that sounds like a little prang that the local lads can deal with; I would have gone to it if it had been half an hour earlier but we don't want to get tied up so near to coffee and bacon sandwich time (male PC, 1995).

His estimation was right because a few minutes later the call came from the Central Task Force control for all 'SS' units, which is their call sign, to return to base for 'further instructions'. We drove back to the centre of the operation which is a small, converted house at the rear of one of the divisional stations in the command area. Bacon sandwiches and coffee were indeed available, and the sergeant told the gathering of six male officers that they were to be 'tasked' to a command area to the south of the city and at 10 am they should report to the police station there to be briefed. He also reminded them that it was 'National Arrest Day', so the Chief wanted some 'good results' to publish in the press for the occasion. On the way out into the cars one of the officers remarked to the others,

> Oh great, I like the sound of this 'National Rest Day' – I'll certainly be taking it easy then (male PC, 1995).

As the morning progressed the working of the 'SS' team was explained by the officer driving the car.

> We're called the 'Cruisers' by the prigs because they know we're a bit more special than the usual traffic lads. For one thing, our cars are much more powerful and the people we're chasing they say 'Hey, they've got cars as fast as ours, we'd better watch out' (male PC, 1995).

In general, the main objective of the day seemed to be to pick up an 'intelligence package' from an area crime team, which consisted of a folder with photographs of local, wanted 'toe-rags', their addresses, details of their cars and their 'modus operandi'. After a briefing in the local police station we began the 'cruising' for which the Central Task Force is known; this involved driving slowly around numerous council estates, finding addresses and seeing if anyone was walking about. It began to snow and as it was only 11 in the morning, hardly anyone was on the streets. Despite this lack of action, the officer did not seem worried that arrests were not imminent. He explained,

> All the prigs are still lying in their beds at this time, after a night's burglaring and thieving. It's no good looking for them before lunchtime (male PC, 1995).

Whilst waiting he outlined the organisation and structure of the task force, saying that it had been set up about two years previously, operated on a dual shift system which meant officers were either on 'earlies' or 'lates', and across the force was regarded as a terrific success.

> Yes, we're the Chief's blue-eyed boys. At first the department was set up as an experiment, but after six months, the word came down from headquarters that we had *more* than fulfilled expectations and we were permanent (male PC, 1995).

As a follow-up question he was asked about his opinion of the Chief and he said,

> Oh yes, a well-respected man's man, gets stuck in, understands our problems and gets us the gear we need. He always listens to the radio when he's being driven about in the car and once, he said to his driver 'We're nearest to that incident' and he got the driver to go to the job. He was jumping over hedges and everything; anyway he caught someone and took him to the nearest nick to personally book him in. When the desk officer asked the Chief for his number, and put it into the computer, he was so surprised he asked him 'Do you realise who you are?' (male PC, 1995).

References to 'blue-eyed boys' and their Chief Constable being regarded as a 'man's man' tend to support Brittan's argument that the 'independent existence of patriarchy is based upon the social construction of men and women into two separate, but unequal, categories' (1989:17). Similarly, Young describes policewomen as an 'anarchic presence' following their integration into mainstream policing, who were only 'grudgingly admired for their qualities of self-possession' (Young, 1991: 240). Another example is the way that Halford described her exclusion by her male colleagues as they 'operated as a cosy group of "lads" ' (Halford, 1993: 114) and how she had discovered, whilst working in the CID earlier in her career, that 'if you ever fell out of favour by not playing by the rules of the pack, you were finished' (ibid: 112).

Shooters and divers

In a similar routine to the early morning procedure at the Central Task Force, on arrival at a command area base to spend a day with the firearms team on court protection duties, bacon sandwiches and coffee were again the first item on the agenda. I had been told to arrive at 8 am and was taken into an underground firing range, where the daily briefing would take place. It was an opportunity for the superintendent to check all was well with his sergeant before leaving them to it, and for the team to chat about the previous day's exercise, one of them remarking,

> Yes, the jury are definitely getting twitchy now they're hearing what the defendants have been up to. I think that's why the judge has told us we have to be less obvious about our weapons (male Sergeant, 1995).

He explained that the judge had complained that the officers guarding the trial, which was a kidnapping linked to gangland killings, were making the jury feel threatened and so they had to be more discreet. In their role as protectors of the jury, judge and defendants from possible 'revenge' attacks, they had to wear plain clothes, unobtrusive radio equipment and firearms which were reassuring by their presence, but not threatening. One of the problems which the judge was concerned about was that in the interests of 'justice' the defendants should not be labelled as dangerous in the eyes of the jury. However, the sergeant who was explaining this to me was cynical about this approach.

> You see the problem is, these two brothers, they've been saying how they've been going around blowing lumps out of all and sundry, and the jury's getting jumpy. Two of the women have already gone off with 'nerves'. If another one leaves, that's it, there'll have to be a retrial (male Sergeant, 1995).

He went on to argue that he thought they were being as discreet as possible in the circumstances, their guns being neatly unobservable, and their radio contact being maintained by invisible earpieces. He explained,

> You see, we have them on holsters around our waists with a spare magazine at the other side. We don't wear the American type which go over your shoulder, so we need to wear jackets which will disguise the thing (male Sergeant, 1995).

He patted the gun through his jacket as an illustration of how it was 'invisible' and then showed me his quick access to his holster, with one hand, explaining that his clothing had to be of a suitable design to allow this to happen. He did a couple of one-handed 'quick draws' and then handed the gun to me, explaining it was loaded but still had the safety catch in place. He showed me how quickly he could replace the spare magazine, which was a 'slot-in' cartridge, and laughed when I said it looked like a child's plastic toy.

> Yes, they are plastic; they're made of a high performance composite, all except for the firing mechanism, of course; we call them our 'lethal Tupperware' (male Sergeant, 1995).

After coffee, at about 9.30am, we crossed the river and arrived at the rear of the city's crown court to watch the vans containing the suspects who were to spend the day in court. Police officers acting as firearms protection were stationed all around the building and on the roof. Hovering overhead for the whole journey from the prison about 20 miles away was the police helicopter. Traffic in the centre of the city had to be stopped and high-powered police cars with anti-ballistic reinforced body panels, which had 'protected' each motorway junction along the entire route, were now waiting to clear the way for the cavalcade. As this elaborate procedure had to be carried out every morning and evening for the duration of the trial, which was expected to last at least two weeks, it might be expected that the officers would be reasonably bored, cynical and exasperated with the event. On the contrary, however, it seemed that the process had certain exciting and dangerous elements which kept their interest, and the sergeant accompanying us listened avidly through his earpiece to the progress of the prison cavalcade as it passed each motorway junction. As the procession came into view, with the helicopter appearing over the top of the bridge just across the river, we were standing outside the front of the crown court building and he said,

> OK, I'll just stop talking to you for a few moments now, this is the dangerous part; I'm watching out to close anyone down who might look suspicious – bouncer types. If I have to pull the gun, get away

from me and go into that doorway and then into the building for protection (male Sergeant, 1995).

Later, with the defendants, jury and judge safely installed in the court building there was time for a tour of the 'public' areas and the 'sterile' parts of the building. In some places, only certain specially authorised police personnel could have access, and the centre of this operation was a suite of offices with 'Gold', 'Silver' and 'Bronze Command' on the doors. Upon entering through the 'Gold' door there was a room stacked with rifles in filing cabinets and a small desk with a phone. It was explained that this line had to be monitored constantly because if something went wrong, it would be the first point of communication.

At the rear of the jury's retiring room, a 'spy' hole allows the police firearms team to see and hear how the proceedings are progressing. As the jury must not feel threatened by the police guarding their 'private' space at the rear of the court, a 'discreet presence' is maintained. Sitting at the rear of the access to the jury room were two plain clothes officers, and one was the only armed female officer in evidence. When asked about any special problems with being a woman on an all-male team, she smiled politely as her sergeant answered for her,

> No, no, not at all. Jill fits in with everyone else – she's just like one of the lads (male Sergeant, 1995).

With a wry smile and meaningful look, she added to her supervisor's remark,

> It tells you something that he thinks *that's* a compliment (female PC, 1995).

In addition to the fieldwork with operational specialists carrying out their 'normal' duties, a few days were spent observing the work of departments which train officers for these tasks. Two of these were the Marine Unit, which provides courses on underwater and surface searches, and the firearms trainers. In each case this provided a combination of experience of their general work, an assessment of the entrance requirements and time getting the 'feel' of the department by meeting the officers working there. Time was spent with the Marine officers who were patrolling the coastline and quite willing to allow a researcher to take control of a large support vessel in the open sea in rough weather, to take part in exercises involving inflatable craft on the river and observe and support an underwater search training exercise.

As a contrast, in the Firearms Department an assessment day was undertaken at an outdoor firing range, which involved gaining experience with numerous handguns, shotguns and types of ammunition. Procedures which are used to assess suitability for the work of the teams were explained and a 'test' was enacted to see whether I would be able to reach the accepted level of accuracy, with training. In both departments facilities for female staff were no less adequate than for male officers. Although the facilities were basic, for example the toilet at the firing range was frozen, it was difficult to assess whether this would represent a significant deterrent to women joining the firearms squad. Following the morning at the shooting range, members of the team who were training that afternoon were assembled in a local country pub. As an all-male group they were extremely polite and helpful, but there was a definite aura of testosterone and being 'manly'. Discussions about 'shooters' rather than guns, and their heavy boots and police overalls with prominent 'POLICE' logos gave them a certain undeniable male status in the dining room at the pub as they ate lunch, where they were obviously well known. Indeed, in this far-flung corner of the northern moors their collective comradeship provided them with a sort of Wild West cowboy, homosocial ambiance, which excluded bystanders, of whom they seemed oblivious. One of the questions which was asked when they turned to me after the lunch with the usual, 'Well what do you want to know?' was about the lack of women on the teams, and several observations were offered,

> Well, you've seen for yourself today, it's cold enough to freeze the balls off a brass monkey and there's no facilities (male PC, 1995).

> Personally I can't understand it, why there's not more women on the teams (male PC, 1995).

> It's very stressful this job. We had a psychologist, from the University, to assess what we do up here recently, and she said the constant, high levels of stress were unbelievable (male PC, 1995).

> Yes, because that's another thing, your partner has to agree to you being on firearms and maybe they're not very keen, the husbands (male PC, 1995).

It might be expected that some responses would be based upon physical factors – perhaps the long hours they spend watching premises or the weight or size of the guns, the power exerted through the recoil and so on.

But their answers seemed much closer to Brittan's explanation of the way clearly demarcated sexual divisions of labour shape male and female roles. In his explanation of 'socialisation thesis', Brittan explains that gender identity is thought to be acquired through roles being added to biology (1989: 19-21). Although none of the men from the firearms team were using explanations that were simply based upon roles or essentialist biological theories for the unsuitability of women to use guns, as Heidensohn has argued, in order to gain acceptance perhaps female colleagues would feel they would have to ' "prove" their ability and sometimes their "bottle" or their manhood' (Heidensohn, 1995:143). She goes on to suggest that although men have to do this too, women have more difficulties because they start from a position of 'not belonging' and have more to 'prove themselves as "men" because that is what they are precisely not' (ibid). As the firearms sergeant told me, following our walk across the roof of the Crown Court building, which was slippery with frost and ice, sloping down to a narrow leaded guttering,

> Yes, well, you did alright up there. I don't really like heights myself, but was told by the lads to test your bottle. I think you passed when you went to the edge, and leant over (male Sergeant, 1995).

As an outsider, of course, a 'non-police' identity would ensure that a researcher would not normally be a threat to this group of men in terms of their specialist skills with firearms. As the iconography of shooting and guns is clearly male, however, it could be argued that women officers might raise insecurity. Because competition for places on the firearms squads was said to be 'tough', the constant need to update, practise and prove their skills every few weeks caused many officers to be anxious about their performance. Requirements to pass the eight-weekly assessment of suitability to carry arms were getting more stringent; a 'moving target test' had been introduced recently, which involved a timed shooting of numerous targets, which have to be assessed, aimed at and shot accurately whilst running to the next firing position. A popular, long-standing member of the firearms team had failed this exercise, even after a second chance, which is not strictly allowed, and had to 'retire' from the squad. On the other hand, one of the instructors explained,

> When the Chief came up to do it he was struggling with the new moving targets, so after a bit he just said, 'Oh that'll do, won't it?' I couldn't really argue, just signed his authorisation – couldn't really leave him without his protection, could I? (male Sergeant, 1995).

The sergeant expressed his dislike at having to fail his 'mate', especially as the officer in question had been 'devastated' at having to leave – going back to normal divisional duties with all his colleagues knowing that he was a 'failure' in his chosen expertise. As the firearms trainer went on to explain, rather ironically in the light of the story about the Chief Constable, normally the regulations on firearms authorisations were very strict, 'for obvious reasons'. In terms of Brittan's explanation of 'masculine crisis theory', in which the successful negotiation of gender identity can be compared to an 'obstacle race', run according to rules which are being continuously rewritten and reinterpreted (1989:27), the casualties are potentially men such as the firearms 'failure'. As he suggests,

> Today, if there is a race, then it is no longer a straight run to the finish. Everybody seems to be under different 'starter's orders'. Everywhere there are casualties ... Now, all we can see is the spectacle of countless millions of men experiencing acute gender anxieties (ibid: 27).

As a result, men have lost their 'gender certainty' due to the 'erosion of male power in the workplace and in the home' find it difficult to find male role models and no longer know who women are 'supposed to be' (ibid:25). It could be argued, of course, that men working in the specialist units described here are constantly having their masculinity reinforced as a result of the relationships in which they interact, and this leads to a mutually constructed and reinforced sense of gender identity. Women officers, however, who are often believed to have access to 'special privileges' in the police because they are a minority competing for a small number of prized places, might be viewed as a threat by some male team members. As a uniformed constable who wanted to join the firearms squad said,

> I've got no chance for the foreseeable future. Force Orders have just come round and it says that any woman who wants to have a two week attachment with any department can have it within the next six months. That's illegal – it's positive discrimination. It means all the places will be full up for ages (male PC, 1996).

A professional body

In the previous chapter on uniformed patrol work the notion of competence in the police was explored and conclusions were related to the way certain arrests confer status and occupational credibility. This data will now be compared with the material just presented from the specialist teams about some of the ways uniformed officers achieve and maintain their personal status. One of the terms which is used by officers to express that which they aim to achieve is 'professionalism', and used as an adjective, the term 'professional' is a general category which confers praise and a group acceptance upon an individual. In some situations the term appears to be used as a management tool, as one officer complained during the fieldwork,

> I don't know what's wrong with the new boss, but he's said we're not allowed to get the leftovers from late night takeaways any more on night shift, and at parading on, we're not to have a cup of tea. Apparently it's not *professional* (male PC, 1997).

At one of the police training days attended in the course of the fieldwork, officers were being reminded about the force policy on arresting the perpetrators of domestic violence. However, some points of law were disputed during a discussion because senior officers seemed to be proposing that '...the man should always be locked up if there was any evidence of abuse' (male PC asking a question from the floor, Command Area Training Day, 1995). In addition, the trainers were suggesting that there should be 'more arrests' but PCs were arguing that they could not overstep their 'normal' powers. Frustrated by the challenge to their transmission of 'force policy' message, one of the senior officers jumped to her feet, interrupted the speaker and announced to the assembled audience,

> Look, we're expecting your normal, high levels of professionalism. Don't forget that, it is paramount (female Superintendent, 1995).

From their frequent reference to the concept, especially by those relatively new to the organisation, such as probationers, officers often seem to internalise this ideal of professionalism. At times this encourages them to attempt the maintenance of an appearance or 'front' of expertise which cannot always be achieved. Faced with 'outsiders', particularly those whom they feel the need to impress, an apparent lack of competence causes obvious embarrassment, and expressions of anger or frustration. Sometimes this is due to practical difficulties which seem to be largely within the control of individuals, such as missing equipment and errors due to lack of preparation prior to going on patrol. In some cases systems failures or lack of information being passed between officers can cause an obvious breakdown in 'professional policing'. An example of this, which was witnessed during fieldwork, was when a male officer apologised to a house owner who suspected intruders upstairs in an unoccupied house next door to his own. As there was no electricity in the house and the floorboards were either missing or rotten, it was considered dangerous to proceed and the officer could not find the spotlight he thought was in the patrol car, so he said,

> Yes, oh dear, we seem to have left our torch back at the nick (male PC, 1995).

Upon looking for it he had quickly realised one of his colleagues must have taken it and although he knew it was no longer in the boot of the car, he made an obvious attempt to search for it in front of a waiting group of local residents. At this point one of the other neighbours came out to ask what was happening and offered to lend the officer a torch. Clearly embarrassed, he replied,

> Oh, yes thanks very much; the great British police, eh? Never have any gear (male PC, 1995).

At another police station a group of officers had collected together some money to buy their own torch, which was locked away when they were off duty. As it was of a superior design to force issue, and always available when needed, one of the participating officers explained,

> It makes you feel better on the streets if you've got the proper gear – much more professional and safer. Mind you, the bosses won't pay for the batteries. We have to buy them out of our own pocket because they say it's our own responsibility. Mean bastards (male PC, 1995).

On another occasion an officer needed to write down the registration number of a passing car and borrowed a pen. Later that evening, in the presence of a number of members of the public, he had to take a statement, and he asked, apologetically,

> Er, can I borrow the 'team' pen again please?

Adding to the people he was taking details from;

Sorry, not very professional is it? (male PC, 1995).

In some more serious cases, equipment failures such as a car or van refusing to start would be blamed upon the 'management' for inadequate spending on 'essentials'. A serious issue of contention, particularly for the CID, was the cost cutting exercise which had led to the purchase of diesel powered cars for the department. As they were believed to be more economic to run and the squads did not need, apparently, to have high performance or speed, it was decided 'at headquarters' that these would be a good idea. Subsequently numerous problems occurred, due to this 'short sighted' economy, as one DC explained after one of the cars had to be push-started,

> These bloody diesel cars, they're dirty, noisy, won't start and there's absolutely no poke to them at all. We sometimes need to cruise quietly and slowly, and you've seen yourself about the starting – we use lots of battery in our normal operations: radios, lights. They're totally inappropriate, and as for chasing after prigs, well, we might as well get out and do it on foot (male DC, 1995).

Later that night, driving around during observations in the same vehicle, a car which had been reported stolen earlier, and which the police suspected would surface on the estate we were patrolling, was spotted. As the car was followed at speed, a long sweeping hill was encountered, and despite the efforts of the driver, who was a trained pursuit officer, the stolen vehicle disappeared at a crossroads just out of our sight. Naturally, the officers were very frustrated, saying,

> Typical – we could have had him! We're working with one arm tied behind our backs. Bloody diesel cars! What good are they to us? (male PC, 1995).

When the officer had finished complaining to his colleague he turned around and explained,

> You see, *they* can go across junctions, not bother if anything is coming. When he got to the top of the hill he probably went straight across. Anything could have happened but they don't care, it's not their car and they don't give a damn for any innocent road users (male PC, 1995).

The combative nature of 'crime fighting' is illustrated by the officer who explained that he had to play by the 'rules' as a professional, but also had to justify losing his quarry. On another occasion during the fieldwork a large patrol van failed to start and a group of officers were attempting to push it, but were struggling to get enough speed to start the engine. At one of the more annoying moments, when the engine had just failed to fire at the third or fourth attempt, a car drove past at speed, and some young men – so-called local 'prigs' – shouted disparaging comments, hanging out of the windows laughing loudly and sarcastically. Everyone stopped pushing and the car number plate was noted, one of the officers stating,

> I know who that is Sarge; it's a little scumbag from the Whitemoor estate. I'll have *him*, don't worry (male PC, 1995).

On the following nightshift two of the people in the car had been arrested and the vehicle impounded as a suspected 'ringer'. One of the officers said,

> Those ringed vehicles, we've been told that late registration 'Q' plates are almost certain to be nicked, so I say we should take them to the crushers and have them made into a small metal cube. Take it round to their house saying 'Here you are, Sir, this *was* your car' (male PC, 1995).

Another PC was listening and he laughed, saying,

> No, even better, make them *watch* their pride and joy being crushed up into millions of little pieces, that would teach them some respect (male PC, 1995).

It has been argued previously that the visible players in the enactment of criminal justice are mostly men and, as Morgan has suggested, gendered connotations are attached to police work, which is considered 'dirty' and therefore male (1992:85). In addition, car chases and the notion of triumphing over the enemy are all stereotypical male activities that lead to the perpetuation of the idea of one group of men policing another, whilst the latter attempt to resist their control.

In the next section of this chapter the interaction of masculinities and professionalism in a discussion of competence and expertise will be explored. Rather than simply suggesting that men reinforce their occupational status by using their masculinity as an operational advantage, it will be argued that their masculinity is being maintained and enacted through tasks associated with policing. However, this will not simply be a tautological argument, suggesting that men are masculine, most police officers are men, and therefore policing is infused with machismo. Rather, the discussion will be supported by evidence of numerous instances where a smooth and effortless performance, which combines being a man and a police officer, is problematic and, arguably, sometimes unobtainable. In the following two sections this discussion will be extended by looking at the problems encountered in the maintenance of masculinity, analysing the way police officers attempt to preserve their sexual and 'heroic' identities when caring for and serving members of the public. Such evidence is concerned with the explanation for rather than justification of actions, values and beliefs, and a discussion of the appropriation or rejection of the 'masculinity package' by women officers will also be conducted. Throughout, the analysis will focus on the effect of gender in the research process and the way a female researcher, entering a male-dominated world, may be subjected to attempts at manipulation and control through a culture of masculinity.

Competent men

As in other fields of social life, problems arise when police officers try to reconcile the practical needs of policing and the maintenance of their gender identities. One of the reasons this is significant is the importance attached to personal and occupational status in the police. As police work is organised to a large degree on shifts or reliefs, individuals are continually subjected to group interactions and processes which reinforce these values and beliefs. Despite the apparent importance placed upon arrest rates and the need to achieve status by organisational or managerial objectives, as explained in the previous chapter, a more tenuous and yet vital occupational credibility is achieved through peer critique. Very few posts in operational policing involve being alone continually – even activities that are conducted by one officer, away from the gaze of superiors or colleagues, will be open to scrutiny. As a result, criteria such as 'bottle', knowledge of internal rules and standards of efficiency are used to include or exclude members of the shift.

Membership of the group relies upon individuals being accepted by the consensus of the majority, and various measurements are employed to judge the suitability of the candidate to gain full insider status. 'Good' quality, high-status arrests, in addition to certain aspects of physical appearance and the ability to run, catch and fight when necessary, are vital criteria. Quantitative performance records, however, seem less important to members of the shift than being able to 'talk a good arrest' or to fight and the ability to withstand public humiliation by peers and supervisors. Indeed, being able to 'take it like a man', in addition to being reliable in terms of loyalty and 'bottle' seems to ensure group respect and have a powerful effect upon behaviour. In his discussion of the attractiveness of group membership during his National Service, for example, Morgan says that despite having reservations about the cultural values which were espoused by his peers 'fear of exclusion from the group became perhaps an even more powerful force than wishing to join it and be accepted' (Morgan, 1987:48). One of the ways he illustrates this point is by reflecting upon the various ways of 'doing masculinity'. He describes how he had to accept being referred to as a 'great big poof' whilst carrying out his National Service (ibid:75) because he liked classical music. However, he was also able to move between 'different worlds'- being a member of the 'music circle' and yet 'join the lads from the block at meal times' (ibid:76). Similarly, sustaining a competent male and police officer role on duty requires officers to integrate various ways of being a man and professional competency, which leaves both elements of self identity open to threat.

In one case witnessed during the fieldwork for this study, a male PC was accompanying his sergeant to investigate a burglary. As the young woman whose house had been ransacked was very upset, the sergeant, well known on the shift as a 'charmer', was using his skills to calm her down. In reality, he was trying to get some information about the suspected burglar, who had just been arrested, and so he was 'softening her up' to find out as much as he could, saying,

> Now look, Michelle – is that your first name? We want to catch these people, I know your mum's just died recently and you're very upset, but we need some vital information off you. Just take your time and think of anything you can tell us (male Sergeant, 1995).

Her distress had been made worse because the stolen property was jewellery given to her by her recently deceased mother. Meanwhile, the PC accompanying the sergeant was called on the radio by the CID duty sergeant back at the police station, asking for some detailed evidence to put to the person in custody. Although usually a fairly brusque, no-nonsense officer, he replied over the air, taking his cue from his uniform sergeant,

Yes, there's problem with taking a formal written statement at this time. IP (injured party) is very distressed and it may have to wait until the morning (male PC, 1995).

Of course this message did not satisfy the CID, who were waiting to interview their suspect before he had time to 'concoct' a story, and then they could go home or back to the pub. A problem existed for them, however, with the amount of authority that could be exerted via the personal radio system, and so the uniform sergeant at the scene was contacted, and he told the PC to take the statement. Upon our return to the station, however, the PC who had mentioned the woman's 'distress' was being severely denigrated, firstly in his absence,

Too distressed, too *fucking distressed;* what does he think he's playing at? Would it be alright, could he please take the statement – if it's not too *distressing* for him? (male Detective Sergeant, 1995).

Shortly after this the 'offending' officer returned to the police station, giving the custody sergeant the necessary information for the charging of the suspect. In full hearing of all police staff on duty, civilian workers and people waiting in the reception area, he was publicly reprimanded by the CID Sergeant, who said to him,

Now look laddie, it's no good saying things like that. I need that information and I need it now – not in fucking three days' time when *you feel* like it – right? (male Detective Sergeant, 1995).

As the officer on the receiving end of this was fairly experienced, with about five years service, not young and certainly not regarded as one of the physically passive members of the shift, this was especially humiliating. He had to stand in the 'public' gaze and tacitly admit he was wrong by not offering any excuses or blaming anyone else. An important element of the police 'code' of manliness demands the ability to accept these sorts of incidents, and knowing that to question or 'bite back' will merely attract more humiliation. Obviously 'feminine' sympathy for the distressed victim of a crime needs to be kept at the scene, and not allowed to be transmitted over the air or interfere with the progress of a CID investigation, especially when the pubs are still open.

In another case witnessed during the fieldwork, a youngish graduate police officer, not long out of his probationary period, was castigated by his sergeant. On the way to a reported pub fight in an unmarked CID police car (as all the marked vehicles were in use) a collision was narrowly avoided. At a roundabout with a narrow access road, a bus coming in the opposite direction blocked the path of the police car, and the officer flashed his lights and shouted out of his open window at the bus driver,

> *Police* – you stupid bastard (male PC, 1995).

As he did this he held up his jacket collar showing the metallic numbers to the bus driver as proof of his supposed right of priority. After the pub incident was resolved, a call came over the air for the driver of the CID car to report to the 'inside sergeant'. Upon hearing this the officer said he 'knew what this would be about' and we went into the custody area of the main station. On the way there he was asked what he was going to say. He made a vague reply and back at the station when he was asked by the sergeant whether he had been the driver of the car in question and if he remembered an incident with a bus at a certain roundabout, he simply admitted he was, didn't query the report, and just said 'Yes, OK' when told there should be no further repetition of this type of behaviour. Back on patrol he explained,

> See? You're much better off just taking it, however wrong the details are or however justified you felt you were in your actions. If I'd questioned that, it would have been written down (male PC, 1995).

As having such incidents 'written down' involves a formal recording on a staff appraisal document, including paperwork for the officer and unfavourable remarks which may affect promotion or movement to specialist posts, this is to be avoided. Better to 'take it like a man', which may involve losing face in terms of the incident itself, but is compensated for by not losing anything in terms of masculine status. In this way, support and admiration are received from colleagues following a reprimand by the 'bosses' which outweigh the injustice. In any case, the officer did not see himself to be in the wrong, as he observed,

> What do they (the public) want? They want fast response – someone might have been stabbed in that fight, but they want safe driving as well. Well they can't have both (male PC, 1995).

Later, upon our return to the police canteen, other members of the shift who had heard the sergeant calling for the PC to report to the station asked what had happened. He was able to act very cool and unconcerned, stating he got a telling off, but there would be no further action. When the incident was recounted to the shift later, it had become a very fast driving incident and near miss, which gained added value in terms of the reinforcement of masculinity. Standing in the doorway of the parade room, casually lighting a cigarette, he told the assembled incoming shift,

> I just coughed for it. What's the point in arguing? There's fuck all he can do about it (male PC, 1996).

Sexualised power

In her study of the oppressive sexual behaviour of men, Stanko observes that women often describe feelings of helplessness in their encounters with men, and they read a great deal of male behaviour as threatening, whilst men do not consider acts such as 'flashing' as abhorrent or potentially violent (1985:11). In a similar way the male police officers described here when accompanied on patrol did not regard their overt objectification of women as particularly demeaning, although in the early days of my fieldwork sometimes police officers would admit to having 'toned down' their remarks and language, apologising for swearing and denigrating women. Remarks about 'women drivers' or female colleagues' inability to use technological equipment and discussions about the relative merits of various pornographic material they were exchanging between themselves would sometimes be prefaced with 'Excuse us' 'Sorry about this' or a qualifying statement which indicated they did not include a researcher in this derogation.

Evidence of sexual behaviour and attitudes was most apparent at one of the subdivisions where the shift were policing a busy nightclub area in the centre of the town. A number of pubs and clubs had their entrances on the main road and a regular part of weekend evenings would be to spend long hours at busy junctions, waiting for something to happen. Perhaps two or three hours would be spent at various crossroads, occasionally speeding off to suspected fights, which usually turned out to be minor disagreements, or drunks falling over. On one occasion three vehicles drove at high speed down a pedestrian precinct to find one man sitting on top of another, punching him rather half-heartedly. About a dozen officers surrounded them and the participants were pulled apart and then asked, 'What's this all about?'. Both men were fairly drunk, and the one who had been sitting on top when we arrived said,

> I don't know – I was just waiting to ring my girlfriend but there was someone in the call box (fieldnotes, 1995).

All the officers surrounding them seemed rather nonplussed at this, and so one officer replied,

> So you just thought you'd have a fight whilst you were waiting? Well, I've heard everything now! Get on your way home, both of you (male PC, 1995).

Regular and yet ultimately unimportant incidents such as this provide minor, short-lived and often humorous diversions for officers hanging around the town centre. In terms of human resource management, it is regarded as necessary to have a certain level of 'cover' in case some major incident occurs on weekend nights. However, in town and city centre environments, there are very few standard 'filler' calls to pass the time between public order related offences. In residential areas there are routine incidents such as domestic assaults, burglaries and car crimes, but in the centre it is simply a matter of 'waiting for the town to kick off' (female PC, 1995). As these long periods of inactivity become extremely boring, just sitting in the van on street corners, male officers tend to spend their time watching, comparing and discussing the bodies of passing young women. In 'van culture speak' this is referred to as 'floating down the town for a letch' and involves 'admiring' the bodies of young women by the size and shape of their breasts, legs and their lack of clothes. Various sexual acts the male officers would like to perform with the women they are watching are explicitly described. In most cases the women are admired from afar and yet denigrated.

> Oh God! Look at those (breasts). Very nice – not the sort of girl you'd take home to meet your mother though (male PC, 1995).

> Look at her – she can't be a day over sixteen, I'm sweating like a paedophile in a toy shop (male PC, 1996).

> Oh, please! Can you imagine those (breasts) on top of you?(male PC, 1995).

In most cases the women attracting their attention would be wearing short revealing dresses or tight jeans and summer tops in sheer materials. Even in the middle of winter, whilst everyone in the van would be wearing jumpers and jackets, people outside on the street would be walking from venue to venue dressed as if it were a hot day. Opportunities for remarking on the inadvisability of this type of clothing would sometimes provide an outlet for their comments.

She hasn't taken her mother's advice – no vest on. Proves her nipples were working though (male PC, 1995).

Look at her – I bet her parents think she's round at a friend's for the night, she's only got her nightdress on (male Sergeant, 1995).

In most cases the officers' admiring glances would be acknowledged by women walking past with a smile or a nod, although others would scowl, shouting back 'What do you think you're staring at', or simply ignore the attention. It could be legitimised, if challenged, as 'normal' police interest in passersby, as the gaze of admiration could be quickly supplanted with the hardened police stare. In some cases encounters would be initiated by women themselves, coming over to the open windows of the cars and vans and leaning provocatively into the vehicles, asking for 'policeman's knock' (a kiss) – and whether the officers are married, asking their names, where they drink and if certain officers they know are on duty. A common request would be whether a local officer, famous for his sexual exploits and also as the singer in a local band, was on duty. On a few occasions each evening, young women would come up to the van or patrol car and ask, Is Paul on tonight? In reply, depending on their mood, and the attractiveness of the women, officers would reply,

Paul? We don't know any cops called Paul. What's he like? (male PC, 1995).

Obviously knowing perfectly well who they were asking about, the officers would entice the women to recount how well they knew him and what he had done. Sometimes officers would reply to the initial request with,

No, he's not on tonight (even if he was). You'll have to make do with us instead (male PC, 1995).

On rare occasions a drunken stare would be directed towards the researcher, sitting in the back of the car or van, and the women would ask 'Here – who's that? Have you arrested her? In reply the officers would usually make some well-practised amusing comments about not paying my fines or being in special branch or other impressive and apparently hilarious remarks.

As each group of women finished their conversations and moved on in the direction of the next pub or club their relative merits compared to the last ones would be discussed. If unattractive, or 'fat' women approached the car, quite often the window would be wound up and sometimes the officers would drive around the block. Depending on the inexperience of the officers, occasionally someone would be 'trapped' by a woman leaning into the car, invading his space, and he would be unable to escape without the compliance of his partner, saying, 'Well, we've got to go now, urgent call' and starting the engine. During these interchanges reference would sometimes be made to the fact that a female researcher was in the van or car, with remarks about whether they could find a good looking man. On a couple of occasions when I joined in their conversation by agreeing that certain women they were admiring were attractive, this resulted in teasing, jokes and professed puzzlement. On one occasion, when we returned to the station for a cup of tea, an officer told the rest of the shift he had 'caught' me looking at a woman they were admiring, which they found highly amusing, with one of them asking,

> Well, weren't there any decent blokes for her? We'll have to find one for her, if that's what she wants (male PC, 1995).

In a similar way, Smith and Gray discuss an incident where police officers were being overtly homophobic, expecting them, as male researchers, to collude. In response Smith decided to purposefully respond in a contradictory way, inferring that he was not colluding. He reports that, 'after listening to a tale of local paedophilia, DJS experimented by refusing to condemn the offender' suggesting that he thought such impulses fairly common, and as a result 'officers became disorientated; when they did not obtain the usual response they seemed to be forced to ask themselves why they were telling the story in the first place' (1983:93). Although my responses were never made with the intention of challenging their remarks or colluding, my agreement that a woman was attractive had the effect of causing some consternation, one of the officers remarking,

> Hey – you shouldn't be looking' (male PC, 1995).

Upon discussing their behaviour with some of the women officers, it was discovered that the women had reservations about their behaviour, which they confided away from their male colleague's hearing.

> You know, if it wasn't for the uniform, most of these lads wouldn't get a second glance by those sort of women (female PC ,1995).

> Yes, they're supposed to say 'Move away from the car please,

madam', when women come over to them; Huh! Not very likely (laughs) (female PC, 1995).

If their wives knew what they said and did! If ever their wives are out on the town they're very careful on duty. I've got a good mind to tell them, some of them, they'd have a fit (female PC, 1995).

By way of comparison, a female officer accompanied during the study, in a van with a male sergeant, was asked by the control room to deal with a male 'streaker'. It was the middle of winter and a youngish man had been chained to a lamp post, completely naked, apparently because it was the eve of his wedding. On arriving the woman officer got out of the van quite enthusiastically and walked over towards the group of the naked man's friends, smiling and saying,

Look, I'm sorry but you'll have to untie him (female PC, 1995).

She was looking very directly at the man's naked body, grinning at him, and waited for his friends to find the key to the lock they had used on the chain around his feet. As this was taking some time, and they were drunk and joking with the women officer, the male sergeant jumped out of the van and came striding over, saying very impatiently,

Look Sally, get him to put some clothes on, *now*! (turning to the friends) I'm warning you – you're all going the right way for being locked up (male Sergeant, 1995).

Getting back into the van the sergeant was still annoyed, with a grim expression, but Sally took no notice of him, remarking,

He was a bit of all right. Well endowed – did you see the size of it? (female PC, 1995).

In his discussion of sexuality and power Brittan uses an example of the phallus locating men in the 'social relations of gender and, by extension, legitimating the male view of power over women' (1989:56). He goes on to argue that, although some men define their sexuality in terms of 'sexual athleticism', most find this difficult to achieve, leading to 'a disjunction between the representations of male sexuality and its actual expression' (ibid:57). In a comparable discussion of the way power and sexuality are linked, Hoch suggests that due to the competitive threat of other men, it is necessary 'to constantly "demonstrate" manliness in every area of life' in order to prove themselves, because 'absolutely the worst thing a man can be is impotent' (1979:65). To further this explanation Hoch describes sexuality as a 'trial and performance' and talks about the paradoxical situation whereby 'virtually every man in our society can expect to experience one or more occasions of impotence' and yet it is regarded with tremendous anxiety 'amounting almost to hysteria' (ibid: 66). However, as Smith and Gray report, police officers' disgust with sexual 'perversions' does not seem to extend to their own behaviour. In one example they describe the way some young boys were reprimanded for exposing themselves to a neighbour. A Chief Inspector told the boys, in the course of a 20-minute formal caution during which they were shouted at and denigrated, that they should be castrated for what they had done and asked how they would feel committing such an offence against their mothers or sisters (Smith and Gray, 1983:76-77).

The apparent bravado of male officers towards women within the safe homosocial environment of the van or patrol car does not seem to extend to other sexual issues. In several observed instances male officers recoiled during cases involving discussions of intimate matters or parts of the body. Examples of this included a woman who reported a man exposing himself and a mother who reported her suspicions about her daughter having under-age sex. In both cases male officers said they would send a policewoman to take a statement, but would go to interview the (male) accused. When a young male police officer was taking details of one of these cases – a man who had masturbated in front of a girl of 16 on a bus – his discomfort was obvious. The officer asked what she had seen, and blushed and shifted about in a very uncomfortable way when she illustrated the actions she had witnessed. As a result he said, 'I can see you're embarrassed so I'll get a specially trained policewoman to interview you in the presence of your mam'. When we got outside he said how relieved he was to have found an excuse to leave the house. When the young woman said she had reported the man to the bus driver and he had dismissed her plea for help, the officer said,

> Well! I think I'll go to the bus station and find his number – he should be spoken to (male PC, 1996).

On another occasion, a case of a girl missing from home, the policeman wanted to know if the mother had any evidence of sexual activity on the part of the missing daughter. He asked the mother if she

...thought there was anything going on, you know, that shouldn't be? (male PC, 1995).

However, he did not broach any specific sexual matters or talk about the possibility that the youngster may need medical help or advice. A woman detective constable who was accompanied during the research had firm beliefs about the necessity of a female officer to take a rape statement, as she said,

> You see, if you've just been raped, the last thing you want to do is to talk to a man. A woman knows how it well, feels ... take oral sex for example, lots of women don't like it, but men don't see a problem with it. Another thing is, we need to take the samples from the doctor during the examination, so we need to be in the room to take the swabs and label them, and the same officer has to deal with the case the whole way through so it has to be a woman. You can have a male officer as Officer in Charge though – they usually deal with the rapist, interview him and that (female DC, 1996).

In this way, beliefs about the 'genital' nature of sex and the 'erotic' identities (Wilton, 1996:104) of officers being linked to their work include assumptions about the 'fixity and uniformity of sexual identity' (Weeks, 1995:88). Cultural norms are also reinforced by female detectives who take on the work as 'gendered' experts, and complain that they get 'sick to death' of sexual investigations and are reported to be 'leaving the CID in droves' (female Superintendent, 1997).

Masculine heroes

Some evidence of officers enacting displays of 'heroic' masculinity will be analysed here, reflecting upon the reasons for this behaviour being perpetuated and reinforced. As this will show, during the fieldwork there were constant reminders that the police are often regarded as the last resort in times of some types of trouble, such as intolerable domestic situations, and the first in others such as road accidents. Whether they are the first or last option, the police seem to be regarded by the general population as the answer to many of their troubles. Indeed, when officers fail to live up to this perception, and reveal themselves to be simply 'human' and unable to provide an answer in an heroic and all-powerful way, anger is sometimes directed towards them. In addition, officers often express dissatisfaction after attending these incidents because they feel they have not fulfilled their function.

An example of this was a violent domestic incident, where a woman had been assaulted by her husband. He had attempted to strangle her and he had given their daughter, aged about 16, a black eye. He then threatened to 'smash the whole house up'. Upon arrival at their house, the two officers had to restrain him as he was beginning to pull at the kitchen cabinets to remove them from the wall. He announced, upon seeing the officers,

> This is *my* house and I'll do what I like in it and *you* aren't going to stop me (fieldnotes, 1996).

At first one of the officers tried to reason with him, saying maybe he should calm down, pack an overnight bag and they would take him to a relative's for the evening. As he ignored this and carried on with his destructive mission, a nod was exchanged between the two officers and he was physically removed from the house. As he protested his rights to behave as he wanted 'in his own home', he was informed that he was being arrested for breach of the peace. Upon returning to the house to take some details from the victims with which to charge the husband however, problems arose. He had talked one of the arresting officers into dropping the charges, as he had 'calmed right down' once they had got him into the cells, and explained he was about to start a new job, and his boss was expecting him to take the lorry out with a delivery at six the next morning. As it was now approaching midnight, the officer agreed to go back to his house and collect some things, persuading his wife to drop the charges if he agreed to hand over his house keys.

When this was put to the woman and daughter, however, they were both adamant that he should be charged, the woman saying,

> Look, this isn't the first time, you know. He can do what he likes to me, I don't care, but when he starts on *her*, that's different (fieldnotes, 1996).

Sitting around the kitchen table discussing possible courses of action, the officer was patient at first but soon became frustrated at her for being so determined to proceed, saying,

> Yes, but two problems: first, you haven't given me any evidence of actual assault to go on – it sounds like a bit of push and shove from both sides, and second; he's down in the cell right now, calmed *right*

down, saying that if you pursue this complaint of assault he'll make a counter charge – a Mickey Mouse one – saying that *you* assaulted *him*. I'll have to arrest you and your daughter and take you down to the nick to take statements (male PC, 1996).

At this, the mother, a rather dishevelled but determined middle-aged woman, seemed to collapse emotionally. Resigned and defeated, she started crying and saying she did not want her daughter put through this process, as she was only 16. She was angry that the policeman could solve her problem, saying,

You're only doing it this way because you're a man. You don't understand, it's different for women (fieldnotes, 1996).

At this point she turned to me for support but I could not say anything to undermine the officer, who went on to say that the best solution was to allow him to have some belongings, get the house keys off him and drop the charges, concluding,

In that way you get what you want – him out of the house and some peace and quiet – and in the morning you can see your solicitor (male PC, 1996).

As a result of this discussion, the case would attract 'no further police action' and 'unnecessary' paperwork could be avoided. On another occasion two officers were called to the house of a woman who showed us into the kitchen where her younger sister was standing, looking nervous and upset, clutching a housecoat around herself. She explained that she had just escaped from her boyfriend's flat, where she had been kept captive for 24 hours, threatened, had her clothes cut off, her sunbed 'smashed up with an axe' and warned not to leave. When the boyfriend went out to the club for a drink, she managed to climb out of an upstairs window and onto an outhouse roof, as the doors and windows downstairs were locked with keys, which he had taken with him. She was now worried because he might come to find her at her sister's. As she was speaking, the two male police officers listened in silence, with grim expressions on their faces. When she paused, one of them asked,

Well, what do you want *us* to do? (male PC, 1995).

She was a bit taken aback, having just poured out her story, talking quickly and on the point of tears.

> Well, I don't know really, I'm just frightened he'll come round here because he knows where I would go (fieldnotes, 1995).

For a moment they paused and then said,

> Do you want us to go and speak to him, or we can lock him up on what you've just told us (male Sergeant, 1995).

On consideration, she thought this was unwise as she realised that the police would not be able to keep him in custody, she said,

> Well, that might make him worse – when you let him out (fieldnotes, 1995).

For a while they discussed the advantages and disadvantages of various forms of action, and then the sergeant suggested they leave her to talk it over with her sister and ring them later when she had decided whether she wanted any police intervention. Despite their seemingly abrupt, initial 'What do you want us to do?', throughout the whole procedure both officers were serious and 'professional' but sympathetic. They made reassuring noises and said that if her boyfriend did come round to the house she was staying at, she should ring them immediately.

> Thanks very much for coming, I mean, I didn't think you'd believe me, it sounds so unbelievable (fieldnotes, 1995).

To which one of the officers replied, looking down, still with a serious expression,

> Oh yes, we always believe people who wear pink fluffy slippers (male Sergeant, 1995).

She was standing in the kitchen in a housecoat and mules and as the tension broke everyone laughed and the police officers started making signals to leave, giving more reassurances about their swift response if her boyfriend came to the house. So the police have to seem to be 'heroic' – protecting a woman who appears vulnerable; caring – they accept she is distressed and provide comfort; 'professional policemen' – they are ready and willing to take legal steps to lock up the perpetrator; but also 'manly yet human' – by making jokes about her slippers. In the course of the fieldwork a number of similar incidents were witnessed, domestic fights and disputes where the police officers tried to resolve difficult situations to the satisfaction of several opposing parties. As previous studies of domestic violence have shown, their levels of concern are often mediated by their assessment of the 'deserving' and 'appropriate' victim (Dobash and Dobash, 1977). At one call which two male officers attended, a young and apparently deranged son had attacked his mother whilst his father, a fireman, was at work. Her request was treated sympathetically because she explained she knew the police could not take effective action, but she had called them as an emergency intervention, and also as evidence to support her campaign for help from other agencies such as social services. As this was viewed as a sensible and rational course of action, in the view of police officers who were critically aware of their limitations in such situations, sympathy and support was offered, with one of them saying,

> No, don't worry about calling us out, that's what we're here for (male PC, 1995).

On the other hand, at a call where a woman claimed she had been attacked by her partner and officers arrived to find her drenched in beer, one asked,

> Yes, but what has he actually *done* to you? (male PC, 1995).

When she explained that she thought his behaviour was 'out of order' they replied,

> Well we're not here to tell people off for little arguments – that's not our job (male PC, 1995).

To fit the criteria of the enactment of heroic masculinity, therefore, it seems some threat to life, safety or dignity must be present. It has been suggested that the form rescue stories take in any society is revealing, as power is not normally used to dominate, but to help the weak or disadvantaged. As Lash argues, 'the hero is always saving someone or something' and acts as the 'redeemer who acts to preserve cosmic law and eternal justice' (1995:6). Indeed, as Williamson suggests, the mass media, and in particular, advertisements, are 'selling us ourselves' because 'being a man' is not only made necessary but also perpetuated by the need to belong, to have a social 'place' (1997:190). On the other hand, as Steinman argues, when male movie stars are eroticised, their masculinity must be preserved, and although making them appealing to women may involve a certain amount of 'feminisation', they cannot turn out to be, say, 'a cokehead, or a spouse- or child-abuser' (1992:207).

As indicated in the introduction to this chapter, competence, sexuality and heroism are three closely-related concepts in police culture, which all seem to contribute to this notion of masculinity and what it is to 'be a man'. In times of crisis, trouble or family difficulties, it is often the police who are called, and they are often regarded as the uniformed problem solvers. In the following section, which contains examples of death, emergency and danger, the way public perceptions of the police create and reinforce expectations of heroism is explored.

Mortal heroes

It is particularly obvious in emergency situations such as road accidents that the police are expected to fulfill high levels of public confidence. When they arrive at these incidents the faces of those waiting at the scene show relief that someone has arrived to 'sort things out'. Even when other professionals such as ambulance crew are already there, the waiting public see the police officers as the scene directors for several reasons. First, they usually arrive at speed and quickly portray an emergency 'We're in control now' image that Herbert (2001) explains is so important to the police. On arrival, officers ask 'Who's injured?', 'Any other casualties?' and 'Did anyone see what happened?' Almost immediately clipboards are produced and people who come towards the officers are prioritised, calmed, recorded and placed in queues relating to their importance, such as the injured, relatives of those hurt, passengers in vehicles, and eyewitnesses. As these procedures seem controlled and yet urgent and decisive, the people who have been in turmoil waiting for the arrival of some form of help and reassurance now have a focus for their concerns. Police officers are generally expert and practised performers of this ritual, and their apparent heroic demeanour, combined with competence and experience, overcomes any doubts they may feel upon arrival at a scene which they may find upsetting. A sense of competence and experience of death reflected in the obvious expectations of the bystanders quickly seems to replace any other feelings or emotions, as witnessed when two experienced officers arrived at the scene of a fatal road accident. At first the call was simply to an early evening road traffic accident or 'RTA', which could mean a small knock between two cars. However, as we drew near to the scene, the officer who was a passenger said to the driver,

Over there – on the right, the ambulance is there already (male PC, 1995).

Upon coming closer, pulling up quickly at the side of the road, their reactions quickly changed, with one of them saying,

Oh dear, God, no. It's a kid (male PC, 1995).

As they both jumped out of the car they walked swiftly to where a small body was lying at the side of the road with an ambulance worker pumping an inflatable bag over the face of the casualty. Both police officers had grim looks on their faces, and the ambulance officer shook her head almost imperceptibly at them as they approached. At this signal, without speaking, they split up, one of them saying to the ambulance driver,

Right, I'll be continuity officer then – anything you want me to do? (male PC, 1995).

As he knelt down on the pavement beside the body, without any verbal arrangements being made, his partner reached into the patrol car for a clipboard and started to move back the small group of people who now seemed to be a little too near the action, announcing,

Let's give them some space to work. Right, now let's see who can tell me what happened – where's the driver of the car? (male PC, 1995).

Of course, the actions which these officers carry out and the style and manner of their approach are completely in keeping with all expectations. If their 'private' reactions, the ones they had expressed as they neared the accident, were revealed, it would be impossible for the public to believe in their performance. It would be unworkable if officers arrived and announced to the waiting crowd that they couldn't cope with death, or their emotions; they have to do 'being ordinary' cops, as Sacks explains (Atkinson and Heritage, 1984), according to the expectations of the watching crowd. In addition, their self image and perceptions of 'men as heroes' are reinforced by contact with mortality, bodies and gore. After the casualty in the road accident described above had been removed to the ambulance, one of the officers took his torch and shone it where the person's head had hit the side of the kerb stone. In the gloom a beam of light shone through the small heap of red coloured jelly which was sitting, glistening on the pavement, and he said,

> See that – that's how you know its a fatal, when that comes out. You're really very lucky to have seen a fatal – I'm off to the hospital to act as the officer managing the body, possessions and informing the relatives and getting a formal identification (male PC, 1995).

As he spoke he was holding a large torch in one hand and in the other he had a pair of court shoes and a handbag, as the person who had died had not been a child as they had first believed, but a very small old woman. It seemed an incongruous mix of 'male' police equipment and signifiers of femininity. Following the accident, we waited at a road junction to keep traffic away, as the scene had to be kept closed while the serious accident team made measurements and took photographs. It was a Saturday evening and now approaching 10 pm, which is the time when the night shift 'overlaps' with the late evening shift at weekends. It was usually an opportunity to order a curry from the local takeaway and watch the results of the day's sports on television in the canteen. However, the next shift could not relieve the officers awaiting their break because all the vehicles were out of the station controlling the traffic. When we returned to the station, and explained to an officer from the next shift why we had not yet eaten, he presumed it was because of the rumoured 'gory' nature of the accident we had attended, saying,

> Nothing like a head injury to put you off your chicken supper, is there? (male PC, 1995).

At another fatal road accident which was witnessed during the research, certain logistical problems meant that it was much harder for officers to maintain a smooth continuous performance of heroic masculism. Although it is argued here that officers generally combine both roles, under stress in this situation, police heroism was sacrificed for masculinity. It was a cold night between Christmas and New Year's eve, and a man had been crossing the road, leaving a minibus which had just dropped him opposite his house, when a car had come in the opposite direction at speed, knocking him into the air and over the bonnet. A few minutes before the accident had been reported, an experienced woman officer was being observed, when an ambulance was seen driving in the opposite direction. She radioed the control room to alert them to the fact that their back doors were open, and control replied that there had been an accident on the coast road. Following their directions we arrived to find a group of distressed people surrounding a man who was lying on the road, groaning and calling out in pain. As the officer stopped the car and walked towards the casualty, everyone turned to her, asking 'Where's the ambulance?', concerned that we had arrived but not the service they needed. She ignored all requests for information and walked briskly to the injured man, asking a young woman who was kneeling on the ground holding his neck,

Is he the only casualty? Are you a nurse? (female PC, 1995).

She confirmed she was, saying,

Yes, and he's really bad – we need an ambulance straight away (fieldnotes, 1995).

Upon hearing this the officer turned away from the crowd, using her radio to contact the police control room to ask them to ring the ambulance controllers to 'hurry them up'. More minutes passed and the casualty was starting to lose consciousness, which was making the nurse attending him become quite desperate, encouraging his friends who were standing around him to talk to him and encourage him to stay awake. One of the people from the minibus which had been transporting them all home used his mobile phone to ring the ambulance service again, as it was now 25 minutes since his first call. We knew it had been ahead of us, but could not say anything which might inflame the situation, although the officer called the control room again with exact and precise instructions of where the accident had occurred. At this point another two police cars drew up and everyone turned to them expectantly; it was a dark and foggy winter night, about 12.30 am, and each time a vehicle approached an even more anxious and tense atmosphere was created. One of the male officers in the next panda car to arrive was asked by the bystander with the mobile phone,

How come all you lot keep coming? Where's the ambulance? We've been waiting over 25 minutes now – he's going to die (fieldnotes, 1995).

By now his friend had lost consciousness and was making distressing gurgling noises, a sort of rasping, snoring which sounded rather like someone taking a long time to drown. Waves of tension built up again and again the man with the mobile phone started shouting at one of the more 'tough' male officers, a weight trainer, poking him in the chest saying, almost in tears,

Look, get us an ambulance! My mate's going to die (fieldnotes, 1995).

As the weight trainer objected to having a finger poked at him, he squared up to the man and pushed him backwards a few paces, saying,

Yes, alright, we're doing our best mate – it's on its way (male PC, 1995).

As he spoke the police officer was sticking his chin out and flexing his arms whilst moving forward, and the man thought better of starting anything more physical and backed down. Observing the scene, and in order to diffuse the tension, a woman officer walked to her car and got a clipboard, going up to the man to distract him, saying,

Right, let's get some details from everyone while we're waiting. You'd all been for a night out together I take it? Do you know his name and address? (female PC, 1995).

As these descriptions show, it can be problematic for some officers to combine masculinity and the need to be seen as 'caring'. When someone has died, a child is missing from home or they have to deal with something concerning sexual behaviour, it can be difficult for male officers to assimilate gender and policing. In these cases they have to adopt an empathetic attitude, often far removed from their normal way of working or experience of life. It seems that violence in the home, however, contrary to some previous analyses which have alleged that it is 'rubbish' work, to be avoided at all costs, provides an ideal forum for officers to get involved in physical situations which they can usually 'win'. By arresting male perpetrators in their homes, they usually also gain the approval of the other family members and bystanders such as the neighbours. Moreover, following the arrest of the perpetrator, in one of the cases reported here, the 'paperwork' could be avoided by suggesting that the victim used 'civil remedies' to resolve the problem.

Summary

This chapter has explored the way police officers behave in various occupational situations by comparing their behaviour and attitudes in certain male-dominated specialist departments with patrol work. As the focus was to analyse police officers' cultural beliefs regarding their sense of self and masculinity, this has concentrated fairly heavily upon male officers in traditionally masculinist situations such as driving, shooting and fighting. The way in which gender is 'accomplished' (Brittan, 1989:40) is revealed by men in the police through their activities at work. Of course this raises problems regarding the position of women officers in the debate. As described in the section on sexuality, they expressed their disapproval of some misogynist activities of their male colleagues, apparently regarding them as 'sick' or 'pathetic'. Women officers did not, however, seem to be in a position to challenge the behaviour of the men. Their attitude seemed to be that the men were acting in a juvenile manner from which they chose to distance themselves.

The aim was to provide some empirical evidence with which to reflect upon the assumption that the 'cult of masculinity' (Smith and Gray, 1983:83) has led to the existence of 'hegemonic masculinity' (Fielding, 1994:47) in the police. In addition it was necessary to provide some form of explanation for the findings described in previous chapters about perceptions surrounding the differential deployment of women compared to their arrest records. It is this kind of discrepancy to which Heidensohn refers when she identifies the need to explain, rather than justify, the existence of cop culture (1995:13). This has proved to be a very difficult task and one which further research could pursue. One of the problems with explaining why gender is enacted in a certain way is the way male structures and belief systems are so pervasive in the police. For example, it is often assumed that certain 'core functions' of policing, which Bayley describes as 'authoritative intervention and symbolic justice' (1996:29), require 'male' attributes such as force and strength – or challenging what men think policing is about (Walklate, 2001:142). In the final chapter these issues will be explored in more depth.

Chapter 6

Masculinities, the body and policing

This final chapter summarises and develops a number of themes that run throughout the book, such as embodiment, the gender of police work and the tasks men and women carry out in the police. Much of the empirical evidence throughout the study has shown how officers' gendered bodies define suitability for certain aspects of their work. Hence, the following discussion analyses what is specific about so-called 'maleness' or masculinity and policing. Furthermore, as the following overview of masculinities and the body suggests, many of the current debates about corporeality and gender are relevant to policing, although not explicitly linked in previous studies. The study of the body has tended to be conducted in a theoretical, rather than empirical way, although there are exceptions (see for example Nettleton and Watson, 1998, Twigg, 2000). Such studies include the study of careworkers and the body, medicalisation, body building and issues relating to emotions and the maintenance of a healthy body.

The 1990s saw, amongst other academic trends, an increasing interest in the body from at least three different perspectives associated with gender. This is in addition to studies concerned with a more general approach towards embodiment and social theory, such as Shilling (1993) and Turner (1996), which make reference to gender but do not have it as their central focus. The first of the three approaches linked to gender to be noted here is embodiment and the medicalisation of the body, illustrated by studies of the 'menstruating, pregnant and lactating' body (Longhurst, 2001:66) or the changes in the body associated with the menopause (Greer, 1992, Martin, 1997) and the objectification of women's bodies leading to the desire to become impossibly thin which can produce eating disorders (Bordo, 1993, Urla and Swedlund, 2000). There are also discussions about the 'disabled' body, such as Benson's exploration of gender, impairment and sexuality (1997) and the 'disabled woman' in the workplace (Chouinard, 1999). Many of these approaches, specifically those relating to medicalisation, which became prominent in the 1990s, originated from Oakley's work on pregnancy and childbirth. Oakley argues that there has been a merging of 'the pregnant female body with the high-powered technology of modern obstetrics' so that 'women lack the capacity to know what is happening to their own bodies' (1993:21). Hence they are turned into cases for intervention such as 'uterine dysfunction', 'incomplete cervix' and 'bad producer' (ibid) or 'in a condition' requiring 'professional' advice (Longhurst, 1999). Hence it is agued that pregnant women become passive or anonymous 'bodies', just as police officers are shown in this book to regard their suspects and arrestees.

A second aspect of embodiment and gender that became more popular in the 1990s is corporeality with reference to Cartesian dualism or the 'thinking body' (Burkitt, 1999). Here, emotion and epistemological concerns particularly associated with feminist theories are considered. This area was discussed in some depth in Chapter 1, where the link between mind and body was analysed, which some feminists have argued challenges traditional 'male' theorising about gender and sexuality. It is relevant for policing because it is linked to agency and control, and what Maher describes as the 'myths about women's passivity and submissiveness – whether "natural" or socially induced' (2000:2). She discusses the role of women in the drug market and argues that although women have been believed in the past to lack the strength or 'muscle' to be 'successful' dealers, confining them in a minor or supporting role to men, in fact, the women she encountered in her research 'perceive themselves neither as powerless victims nor as emancipated and independent, nor, as their own accounts demonstrate, are they without agency' (ibid:19). Similar findings have been analysed here. Although in the police women are on the opposing 'side', as crime fighters, their representation as passive accomplices to men's active participation in the 'war' is comparable.

The third area of embodiment and gender, which is to be the main focus of this final chapter, is masculinity and the body. In one form or another this area has been analysed from the perspective of sport (Pronger, 1990), men in film (Kirkham and Thumin, 1993) and the media (Craig, 1992), consumerism (Edwards, 1997), homosexuality and Aids HIV (Benson, 1997), health (Watson, 2000), and the law and crime (Collier, 1995, 1998), although not in relation to policing due to a general lack of empirical research. However, as theorists who work within this paradigm explain, the terms masculinity, masculism and even maleness are ambiguous. Hearn argues for a return to the word 'men', suggesting that the others can distract from the emphasis on 'social relations between women and men' (1996:203). Taking up this discussion, MacInnes suggests that to use 'masculinities' in the plural implies that there is something about all men, or 'that these masculinities share' (1998:63 original emphasis) when the only thing they have in common is a penis. The importance of the penis, its size and the ability to perform sexual functions as a definer of self esteem was an issue discussed in Chapter 5 of this book, which began with a discussion of terms such as 'masculism', the crisis of masculinity and the competition which men face in an age of uncertainty to prove their 'manhood' (Britton, 1989). Later in Chapter 5, ways of 'being' a man in the police, such as being heterosexually active, 'professional' and heroic were analysed, and the difficulties for male officers in maintaining a masculine image of themselves which can also be displayed to colleagues. There are other problems associated with the definition of terms such as masculinity and using them to explain male behaviour, according to Collier (1998). He argues that not only are 'masculinities' politically ambiguous but they are also conceptually imprecise in terms of, for example, crime and the life course of men. If 'maleness' and 'being a man' leads to conceptualisations of '*masculinity* as something which impacts on men so as to induce *criminality*' then, he asks, how can this explain at what age men become or cease being ' "wild", "dangerous" and "maverick" '? (1998:17).

Aside from these discussions about masculinities, this book has been concerned with the analysis of evidence which contradicts much of what has been published previously on women in the police. Throughout the discussion there is also much that confirms what we seem to know about men. One of the main arguments tested by the study is the concept of 'differential deployment', an insidious means of keeping women in their place, which is said to prevent women from gaining promotion in the police. This has been alleged to be through the allocation of certain 'low-status' tasks to women officers and the more 'promotion worthy' work to men. As explained in Chapters 2 and 3, in the past it was said that this was done to 'keep women safe', leading to their exclusion from 'real' policing involving violence, the use of force and strength. Thus women officers lose confidence in their own ability to use their bodies as part of their policing function, and when required to do so, are hesitant or less competent due to lack of practice and so are regarded as incapable and further kept out of the firing line. One of the reasons for this is that women do not 'put their whole bodies into engagement in a physical task with the same ease and naturalness as men' according to Young (1990:145). So although men and women undertake tasks that require force and strength differently, and they have physical differences, the differences in the 'performance of tasks requiring coordinated strength, however, are due not so much to brute muscular strength as to the way each sex *uses* the body' (Young, 1990:145 original emphasis).

This vicious circle of incapacitation is well documented to have begun in earnest after the integration of male and female police departments in the UK, the US and some other countries across the world. In the UK the combining of male and female departments in the police was seen by many officers as an unwelcome move. It happened in the 1970s, when sexual equality employment laws were passed from which the police could not be exempt. Central to these debates is the concept of em-bodiment, or more specifically sexual embodiment. This refers here to the way the physical appearance of the body, designated 'male' or 'female', can be a determinant to which tasks an officer is most suited. It is associated with concepts such as Butler's 'genital identity' (1990) and related not only to force and strength, but also to something more difficult to quantify, an essential ability to be either 'tough' or 'empathetic' for instance. In Chapter 2, for example, the notion of 'gendered' specialists was examined in relation to dealing with women and children in specialist units and more generally on patrol. Domestic abuse, child runaways and young suspects being dealt with by women officers was explored. It was shown, contradicting to some extent what has been alleged in the past, that male officers did not pass this work to women. Although many more women, in percentage terms, were working in the Child and Family Protection departments, the reasons for this were explored and many were not necessarily linked to notions of it being their 'natural' place. In focus group discussions, women claimed that they had agency and the ability to choose when they explained that there were reasons they were working, or not working, in this type of department.

Similarly, contributions from men who attended focus groups were analysed, as they expressed doubts about their ability to deal with young children, and described the inability of their female colleagues to deal with firearms incidents as competently as men. This seems to be a problem of men, rather than women, however, because it is argued here that many women in the police seemed to be managing their lives and careers quite adequately. They did not feel particularly coerced to enter fields such as child and family protection, and they were not given disproportionate amounts of work to do with women and children. Many were in the specialist departments because they had chosen this type of work and it was men who were having difficulties with accepting their role. In the discussion groups they complained that women got all the advantages of being a minority and none of the disadvantages of being given the bulk of the boring, time consuming, no visible outcome calls such as domestic violence incidents. When women were asked whether child protection was 'low-status' work, many replied that if the men saw it as such, then it was their problem.

This is not to say that the picture for women in the police is without problem or prejudice. Some of the women interviewed and contributing to discussion related in Chapter 2 stated that they were regarded as 'child specialists' and in Chapter 3 the differential deployment argument was recognised as being valid relating to sexual assaults. This was seen in the way that women had to conduct their normal duties in combination with being the 'gendered expert', whereas men did not. The problem here is separating the gendered body and its connotations of expertise from traditional structures, practices and beliefs. To return to Chapter 1, it was argued that sexual identity has an 'erotic' aspect that it is difficult to separate from the simple possession of male or female genitalia. This is taken up again in Chapter 3, describing how women are the experts in a field demanding expertise. Structures and training have placed them in this position, but then so have understandable demands from female complainants who wish to have a woman present at an intimate examination. One of the few existing empirical studies of the body and work also makes this point when Twigg explains that the women care-workers she interviewed preferred to wear rubber gloves when washing male patients because they protect 'the worker from a contact that is too direct and too intimate' (2000:151). Moreover, dealing with unwelcome sexual advances, such as requests from the male clients to 'wash their private parts' and attempting to touch the careworkers in a sexual way were 'taken in their stride' with jokes and references to the lack of threat presented by 'old' men (ibid:154–6). A more serious matter, however, was revealed in a study of men working in nurseries and paid childcare. Personal care of young children and babies involves touching their bodies in various intimate situations such as nappy changing, using the lavatory and cuddling and comforting them (Cameron, Moss and Owen, 1999:140). Strategies have to be in place to avoid the abuse of children and allegations being made against the staff, but to have rules insisting that a careworker is never alone in a bathroom with a child can involve two members of staff taking a child to the toilet, which is impractical, or several children being taken at once. So although men and women are employed in nurseries covered by equal opportunities policies, one of the male teachers was advised by a colleague that he should never 'be in a class alone with a girl' (ibid:142).

Hence, 'masculinities', or something that is specific to men, but impossible to define and not usually possessed by women, has been portrayed recently as one of the 'answers' to why men commit brutal crime. Specifically, masculinity or masculinities have been associated with violence and crime in the sense that it is this aspect of men that is thought to drive aggressive behaviour. But it has been argued that masculinity itself is not necessarily a bad thing, any more than 'femininity' is good one, nor that 'masculinity' is confined to men. As discussed in the early sections of Chapter 5, policing is an occupation which allows men to express and enact many of the characteristics that are central to their sense of self as men. Given that most people feel that their gender is fairly central to their sense of identity, this produces a potential conflict when asked to be 'gender neutral' as a police officer. Evidence from the fieldwork observations of police behaviour illustrates the difficulties the police face in operating within an equal opportunities framework when some of the required tasks are gender and body specific. The ethnographic data recording interactions between police officers and between police and the public showed that although much of the work that was previously believed to be 'women's work' was not allocated to them specifically, cases involving sexuality, especially those regarded as 'deviant' such as child abuse, were believed to be outside the professional capabilities of male officers. Violence, or the use of force as it might be described when police officers are involved, is not gender specific, however. Arrest rates in Chapter 4 showed that women were just as likely to be involved in arrests associated with violence or aggravated aspects such as resisting arrest. This focus on the enactment of gendered action on the street and in certain specialist departments throws light on embodiment, force and strength in the police. In the past, research has shown that women are the victims of male violence and that there is a link between being male and committing certain types of violent crime, yet few empirical studies have concentrated on violence between men. In order to examine the way men enact violence, it is useful to think about the type of situations which lead to violent encounters. History suggests that men have always had to defend their 'honour' and this is often linked to sexual prowess in the presence of colleagues, as illustrated in Chapter 4, where male officers commented on the bodies of attractive women, but were protected from challenge in the cocoon of the police car. As Hearn and Collinson argue, 'sexual harassment is usually an instance or a commentary on men's sexualities … often understandable as about violence, power, authority, labour-power, protection of space and wage levels, economic discrimination' (1996:64). As such, this violence is not the result of men's 'natural' or uncontrollable sexual aggression, but a means to exert power over women. In occupations such as policing, however, to be violent or have the capacity to use the body as 'physical capital' (Shilling, 1993) or to threaten forceful resolution of any situation, is to '*be* a man'. As Hollway suggests, 'Violence is often seen as (and indeed used as) the inevitable backstop: "If we/they don't get our/their way, we/they could be violent" ' (1996:73). Indeed, this can illustrate why men are so ready to use violent means to resolve conflict, why they might be violent towards women, and in other situations believe it is their 'right' – not just because 'they can'. As Hearn suggests, 'policing has itself always been gendered … one set of men work against, and sometimes with, another set of men' (1992:133). In terms of embodiment, questions need to be asked about the extent to which gendered bodies are 'controlled' in violent situations, just as they are argued to be in sport.

This type of ambiguity exists for men, and to some extent women, working as police officers when they face violence or threats to their authority. Street encounters between police and public are often resolved by someone 'winning' and from the officers' viewpoint, it has to be the police. In some cases the 'fight for the streets', although not a war conducted using bullets and guns or even fists and feet, is being waged between one group of men and another. As Herbert suggests 'for masculinist officers, the street is a male preserve, and its control the ultimate test' (2001:59). In this book this is illustrated using examples of the police being humiliated. In these cases they are often successful in punishing their tormenters. In one of the command areas where the research was conducted, in the larger research force, a group called the 'Gang' controlled the doors of local pubs and clubs and the drug trade within the establishments. Another group called the 'Anti-Gang' were their rivals, and were challenging their power to control the town. Whilst these rivalries were being played out, the police would be called to attend 'threats to kill' where people were telephoned anonymously and told they were being targeted, or they received 'drive-bys' where the windows of the opposing gangs' houses were blasted out by a shotgun fired as a car was driven past by an accomplice.

Such problems of public and social order sometimes surface and unacceptable levels or types of violence may occur in police subdivisions. At one stage the rivalry between the two gangs mentioned above led to a doorman being shot dead as he came home at the end of his shift. He had reached his doorstep and bled to death in front of his partner and young family. The shooting had been preceded by a number of 'warning drive-bys' and was becoming a problem for the police as it was seemingly out of control. Whilst the town was fairly ordered, and the violence was between the gangs, peace and tranquillity were maintained. Once this became more public, with the doorman being shot, it was perceived to be out of control and action needed to be taken. Similarly, violence by the police can only be sanctioned by the organisation when it is at a minimum level necessary to regain order. This study has analysed the relationship between gender and policing in terms of how this is actually achieved. Thus, how the task of policing is not only enacted but also conceptualised by officers was considered through the examination of gender leading to specialism. By observing how certain tasks appear to be categorised by their status in terms of being 'real' or 'proper' police work, the importance of gendered bodies has been examined in depth. Commonly-held assumptions about differential deployment, hegemonic masculinity, 'macho cops' and the discrimination women encounter, have been analysed in relation to theoretical approaches to gender. Hence the study progressed from focusing upon female officers' roles to the explanation of masculinities as the expression of what it is to 'be a man' in the police.

As part of this expression of manhood it is to be expected that, within an organisation which was traditionally based on male values, created within a quasi-military framework and the product of a specific history, women would be excluded from certain areas of expertise. Furthermore, evidence collected during the fieldwork in the traditionally 'macho' specialist departments reveals that some men consciously remove themselves from any 'feminine' caring roles or activities. Male officers on general patrol have to engage with women as 'equal' colleagues, carrying out a range of 'female' tasks such as caring, sympathy and emotion work, and some leave this general patrol work, to enter the more rarified, almost exclusively male departments – the cars, guns and horses. In addition to avoiding 'women's' work or converting it to something more acceptably male, men in the police use their power as law enforcers to reinforce their own heterosexual identity. In this book evidence collected during field observations illustrates how sexual insecurities are compensated for, and disguised through, homosocial exchanges when observing women from the safety of a police car or van. In addition, delicate or sensitive situations, such as those involving emotional distress, call for certain well-rehearsed scripts to be used in order to cope with the situation in a professional, competent and essentially masculine way. In the examination of structure and agency, as outlined in Chapter 1, the importance of the body as a consuming and representational being is now regarded as an important area of concern. Evidence from this study suggests that the objectification of women's bodies shows how policing is embedded within and imbued with gendered and sexually stereotypical practices and ideologies. Furthermore, the problem of masculinities is highlighted as an area of concern for the study, as it has been suggested that women were being controlled and 'ghettoised' in the police (Jones, 1986, Heidensohn, 1995). This book challenges previously published work on differential deployment and the role of human agency in the police. Empirical evidence analysed throughout the study shows that women are not being differentially deployed on general patrol, that work with young people and domestic violence was not seen as 'women's work' and there is little evidence female officers were not being promoted because they lacked the general experience and 'arrest portfolio'. National UK statistics show that they are being promoted more quickly than men in some ranks and, although the overwhelming majority of applicants to join the police are men, women are twice as likely to be recruited. Indeed, evidence was presented both locally and nationally that women have a better chance of being promoted in some situations. The first rung on the management ladder is becoming an inspector, and there have been significant increases in numbers of women at this rank; the percentage of female sergeants more than doubled between 1990 and 2000 (Home Office, 2001).

This suggests that factors which have been thought to prevent women from being promoted, rather contrary to expectations, are not necessarily having a discriminatory effect. The crux of the debate is the issue of what women actually do in the police and to what extent tasks and duties are being allocated on the basis of gender. Officers' attitudes towards domestic violence incidents is that, although they are not popular, they can provide a 'good pinch' and they see it as the enactment of their 'heroic function' to protect the vulnerable in these situations. It is acknowledged here that certain gender-related controls are placed on women by their male colleagues. Evidence of the sexualisation of the workplace by the male majority, leading to the judgement of women's morals and behaviour are examples of this aspect of a male-dominated environment. Other examples include women being excluded from 'male' specialisms such as the CID and traffic departments and the way some women were moved towards promotable positions, apparently without choice, by simply being told they were to go to certain posts. On the other hand, there were also instances where women were given considerations for 'family' reasons, such as part-time work and shift changes to fit with children or partners.

As the legal definitions are complex and specialised in the child protection field, as in the sexual offences arena, the special rules concerning evidence gathering are described in Chapter 3. Codes of practice, resulting from strict legal rules on admissibility of evidence and procedures in court, result in a few very highly skilled officers being trained to collect video evidence and take statements from abused children. In addition, the two police forces researched for this book provided sexual offences training only for women officers, although towards the end of 1997, the small number of men working in child protection units were given this training. Specialist knowledge as a gendered skill was seen to be an aid to expert status and an advantage for women seeking to avoid uniformed patrol work. It was shown that when officers were appointed to the CID, such knowledge was counted as valuable experience, but it also meant that women were being given virtually every sexual offence to deal with, leading to their dissatisfaction and eventual resignation from this department.

The evidence from these discussions indicates fairly conclusively that policing is gendered in a number of ways, and this was contrasted with evidence collected during the fieldwork on patrol. Throughout these observations it was difficult to find much evidence of the differential deployment of male and female officers. In Chapter 4, which concentrates on these accompanied street patrols, the way officers were sent to incidents on the basis of several criteria other than gender was demonstrated. Use of computer dispatch systems (CADs), the way calls are held in a prioritised queue until an officer is available, and the lack of an individual supervisor's involvement in directing people to certain types of incident was used to contradict the previously argued case for deployment by gender in the police. Furthermore, the data shows that women are achieving the same percentage of arrests as men for 'crime' incidents, although their 'non-crime' rates were slightly lower. In addition, and perhaps most compellingly, arrests requiring traditional 'male' abilities connected with physical force, strength and violence, such as aggravated house burglary and car crime, show, within the limited scale of this study, to be attributed more to women in percentage terms. Finally, the evidence suggests that women and juveniles are equally as likely to be arrested by women as men, although a higher percentage likelihood of male suspects being arrested by men was shown. Overall, the traditional image of the high adrenalin, 'macho cop' arrest being made only by men now seems unsupportable.

In Chapter 5, analysing men and masculinities in the police, this book attempts to provide what Heidensohn suggests has being missing from the literature to date, which is a 'men's perspective' (1995:13). Officers working with 'cars, guns and horses' were interviewed and observed, with the findings discussed. Departments which had a very low percentage of women serving in them were investigated and the way men absented themselves from 'caring' roles in the police was analysed. Whether these officers chose to separate themselves from general patrol work and women colleagues was considered, looking at the synthesis of gender roles and occupational culture. In some of these departments the environment was strongly 'anti-women' and asking why there were so few female officers produced puzzlement and a certain level of hostility from male respondents. Some sharp-shooting, hard-riding men in these departments confessed to being perplexed as to why there were no female applicants waiting to join them. At the same time their description of hard physical activity demanding superhuman stamina and extreme dedication suggested that such work would be repellent to virtually all but the most determined woman. Finally, in the latter part of Chapter 5, four aspects of 'masculinities' or ways of being a man in the police are explored. These analyse masculinities using four aspects that have a special place in police culture, namely competence, professionalism, heterosexuality and heroism. A discussion of men acting 'as men' in the police is conducted, which presupposes there are alternative ways of being one. It illustrates certain difficulties officers encounter in more 'feminised' situations requiring soft voices and sympathetic expressions, such as a sudden death. Chapter 5 concludes that the maintenance of masculinities in these situations can be problematic and various compensatory actions and statements have to be made by male officers.

So, although many occupations can be classified as either pre-dominantly male or female, it has often proved more difficult to define why particular tasks within the work place are regarded as essentially masculine or feminine. In Chapter 1 a discussion of the way 'force and skill becomes a statement embedded in the body' (Connell, 1987:85) leads on to the issue of equality and difference (Irigaray, 1993:84). In later chapters activities such as typing and funeral directing are discussed in terms of self-identity and the expectations of colleagues and supervisors. Indeed, because men and women are given the neutral title of 'officer' or 'constable' in the police, they are technically occupying an ungendered role. As part of an 'integrated' force or service, according to equal opportunities legislation, male and female officers should carry out an identical range of tasks and duties. Ambiguities have been examined here, however, which highlight tensions between police culture and gender and reveal the pervasive influence of masculinities upon the enactment of policing. This final section concludes by discussing how these findings differ from those discovered by previous studies in two ways: first, in terms of the type of data and the way it was collected and second, due to the focus on the relationship between gender and the embodied nature of policing.

In order to analyse the problems involved in defining certain acts or behaviour as male or female, this book examines how policing is carried out 'on the ground' through observing officers on duty, often in situations where stress and danger make it difficult for them to act in anything but a 'natural' manner. As the fieldwork was conducted, it was informed by viewing the lived 'experience of policing and gender – how a woman can become one of the boys' (Fine, 1987:144–5) and how men 'perform masculinity' (Brittan, 1989). In later chapters of this book it is argued that subcultural masculinities in specialist departments reflect particular hierarchies of gendered competence and status. More specifically, in the departments staffed predominantly by men, the 'cult of masculinity' appears to be exaggerated, reflecting the 'officer's sporting club' which Smith and Gray (1983:91) identified as being similar to the police working environment. One of the difficulties with Smith and Gray's analysis, however, is that it relies on the acceptance of the categorisation of 'male' and female' as unproblematic. For example, in their discussion of this issue, they describe some male officers as 'anti-women' and classify 'WPCs' as an homogenous group who complain they are not treated equally in terms of promotion. Dichotomies of this type are evidently the result of beliefs about innate gender characteristics, as one of the women interviewed by Smith and Gray said she 'accepted she couldn't do the same job as the men' and another was described as 'a very good driver' by the authors (1983:94–5). As might be expected, matters are more complicated than this suggests, as the male/female dichotomy provides no explanation to accommodate the 'non-conventional' woman or man – they make gendered assumptions about the acquisition of skills such as driving cars and firing guns. In the type of study which Smith and Gray conducted, women officers are simply regarded as a minority without individual characteristics, opinions or feelings and are described in relation to the male majority.

Hence, it is worth challenging the notion that the application of conceptual gender characteristics, described as binary opposites, can define 'male' and 'female' without any necessity to recognise deviations from 'normal' gendered behaviour. In his ethnography of police life, Young constructs a set of 'semantic rigid dualities' which he uses to discuss women in the police. He begins with two columns headed 'masculinity' and 'femininity' and proceeds to put characteristics such as 'hard', 'soft', 'emotional', 'force' and 'service' into the appropriate place (1991:209). He emphasises the split between male preserves such as patrol work and 'warfare' in the CID, and the typing pool staffed by women officers known as the 'bitch squad' (ibid:258). It seems that this type of clearly-defined dichotomy is often in evidence where gender and policing are debated, leading to discussions of 'what men do' compared with 'what women do' and how this changes over time or remains the same. More recently, there has been a movement towards the notion that the link between sexuality and gender may be quite significant in this area of gender studies. It is suggested for, example, by Jackson and Scott, that although there is an analytical distinction between sex and gender, it must be recognised that they are 'empirically related' (1996:3). Furthermore, in her discussion of anthropological studies, Caplan explores the extent to which sex and gender can be regarded as 'independent variables' because 'in Western society, one's sexual orientation is a very important part of one's identity' (Caplan, 1987:2). Complexity is increased when cultural constructions are analysed in terms of sexual identity (Weeks, 1995), leading to 'categories of identity within the context of radical gender asymmetry' (Butler, 1990:11) being challenged. As a result of the significance attached to the gendered roles which Wilton has described as 'genital identity' or the 'sex-erotic' as opposed to the 'sex/gender' (Wilton, 1996:104), it could be difficult for women officers, in a system which is implicitly male, to consider themselves as gender neutral 'officers'. Furthermore, as Morgan suggests, there are no social arenas which are 'unembodied' or 'ungendered', and policing in particular, 'is an occupation in which it is obvious that bodily skill and deployment will be required' (Morgan, 1993:77–78).

Throughout this study, gender roles, informed by police working rules and culture, have been shown to be influenced by what Fielding has described as 'hegemonic' masculinity (1994) in some specialist departments. In terms of general street patrols, however, differential deployment is shown to be less pronounced than previous studies by Heidensohn (1995), Jones (1986) or Anderson et al (1993) have claimed. This is illustrated in Chapter 5, where an examination of 'artificial unities of genders and sexualities' which include 'relationships of dominance and subordination' were related to policing (Hearn and Morgan, 1995:179). Examples of what might be identified as 'masculine' and 'non-masculine' behaviour are examined in a framework which synthesises gender roles and police culture. In the evaluation of various examples of cultural ideals such as competence and professionalism, beliefs about appropriate 'male' behaviour and the way women are excluded from sites of organisational power show that policing is still firmly regarded as male. As Battersby notes, women and men are involved in a power struggle which 'favours woman, as long as she does not seek to fight man with his own weapons and on his own ground' (Battersby, 1989:122). Indeed, credible threats to male power and competency in the police seem to be largely resisted, as ideological categories of skill (Phillips and Taylor, 1980:79), such as firing guns and being able to drive fast, are controlled by men. In effect, women are being handed 'equality of opportunity' on the streets, where they carry out operational duties in the lowest status areas of patrol work. Where 'masculinity' really counts, however, in the departments where 'men are men', women are absent.

It was discussed above that, as Brittan (1989) Collier (1995) and Connell (1993) have all acknowledged, 'masculinity', 'masculinities' and 'masculism' are problematic concepts to relate to everyday, observed behaviour. It is clear from this study that they are fairly identifiable in some of the more 'public' arenas of policing. In child and family protection departments where the 'invisible' and time-consuming cases, which may never be prosecuted, are investigated by women, the maintenance of masculinity is less evident. Street patrol duties are shown here to be generally allocated without reference to gender and yet women make more arrests for high-status, dangerous and aggravated offences. However, where highly visible, 'proper', 'huntin' and shootin'' masculinity is required, men still predominate.

Bibliography

Acker, J. (1990) Hierarchies Jobs, Bodies: A Theory of Gendered Organizations. *Gender and Society,* vol. 4, pp.139–158

Ackroyd, S., Harper, R., Hughes, J. A., Shapiro, D. and Soothill, K. (1992) *New Technology and Practical Police Work.* Buckingham: Open University Press

Adkins, L. (1995) *Gendered Work: Sexuality, Family and the Labour Market.* Buckingham: Open University Press

Alvesson, M. and Due Billing, Y. (1997) *Understanding Gender and Organizations.* London: Sage

Anderson, R., Brown, J. and Campbell, E. (1993) *Aspects of Discrimination Within the Police Service in England and Wales.* London: Home Office

Atkinson, J. M. and Heritage, J. (1984) *Structures of Social Action; Studies in Conversation Analysis.* Cambridge: Cambridge University Press

Atkinson, P. (1990) *The Ethnographic Imagination: Textual Constructions of Reality.* London: Routledge

Audit Commission (1996) *Streetwise. Effective Police Patrol.* London: HMSO

Baker, A. and Duncan, S. (1985) Child Sexual Abuse: A Study of Prevalence in Great Britain. *Child Abuse and Neglect,* vol. 9, pp. 457–67

Bartky, S. L. (1997) Foucault, Femininity and the Modernisation of Patriarchal Power in K. Conboy, N. Medina and S. Stanbury (eds.) *Writing on the Body: Female Embodiment and Feminist Theory.* New York: Columbia University Press

Battersby, C. (1989) *Gender and Genius.* London: The Women's Press

Bayley, D. H. (1996) What Do the Police Do? in W. Saulsbury, J. Mott and T. Newburn (eds.) *Themes in Contemporary Policing.* London: Policy Studies Institute

Bell, V. (1993) *Interrogating Incest. Feminism, Foucault and the Law.* London: Routledge

Benson, S. (1997) The Body, Health and Eating Disorders in K. Woodward (ed.) *Identity and Difference. Culture, Media and Identities*. London: Sage

Bittner, E. (1990) *Aspects of Police Work*. Boston: Northeastern University Press

Bordo, S. (1993) *Unbearable Weight: Feminism, Western Culture and the Body*. Berkeley: University of California Press

(1997) The Body and the Reproduction of Femininity in K. Conboy *et al* (eds.) op cit

Brewer, J. D. and Magee, K. (1990) *Inside the RUC*. Oxford: Oxford University Press

Brittan, A. (1989) *Masculinity and Power*. Oxford: Basil Blackwell

Brooks, L. W., Piquero, A. and Cronin, J. (1994) Work-Load Rates and Police Officer Attitudes: An Examination of Busy and Slow Precincts. *Journal of Criminal Justice*, vol. 22, no. 3

Brown, J. (1996a) Police Research: Some Critical Issues in F. Leishman, B. Loveday, and S. P. Savage (eds.) *Core Issues in Policing*. London: Longman

(1996b) Integrating Women into Policing: A Comparative European Perspective. *Policing in Central and Eastern Europe*. Slovenia: College of Police and Security Studies

(1998) Aspects of Discriminatory Treatment of Women Police Officers Serving in England and Wales. *British Journal of Criminology*, vol. 38, no. 2, pp. 265–82

Brown, J. and Sergeant, S. (1995) Policewomen and Firearms in the British Police Service. *Police Studies*, vol. 18, no. 2, pp. 1–16

Brown, J. and Gillick, M. (1998) Differing Perspectives on a Police Force's Equal Opportunities Grievance Procedure: Viewpoints of police managers and front-line personnel. *International Journal of Police Science and Management*, vol. 1, no. 2, pp. 122–32

Brown, J. and Grover, J. (1998) Stress and the Woman Sergeant. *The Police Journal*, vol. 71, no. 1, pp. 47–54

Brown, J. and Heidensohn, F. (2000) *Gender and Policing: Comparative Perspectives*. Hampshire: Macmillan

Browne, K. (1994) Child Sexual Abuse in J. Archer (ed.) *Male Violence*. London: Routledge

Burkitt, I. (1999) *Bodies of Thought. Embodiment, Identity and Modernity*. London: Sage

Burrows, J. and Lewis, H. (1988) *Directing Patrol Work: A Study of Uniformed Policing*. Home Office Research Study No. 99. London: HMSO

Butler, J. (1990) *Gender Trouble. Feminism and the Subversion of Identity*. London: Routledge

(1997) Performative Acts and Gender Constitution: An Essay in Phenomenology and Feminist Theory, in K. Conboy *et al* (eds) op cit

Butler-Sloss, E. (1988) *Report of the Inquiry into Child Abuse in Cleveland 1987*. London: HMSO

Cain, M. (1973) *Society and the Policeman's Role.* London: Routledge & Kegan Paul
    (1992) Trends in the Sociology of Policework, in K.R.E. McCormick and L.A.
    Visano (eds.) *Understanding Policing.* Toronto: Canadian Scholars' Press
Cameron, C., Moss, P. and Owen, C. (1999) *Men in the Nursery. Gender and Caring
    Work.* London: Sage
Campbell, B. (1988) *Unofficial Secrets.* London: Virago
Caplan, P. (1987) *The Cultural Construction of Sexuality.* London: Routledge
Cassell, J. (1996) The Woman in the Surgeon's Body: Understanding Difference.
    American Anthropologist. vol. 98, no. 1, pp. 41–53
Chan, J. (1996) Changing Police Culture. *British Journal of Criminology,* vol. 36,
    no. 1, Winter
Chouinard, V. (1999) Life at the Margins. Disabled Women's Explorations of
    Ableist Spaces in E. Kenworthy Teather (ed.) *Embodied Geographies. Spaces,
    Bodies and Rites of Passage.* London: Routledge
Church, J. (1997) Ownership and the Body in D. Tietjens Meyers (ed.) *Feminists
    Rethink the Self.* Oxford: Westview Press
Clatterbaugh, K. (1990) *Contemporary Perspectives on Masculinity: Men, Women and
    Politics in Modern Society.* San Francisco: Westview Press
Cline, S. (1995) *Lifting the Taboo: Women, Death and Dying.* London: Abacus
Cockburn, C. (1991) *In the Way of Women: Men's Resistance to Sex Equality in
    Organizations.* London: Macmillan
Coffey, A. (1999) *The Ethnographic Self. Fieldwork and the Representation of Identity.*
    London: Sage
Collinson, D. L. and Hearn, J. (1996) 'Men' at 'Work': Multiple Masculinities/
    Multiple Workplaces in M. Mac an Ghaill (ed.) *Understanding Masculinities.
    Social Relations and Cultural Arenas.* Buckingham: Open University Press
Collier, R. (1995) *Masculinity, Law and the Family.* London: Routledge
    (1998) *Masculinities, Crime and Criminology.* London: Sage
Connell, R. W. (1987) *Gender and Power.* Oxford: Polity Press
    (1995) *Masculinities.* Berkeley: University of California Press
Craig, S. (1992) Considering Men and the Media in S. Craig (ed.) *Men, Masculinity
    and the Media.* London: Sage

Davis, K. (1996) From Objectified Body to Embodied Subject: A Biographical
    Approach to Cosmetic Surgery in S. Wilkinson (ed.) *Feminist Social
    Psychologies: International Perspectives.* Buckingham: Open University Press
Department of Health (DOH) (1991) *Working Together under the Children* Act,
    1989: *A Guide to Arrangements for Inter-Agency Co-operation for the Protection of
    Children from Abuse.* London: HMSO
Dobash, R. E. and Dobash, R. P. (1977–78) Wives: The 'Appropriate' Victims of
    Marital Violence. *Victimology,* vol. 2, nos. 3–4, pp. 426–42
    (1992) *Women, Violence and Social Change.* London: Routledge
Dunhill, C. (ed.) (1989) *The Boys in Blue: Women's Challenge to the Police.* London:
    Virago Press
Dunne, G. A. (1997) *Lesbian Lifestyles: Women's Work and the Politics of Sexuality.*
    London: Macmillan Press

Edwards, S.S.M. (1993) Selling the Body, Keeping the Soul: Sexuality, Power and the Theories and Realities of Prostitution, in S. Scott and D. Morgan (eds.) *Body Matters*. Bristol: Falmer Press.
(1989) *Policing 'Domestic' Violence: Women, the Law and the State*. London: Sage
(1996) *Sex and Gender in the Legal Process*. London: Blackstone Press

Edwards, S.S.M. and Soetenhorst-de Savornin Lohman, J. (1994) The Impact of 'Moral Panic' on Professional Behavior in Cases of Child Sexual Abuse: An International Perspective. *Journal of Child Sexual Abuse*, vol. 3, no. 1, pp. 103–126

Edwards, T. (1997) *Men in the Mirror. Men's Fashion, Masculinity and Consumer Society*. London: Cassell

Equal Opportunities Commission (1985) *Code of Practice*. London: HMSO

Fielding, N. (1988) *Joining Forces: Police Training, Socialisation and Occupational Competence*. London: Routledge
(1994) Cop Canteen Culture in T. Newburn and E.A. Stanko (eds.) *Just Boys Doing Business? Men, Masculinities and Crime*. London: Routledge

Fielding, N. and Fielding, J. (1992) A Comparative Minority: Female Recruits to a British Constabulary Force. *Policing and Society*, no. 2, pp. 205–18

Fine, G. A. (1987) One of the Boys: Women in Male Dominated Settings in M.S. Kimmel (ed.) *Changing Men: New Directions on Men and Masculinity*. London: Sage

Frank, A. (1990) Bringing Bodies Back In: A Decade Review. *Theory, Culture and Society*, vol. 7, pp. 131–62

Ghate, D. and Spencer, L. (1995) *The Prevalence of Child Sexual Abuse in Britain*. London: HMSO

Giddens, A. (1991) *Modernity and Self Identity*. Oxford: Polity Press

Golde, P. (1986) *Women in the Field*. Berkeley: University of California Press

Golden, K. (1981) Women as Patrol Officers: A Study of Attitudes *Police Studies*, vol. 4, no. 3

Gomm, R., Hammersley, M. and Foster, P. (2000) Case Study and Generalization in R. Gomm, M. Hammersley, and P. Foster (eds) *Case Study Method*. London: Sage

Greer, G. (1992) *The Change. Women, Ageing and the Menopause*. London: Penguin

Gregory, G. and Lees, S. (1999) *Policing Sexual Assault*, London: Routledge

Halford, A. (1993) *No Way up the Greasy Pole*. London: Constable

Halford, S., Savage, M. and Witz, A. (1997) *Gender, Careers and Organisations: Current Developments in Banking, Nursing and Local Government*. London: Macmillan

Hall, E. J. (1993) Smiling, Deferring and Flirting: Doing Gender by Giving 'Good Service'. *Work and Occupations*, vol. 20, no. 4, pp. 452–71

Hammersley, M. and Atkinson, P. (1995) *Ethnography: Principles in Practice*. London: Routledge, 2nd edn.

Hausman, B. L. (1995) *Changing Sex: Transsexualism, Technology and the Idea of Gender.* Durham: Duke University Press

Hearn, J. (1992) *Men In the Public Eye.* London: Routledge

(1996) Is Masculinity Dead? A Critique of the Concept of Masculinity/ Masculinities in M. Mac an Ghaill (ed.) *Understanding Masculinities. Social Relations and Cultural Arenas.* Buckingham: Open University Press

Hearn, J. and Morgan, D. (1995) Contested Discourses on Men and Masculinities in M. Blair, J. Holland and S. Sheldon (eds.) *Identity and Diversity.* Buckingham: Open University Press

Heidensohn, F. (1995) *Women in Control: The Role of Women In Law Enforcement.* Oxford: Oxford University Press

(1996) Making it Even: Equal Opportunities and Public Order in C. Critcher, and D. Waddington (eds.) *Policing Public Order: Theoretical and Practical Issues.* Aldershot: Avebury

(1994) 'We can handle it out here'. Women Officers in Britain and the USA and the Policing of Public Order. *Policing and Society,* vol. 4, pp. 293–303

Herbert, S. (2001) 'Hard Charger' or 'Station Queen'? Policing and the Masculinist State. *Gender, Place and Culture,* vol. 8, no. 1, pp. 55–71

Heward, T. (1994) Retailing the Police: Corporate Identity and the Met. in R. Keat, N. Whitely and N. Abercrombie, (eds.) *The Authority of the Consumer.* London: Routledge

HMIC (1992) *Equal Opportunities In the Police Service.* London: Home Office

HMIC (1996) *Developing Diversity in the Police Service: Equal Opportunities Thematic Inspection Report 1995.* London: Home Office

HMSO (1991) *Aspects of Britain: Women In Britain.* London: HMSO

Hobbs, D. (1988) *Doing the Business. Entrepreneurship, the Working Class and Detectives in the East End of London.* Oxford: Oxford University Press

(1993) Peers, Careers and Academic Fears; Writing as Fieldwork in D. Hobbs and T. May (eds.) *Interpreting the Field, Accounts of Ethnography.* Oxford: Clarendon Press

(1994) Mannish Boys. Danny, Chris, Crime, Masculinity and Business in T. Newburn and E.A. Stanko (eds.) *Just Boys Doing Business? Men Masculinities and Crime.* London: Routledge

(1995) *Bad Business. Professional Crime in Modern Britain.* Oxford: Oxford University Press

Hoch, P. (1979) *White Hero, Black Beast. Racism, Sexism and the Mask of Masculinity.* London: Pluto Press

Holdaway, S. (1983) *Inside the British Police.* Oxford: Basil Blackwell

(1994) Recruitment, Race and the Police Subculture in M. Stephens and S. Becker (eds.) *Police Force, Police Service. Care and Control in Britain.* London: Macmillan

(1996) *The Racialisation of British Policing.* London: Macmillan

Holdaway, S. and Parker, S. K. (1998) Policing Women Police. Uniform Patrol, Promotion and Representation in the CID. *British Journal of Criminology,* vol. 38, no. 1, pp. 40–60

Hollway, W. (1996) Gender and Power in Organizations in B. Fawcett,

B. Featherstone, J, Hearn and C. Toft (eds.) *Violence and Gender Relations. Theories and Interventions.* London: Sage

Home Office (1995) *Criminal Statistics in England and Wales.* London: HMSO

Home Office (2001) Police Officer Strength In England and Wales. http://www.homeoffice.gov.uk/rds/pdfs/hosb1001.pdf

Home Office in conjunction with Department of Health (1992) *Memorandum of Good Practice on Video Recorded Interviews with Child Witnesses for Criminal Proceedings.* London: Home Office

Horley, S. (1988) *Love and Pain.* A *Survival Handbook for Women.* London: Bedford Square Press

Hoyle, C. (2000) *Negotiating Domestic Violence. Police, Criminal Justice and Victims.* Oxford: Oxford University Press

Hunt, J. (1984) The Development of Rapport through the Negotiation of Gender in Fieldwork among Police. *Human Organisation,* vol. 43, no. 4

Irigaray, L. (1993) *Je, Tu, Nous. Towards a Culture of Difference.* London: Routledge

Jackson, S. and Scott, S. (1996) *Feminism and Sexuality: A Reader.* Edinburgh: Edinburgh University Press

Jones, S. (1986) *Policewomen and Equality: Formal Policy v. Informal Practice?* London: Macmillan

Jones, T., MacLean, B. and Young, J. (1986) *The Islington Crime Survey: Crime, Victimization and Policing in Inner-City London.* Aldershot: Gower

Kazanjian, A. (1993) Health-Manpower Planning or Gender Relations? The Obvious and the Oblique in E. Riska and K. Wegar (eds.) *Gender, Work and Medicine.* London: Sage

Kelly, L. (1992) The Connections between Disability and Child Abuse: A Review of Research Evidence. *Child Abuse Review,* vol. 1, pp. 157–167

Kirkham, P. and Thumim, J. (eds.) (1993) *You Tarzan. Masculinities, Movies and Men.* London: Lawrence and Wishart

Lancaster, E. (1996) Working with Men who Sexually Abuse Children: the Experience of the Probation Service in B. Fawcett, B. Featherstone, J. Hearn and C. Toft (eds.) *Violence and Gender Relations: Theories and Interventions.* London: Sage

Lash, J. (1995) *The Hero. Manhood and Power.* London: Thames and Hudson

Lawler, S. (1996) Motherhood and Identity, in J. Cosslett, A. Eastman and P. Summerfield (eds.) *Women, Power & Resistance.* Buckingham: Open University Press

Lawrence, E. (1996) Gender and Office-Holding in Trade Unions in L. Morris and E. Stina Lyon (eds) *Gender Relations in Public and Private: New Research Perspectives.* London: Macmillan Press

Lee, R. M. (1995) *Dangerous Fieldwork.* London: Sage

Liddle, A. M. (1995) Child Sexual Abuse and Age of Consent Laws: A Response to Some Libertarian Arguments for 'Sexual Liberty' in R.E. Dobash, R.P. Dobash and L. Noaks (eds.) *Gender and Crime.* Cardiff: University of Wales Press

Longhurst, R. (2001) *Bodies. Exploring Fluid Boundaries.* London: Routledge

Lyon, C. M. and de Cruz, S. P. (1993) *Child Abuse.* Bristol: Jordan Publishing

MacInnes, J. (1998) *The End of Masculinity. The Confusion of Sexual Genesis and Sexual Difference in Modern Society.* Buckingham: Open University Press

Mackenzie, C. (1998) A Certain Lack of Symmetry: Beauvoir on Autonomous Agency and Women's Embodiment in R. Evans (ed.) *Simone de Beauvoir's The Second Sex. New Interdisciplinary Essays,* Manchester: Manchester University Press

Maher, L. (2000) *Sexed Work. Gender, Race and Resistance in a Brooklyn Drug Market.* Oxford: Oxford University Press

Manning, P. K. (1977) *Police Work.* Cambridge Mass: MIT Press

Martin, C. (1996) The Impact of Equal Opportunities Policies on the Day-to-Day Experiences of Women Constables. *British Journal of Criminology*, vol. 36, no. 4, pp. 510–28

Martin, E. (1989) *The Woman in the Body: A Cultural Analysis of Reproduction.* Buckingham: Open University Press

(1997) Medical Metaphors of Women's Bodies: Menstruation and Menopause in K. Conboy, N. Medina and S. Stanbury (eds.) *Writing on the Body. Female Embodiment and Feminist Theory.* New York: Columbia University Press

Martin, S. E. (1980) *Breaking and Entering: Policewomen on Patrol.* Berkeley: University of California Press

Martin, S.E. and Jurik, N. C. (1996) *Doing Justice, Doing Gender: Women in Law and Criminal Justice Occupations.* London: Sage

Maynard, M. (1997) *Science and the Construction of Women.* London: UCL Press

Messerschmidt, J. (1993) *Masculinities and Crime.* Maryland: Rowman & Littlefield

McLaughlin, E. (1996) Police, Policing and Policework in E. McLaughlin and J. Muncie (eds.) *Controlling Crime.* London: Sage

McKenzie, I. (1996) Violent Encounters: Force and Deadly Force in British Policing in F. Leishman, B. Loveday and S.P. Savage (eds.) *Core Issues in Policing.* London: Longman

McNay, L. (1992) *Foucault and Feminism: Power, Gender and the Self.* Cambridge: Polity Press

McNeil, M. (1987) *Gender and Expertise.* London: Free Association Books

Miller, S.L. (1999) *Gender and Community Policing: Walking the Talk.* Boston: Northeastern University Press

Morgan, D. (1987) *'It Will Make a Man of You' Notes on National Service, Masculinity and Autobiography. Studies in Sexual Politics.* Manchester: University of Manchester

(1992) *Discovering Men.* London: Routledge

(1993) You Too Can Have a Body Like Mine: Reflections on the Male Body and

Masculinities in S. Scott and D. Morgan (eds.) *Body Matters: Essays on the Sociology of the Body.* London: The Falmer Press

Moss Kanter, R. (1977) *Men and Women of the Organization.* New York: Basic Books

Nash, C. L. and West, D. J. (1985) Sexual Molestation of Young Girls: Retrospective Study in D.J. West (ed.) *Sexual Victimisation.* Aldershot: Gower

Nettleton, S. and Watson, J. (eds.) (1998) *The Body in Everyday Life.* London: Routledge

Newburn, T. and Stanko, E. A. (1994) *Just Boys Doing Business? Men, Masculinities and Crime.* London: Routledge

Nicholson, P. (1996) *Gender, Power and Organisation: A Psychological Perspective.* London: Routledge

Norris, C. (1993) Some Ethical Considerations on Fieldwork with the Police in D. Hobbs and T. May (eds.) *Interpreting the Field. Accounts of Ethnography.* Oxford: Clarendon Press

Oakley, A. (1993) *Essays on Women, Medicine and Health.* Edinburgh: Edinburgh University Press

Pahl, J. (1982) Police Response to Battered Women. *Journal of Social Welfare Law,* November, pp. 337–343

Phillips, A. and Taylor, B. (1980) Sex and Skill: Notes towards a Feminist Economics. *Feminist Review,* vol, 6, pp. 79–88

Pringle, R. (1992) Absolute Sex? Unpacking the Sexuality/Gender Relationship in R.W. Connell and G.W. Dowsett (eds.) *Rethinking Sex.* Victoria: Melbourne University Press

Pringle, R. (1993) Male Secretaries in C.L. Williams (ed.) *Doing Women's Work: Men in Nontraditional Occupations.* London: Sage

Pronger, B. (1990) *The Arena of Masculinity. Sports, Homosexuality, and the Meaning of Sex.* London: GMP Publishers

Punch, M. (1993) Observation and the Police: The Research Experience in M. Hammersley, (ed.) *Social Research. Philosophy, Politics and Practice.* London: Sage

Reiner, R. (1991) *Chief Constables.* Oxford: Oxford University Press
(2000) *The Politics of the Police.* Oxford: Oxford University Press 3rd edn

Rich, A. (1977) *Of Woman Born: Motherhood as an Experience and Institution.* London: Virago

Scott, A. (1997) The Knowledge in Our Bones: Standpoint Theory, Alternative Health and the Quantum Model of the Body in M. Maynard (ed.) *op cit*

Scott, S. and Dickens, A. (1989) Police and the Professionalisation of Rape in C. Dunhill (ed.) *The Boys in Blue: Women's Challenge to the Police.* London: Virago Press

Seidler, V. J. (1997) *Man Enough. Embodying Masculinities*. London: Sage

Shapland, J. and Hobbs, D. (1987) *Policing on the Ground in High Wycombe*. Oxford: Centre for Criminological Research, University of Oxford

Shilling, C. (1993) *The Body and Social Theory*. London: Sage
(1997) The Body and Difference in K. Woodward (ed.) *Identity and Difference*. Buckingham: Open University Press

Skinner, T. (2000) Feminist Strategy and Tactics: Influencing State Provision of Counselling for Survivors in *Women, Violence and Strategies for Action. Feminist Research, Policy and Practice*. Buckingham: Open University Press

Skolnick J. H. (1975) *Justice Without Trial: Law Enforcement in Democratic Society*. New York: John Wiley & Sons

Smith, D. J. and Gray, J. (1983) *The Police and People in London: vol. iv. The Police in Action*. London: Policy Studies Institute

Southgate, P. (1981) Women in the Police. *The Police Journal*, vol. 54, no. 2

Stanko, E. A. (1985) *Intimate Intrusions: Women's Experience of Male Violence*. London: Unwin Hyman
(1994) Dancing with Denial: Researching Women and Questioning Men in M. Maynard and J. Purvis (eds.) *Researching Women's Lives from a Feminist Perspective*. London: Taylor & Francis

Stanley, L. and Wise, S. (1993) *Breaking Out Again*. London: Routledge

Steinman, C. (1992) Gaze out of Bounds. Men Watching Men on Television in S. Craig (ed.) *Men, Masculinity and the Media*. London: Sage

Tarling, R. (1993) *Analysing Offending. Data, Models and Interpretations*. London: HMSO

Tolson, A. (1977) *The Limits of Masculinity*. London: Tavistock Publications

Turner, B. S. (1992) *Regulating Bodies. Essays in Medical Sociology*. London: Routledge
(1996) *The Body and Society. Explorations in Social Theory*. London: Sage, 2nd edn

Twigg, J. (2000) *Bathing – the Body and Community Care*. London: Routledge

Uildriks, N. and van Mastrigt, H. (1991) *Policing Police Violence*. Boston: Kluwer Law

Urla, J. and Swedland, A. C. (2000) An Anthropometry of Barbie. Unsettling Ideals of the Feminine Body in Popular Culture in L. Schiebinger (ed.) *Feminism and the Body*. Oxford: Oxford University Press

Waddington, P. A. J. (1999) *Policing Citizens: Authority and Rights*. London: UCL Press

Walklate, S. (1995) *Gender and Crime: An Introduction*. London: Prentice Hall
(1996) Equal Opportunities and the Future of Policing in F. Leishman, B. Loveday and S.P. Savage (eds.) *Core Issues in Policing*. London: Longman
(2001) *Gender, Crime and Criminal Justice*. Cullompton: Willan

Warren, C. A. B. (1988) *Gender Issues in Field Research*. London: Sage

Watson, J. (2000) *Male Bodies. Health, Culture and Identity*. Buckingham: Open University Press

Weeks, J. (1995) *Invented Moralities. Sexual Values in an Age of Uncertainty*. Cambridge: Polity Press

Wertsch, T. L. (1998) Walking the Thin Blue Line: Policewomen and Tokenism Today. *Women and Criminal Justice*, vol. 9, no. 3, pp. 23–61

Westmarland, L. (1999) Women Managing in the Police. *Police Research and Management*, vol. 3, no. 3, pp. 59–68

(2001) Blowing the Whistle on Police Violence. Gender, Ethnography and Ethics. *British Journal of Criminology*, vol. 41, pp. 523–535

Westmarland, L. and Yearley, S. (2001) Unintended Outcomes of Police Selection Procedures: A Study of Rationality in Action. *Police Research and Management*, vol. 5, no. 1, pp. 71–88

Wexler, J. G. (1985) Role styles of Women Police Officers. *Journal of Police Science and Administration*, vol. 12, nos. 7–8, pp. 749–56

Wichroski, M. A. (1994) The Secretary: Invisible Labor in the Workload of Women. *Human Organisation*, vol. 53, no. 1, pp. 33–41

Williamson, J. (1997) Meaning and Ideology in A. Gray and J. McGuigan (eds.) *Studying Culture. An Introductory Reader*. London: Arnold, 2nd edn

Wilton, T. (1995) *Lesbian Studies. Setting an Agenda*. London: Routledge

(1996) Genital Identities: An Ideosyncratic Foray into the Gendering of Sexualities in L. Adkins and V. Merchant (eds.) *Sexualising the Social. Power and the Organisation of Sexuality*. London, Macmillan

Witz, A. (1992) *Professions and Patriarchy*. Routledge: London

Wolcott, H. F. (1999) *Ethnography. A Way of Seeing*. London: Sage

Wyles, L. (1952) *A Woman at Scotland Yard*. London: Faber

Young, I. M. (1990) *Throwing Like Girl and Other Essays in Feminist Philosophy and Social Theory*. Bloomington: Indiana University Press

Young, M. (1991) *An Inside Job. Policing and Police Culture in Britain*. Oxford: Oxford University Press

(1984) Police Wives: A Reflection of Police Concepts of Order and Control in H. Callan and S. Ardner (eds.) *The Incorporated Wife*. London: Croom Helm

Index

absent body, 7
accountability, public, 60, 61
acting tough, 130
activity analysis, patrol work, 99
adrenalin rush, 115
agencies, child abuse cases, 51
agency and structure, 5–8
ages, arrestees, West command
    area, 112
arrested bodies, 3
arrestees, West command area,
    111–12
arrests
    by type, 114–18
    drunks, 97
    occupational competence, 138
    pecking order of, 107
    physical courage, 131–2
    tests of manhood, 6
    West command area, 111–14
    women's achievements, 185
assaults, 115, 116
    see also domestic violence;
    incestuous assaults; sexual
        assaults
assumptions
    about police work, 18, 35–6
    differential deployment, 49

attitudes, to police work, 48–9

Bat phone dispatch system, 120
between-men culture, 8
blue-eyed boys, 144
bodies
    powerful, 96–8
    see also gendered bodies
body weight, 131
bonding, exclusion of women, 137
bravado, death defying, 139
burglaries, West command area
    arrests, 116
    male crime fighting, 115
    statistics, 103, 106
burglars, juvenile, 38
Butler-Sloss Inquiry, 51, 59

calls
    about offending children, 36–7
    adrenalin rush, 115
    daily logs, 121
    deployment of officers, 123
    status allocated to, 106–7
    to assaults, 115
    see also rubbish calls
car crime, West command area
    arrests, 116